REVIEWS OF GINNY KOPF'S THE DIALECT HANDBOOK
by Professional Dialect Coaches and Trainers

THE DIALECT HANDBOOK is a splendid achievement. What a wonderful tool Ginny Kopf has provided for actors, directors, dialect coaches and potential dialect coaches. I've dropped my plans to write a complete dialect resource and preparation manual for coaches and actors. It would be hard to top what Ginny has already done.

> David Alan Stern
> Author of *Acting with an Accent* series

This book fills an existing gap in the literature on stage dialects. The Dialect Directory is a treasure. The author's approach is upbeat, simple, and to the point. The best feature of this book is the author's enthusiasm for dialect work and her ability to address the whole person rather than just speak about sound or pronunciation.

> Bonnie Raphael
> University of North Carolina, Chapel Hill

I judge this to be one of the most helpful, most current and innovative dialect study guides I've ever encountered. It is an excellent resource for playwrights and directors as well. It contains an unprecedented Dialect Directory which alone will save you hours of research time and plenty of money over the years.

> Tyne Turner
> Utah Shakespeare Festival

The Dialect Handbook is a great resource to support the teaching of dialects. My students found it to be an effective, sensible and practical guide to learning, sampling and performing dialects for a role.

> Eric Armstrong
> Roosevelt University, Chicago

The Dialect Handbook outlines a direct and practical method of dialect acquisition, of great value in learning any dialect. The Directory of Dialects is a valuable resource for professional actors, directors, and coaches.

> Mira Kehoe
> The Guthrie Theater

The Dialect Directory is one of the most useful resources I've ever seen.

> Claudia Anderson
> DePaul University Theatre School, Chicago

Ginny Kopf shows that she is comprehensive, knowledgeable, articulate, detailed, and obviously caring about dialects and her readers. She truly wants her readers to succeed, and to be well-informed and confident in doing so.

> Kate Ufema
> University of Minnesota-Duluth

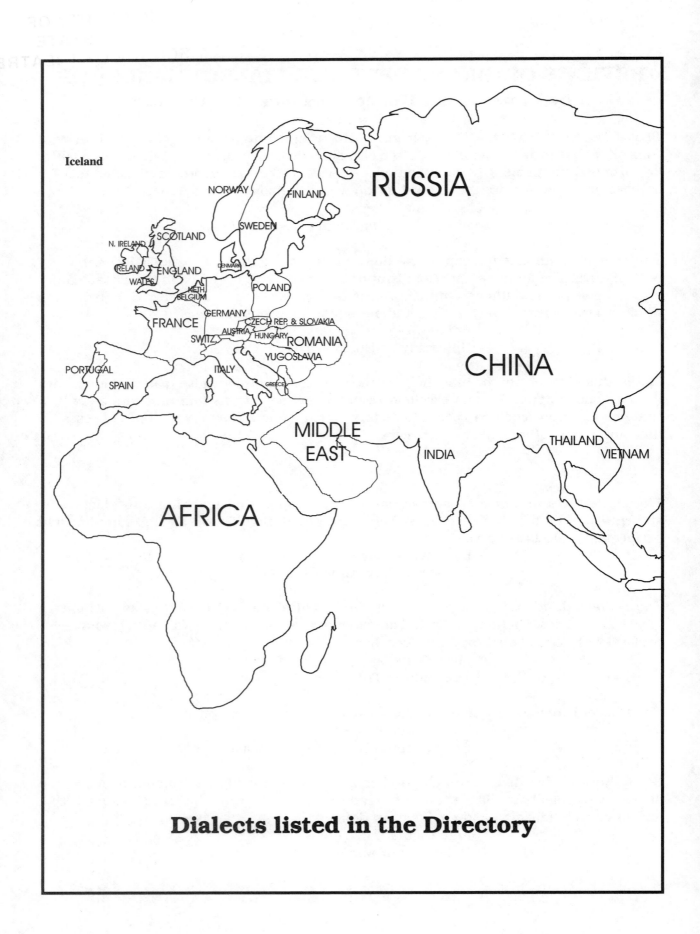

Iceland

NORWAY

FINLAND

RUSSIA

SWEDEN

SCOTLAND

N. IRELAND

DENMARK

IRELAND

ENGLAND

WALES

POLAND

NETH.

BELGIUM

GERMANY

CZECH REP. & SLOVAKIA

FRANCE

AUSTRIA

HUNGARY

ROMANIA

SWITZ.

YUGOSLAVIA

PORTUGAL

ITALY

SPAIN

GREECE

CHINA

MIDDLE

EAST

THAILAND

INDIA

VIETNAM

AFRICA

Dialects listed in the Directory

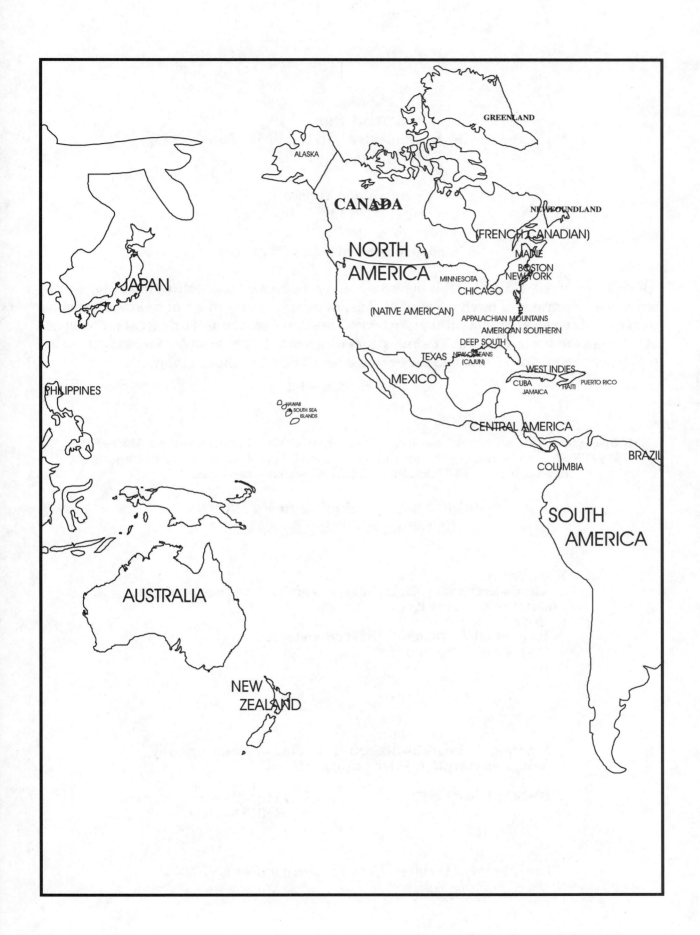

GREENLAND

ALASKA

CANADA

NEWFOUNDLAND

(FRENCH CANADIAN)

NORTH
AMERICA

MAINE

MINNESOTA

BOSTON
NEW YORK

CHICAGO

(NATIVE AMERICAN)

APPALACHIAN MOUNTAINS

AMERICAN SOUTHERN

DEEP SOUTH

TEXAS

NEW ORLEANS
(CAJUN)

MEXICO

WEST INDIES

CUBA

HAITI

PUERTO RICO

JAMAICA

JAPAN

PHILIPPINES

HAWAII
SOUTH SEA
ISLANDS

CENTRAL AMERICA

BRAZIL

COLUMBIA

SOUTH
AMERICA

AUSTRALIA

NEW
ZEALAND

Published by:
Voiceprint Publishing
3936 S. Semoran Blvd., PMB 243
Orlando, FL 32822

2nd edition, revised
Copyright © 2003 by Ginny Kopf
Copyright © 1997 by Ginny Kopf
Printed in the United States of America

Special thanks to:

My colleagues of VASTA (the Voice and Speech Trainers Association), Beth Cunningham, Murry Fisher, Peg O'Keefe, Mira Kehoe, Louis Colaianni, Bonnie Raphael, Ralph Zito, Jani Herbster, Nan Norton, Julie Gagne, Denise Gillman, and especially my husband, Ron Kopf.

Publisher's Cataloging in Publication
(Prepared by Quality Books Inc.)

Kopf, Ginny.
    The dialect handbook : learning, researching, and performing a dialect role / Ginny Kopf
    p cm.
    Includes bibliographical references and index.
    ISBN 0-9655960-6-0

1. Acting 2. English--Dialects. 3. English--Pronunciation by foreign speakers. 4. Voice culture.   I. Title.

PN2071.F6K66 1997   792'.028
                                     QBI97-40039

The Library of Congress Catalog Card Number is 97-60019

THE DIALECT HANDBOOK

~ ~

LEARNING, RESEARCHING, AND PERFORMING A DIALECT ROLE

Ginny Kopf

**2nd edition
Revised and expanded**

VOICEPRINT PUBLISHING

Orlando, Florida

CONTENTS

INTRODUCTION: (DON'T SKIP THIS!)

HOW TO USE *THE DIALECT HANDBOOK*

Actors approach dialects with both delight and terror. The bottom line is, you want to be *believable*. You've probably seen a play or movie recently in which an actor's dialect was really impressive, and you wondered, "How did he do that? How did he make it sound so natural?" You've also seen how distracting a bad dialect can be. To be believable, your dialect must flow naturally, but it must also be clear and consistent. You must meet the audience's expectations of how they think a person from that city and that walk of life would sound. Just as importantly, you have to convince them with your body language—how you walk, stand, sit, gesture, move your head. What you don't want is a dialect that is overly conspicuous, and it will be if it is inconsistent—or even if it is too technically perfect.

You can learn a number of dialects by taking a class at your local college theatre department or at an acting studio. Also, several fine texts and CDs are on the market that teach the "standard" stage dialects. However, these approaches to dialect work are often too generic to be suited to a particular role in which you're cast. In response, then, *The Dialect Handbook* was written to answer all of your questions about preparing for a dialect role, including:

- Can anyone learn a dialect, or do some people just have a knack for it?
- How do I start? Are there practice tapes?
- Can't I just mimic someone else's dialect?
- Which dialects should I learn?
- What can I do to make sure it sounds believable?
- How heavy do I make the dialect?
- Do I need to adapt the "real" dialect for the stage?
- How should I mark the phonetic substitutions?
- Why is it important to research the culture?
- How do I get through an audition in dialect?
- How do I polish the dialect through rehearsals?
- How important is my character's body language?
- How do I keep it consistent?

This book offers a very practical approach to learning dialects that will be believable and accurate. It traces the entire process of creating a dialect role, from pre-production script analysis, through the rehearsal period, to opening night and beyond.

I'd like to note here that my **dialect aquisition method** has an emphasis that may be new to some students and dialect teachers. It directs actors to do in-depth research about the cultural background of the character. This may seem like a lot of work, but the approach has a definite purpose. As I've seen over and over in my work with dialect plays, definite connections can be made between a particular character's cultural background and her manner of speaking and moving. If you as an actor are looking for a "hook" (in other words, something you can use to get into the rhythm and feel of your dialect role), these cultural parallels can be an invaluable jumpstart—and they are readily available to you through careful research. You may choose to disregard this, and learn just the vowel and consonant substitutions of the accent, but you will merely be learning the mechanics of the speech, or trying to trust solely on your mimicking ability. The way your character expresses herself, both physically and vocally, will make *sense* once you study the people and their land. And, I guarantee that you will find that the sounds will come *much* more easily. There are a number of other dialect books that demonstrate the sounds of individual accents. For example, they teach you how to do an Irish accent. This book shows you how to *be* Irish.

The entire process outlined in this book is summarized for you in the **"Actor's Checklist"** which I've included in the last chapter. To demonstrate an application of the process, I've provided a **Dialect Acquisition Form** that has been filled out for a specific role in the Irish play *Dancing at Lughnasa*.

The extensive **Bibliography** will guide you in your research for your acting role. It describes all of the prominent dialect books and tapes/CDs, comparing and contrasting them, so that you will know how to use them. Also provided are addresses, web sites, and tips on how you may find or order these materials. *The Dialect Handbook* was designed to be a supplement to all of the resources available to you as you learn your accent.

With its wide range of dialect source and reference materials, the **Dialect Directory** at the back of the book will become your most vital resource in dialect acquisition. It lists hundreds of films, television programs, and audiotapes or CDs, providing accurate spoken examples of all of accents and dialects you will need. In addition, the Directory lists books and other resources that you can use to research a particular accent and its native speakers' culture. Finally, the Directory indicates which tapes and texts include guided instruction to help you master specific sounds used in the dialects. Be sure to check the **Index** to find all the pages where the topic you are studying is mentioned in the book.

In terms of the *Handbook*'s written style, a few words may be in order at this point. You may wonder about the book's use of the terms "accent" and "dialect." To Americans, an "accent" technically refers to a foreigner speaking American English, and a "dialect" is a variety of spoken language that occurs within a specific country or region. (For example, English spoken by a German, French, or Russian native would be considered "foreign accents," though there are numerous "dialects" spoken within each of these countries.) However, following the example of a number of other speech texts, the words "dialect" and "accent" will be used interchangeably in this text. Also, I have chosen to use "he" and "she" alternately when referring to a nonspecific director, playwright, or actor in order to avoid the cumbersome "he or she," "his or hers."

The entire text is written in a question-and-answer format, so you can easily find the information you're seeking. If you are a director or dialect coach, you will be able to use this book to lead your cast through the step-by-step process I've designed. For ease of reference, I use many examples and terms from popular films and plays. Please note, also, that the approach described is not limited to theatre. It can be directly applied to film, television, voice-overs, stand-up comedy, or any other live performance.

Finally, I'd like to comment on my use of cultural research in dialect acquisition. In this day and age, I realize it may be considered politically incorrect to recommend making generalizations about any culture, region, or group of people; and the kind of research I'm proposing here does indeed require the formulation of certain broad statements (at least initially in the process) to describe cultural or regional traits. However, I hope readers keep in mind that theatre is an art form that seeks ways to bring people together, to share our common humanity. It is certainly not my intention to give the mistaken impression that I see any culture as a mere collection of stereotypical "traits." I urge you to read my "author's notes" throughout this book, and to read the introductory material of the Dialect Directory to help you understand the efforts I'm taking in treading this ground of potential political incorrectness with compassion.

In explanation, then, I can only tell you that I use this focus on cultural characteristics simply because it works, and it can work very quickly. In the world of theatre and film, with their often-tight rehearsal schedules, this approach provides actors and dialect coaches with a valuable tool, one that helps actors to quickly integrate new speech rhythms and patterns, and new kinds of body language and movement, as they work to bring their dialect role vibrantly to life.

The Dialect Handbook will teach you how to research, acquire, and perfect a dialect so that you are able to apply it to a characterization that fits the play as a whole. After all, your dialect should be an organic part of who your character *is*, not a decoration. The audience should focus on the action of the play and its characters, not on your interesting dialect! Aristotle wrote that our craft as actors is to produce "art that imitates life." So, our challenge is to create (or rather, re-create) dialects that will be so believable that they will augment rather than distract from the play's story and message.

CHAPTER 1

AN INTRODUCTION
TO LEARNING DIALECTS

Can anyone learn a dialect?

Many people believe that either you have a "knack" for picking up accents or you don't—that no one really sits down and *learns* them. That's not so. It's true that some people can easily mimic accents they hear, just as some people can play the piano by ear without ever having a formal lesson. But most people are trainable. How long will it take? It depends on your aptitude for learning a new skill. Even if you're not a natural-born mimic, you can learn how to do credible dialects.

What skills do I need?

Learning dialects involves both your right and left brain—intuition, as well as logical analysis. It helps to have a *strong ability to mimic*, yes. In addition, you'll need *flexibility* to form new and sometimes strange mouth shapes for making certain sounds. Think of it as "learning dance steps for the mouth." Dialect acquisition also involves *muscle memory*, so that you can recall those dance steps. It definitely helps if you have an *understanding and recognition of phonetics*, but you can be trained in this. If you have any *aptitude for music*, you will be better able to hear and copy the rhythms and pitch changes of different dialects. You'll need *skill in interpretive character analysis*. Plus, I hope that I inspire in you a passionate *curiosity* about nationalities that differ from your own. While the process is similar to learning a foreign language, you don't have to have an aptitude for foreign language acquisition to be able to pick up dialects.

Overall, learning dialects will take *discipline* and *patience*. Certain accents will be harder for you than others, depending on whether you've developed the skills we've just talked about. But, according to my experience, once you've disciplined yourself to learn a few accents, others come more easily.

I recommend that you take a voice and diction course before you begin studying dialects. You need to become aware of how your speech mechanism works. You'll learn about vowel and consonant placement, resonance, tone quality, breathing, inflection, rate, rhythm, and overall expressiveness in your delivery. You'll discover your natural voice, and how to control it. This will help you to understand how to *change* your voice for dialects.

Which dialects should I learn?

For actors working in the U.S., the most useful dialects to learn, for stage or screen, are the two major regionalisms of American English: Northern (i.e., Brooklyn, Bronx, Boston) and Southern. You also need to know how to differentiate between the several different types of Southern dialects. For example, the dialects heard in Texas, Alabama, Kentucky, and Mississippi have distinctive qualities that set them apart.

The foreign accents most commonly heard in theatre or film are the British varieties, including RP, Cockney and North Country dialects. I also recommend you learn what can be called the Mediterranean accents (including Italian and many varieties of Spanish). Due to the popularity of recent films, Irish, Scottish, Australian, and Jamaican accents have also become important ones to master. Russian, German, and French accents were heard in many films and television shows in past years, particularly during World War II. You may notice that accents seem to come in and out of fashion, often depending on international politics. The past decades saw the emergence of a number of films and plays about South Africa, due to political unrest in that country. For similar reasons, we've been hearing more Middle Eastern accents on stage and screen.

For on-camera roles, where you're more likely to be typecast than you would in stage work, learn the accents of the nationalities that most closely fit your physical appearance. If you're not sure, ask your acting coach, your agent, or even your friends what nationalities they think you could play. For example, if you have dark features, your appearance might suggest that you are of Hispanic or Latin descent. In this case, you should learn an Italian accent and several different types of Spanish. Perhaps you could also play a Saudi Arabian, a Native American, or an Asian Indian.

Although there certainly are infinite variations, many ethnic types have certain physical characteristics that we often think of as being "typical." You must admit that red hair makes us first think of Irish characters. A rounder, more rugged look in the same coloring tends to look Scottish. (Eric Stoltz's natural red hair made him especially suited for his role in the Scottish film *Rob Roy*.) A paler, longer face (like that of John Cleese) may look more British. Do you have chiseled Germanic features? For French, we may think of sharper, thinner, more elegant features (à la Maurice Chevalier). The Swedish stereotype is one who is fair and blonde.

Be painfully honest with yourself about your own look. Just because you find a Japanese accent fascinating, there's little point in learning one unless you look Asian. For film, more than for stage, the actor with the true ethnic look would be cast. African-American actors would be wise to learn the Jamaican and African dialects, several Southern regionalisms, and the "urban dialects" or Ebonics, the much debated "Vernacular Black English." Don't trap yourself into one type of role in casting. Learn at least one other dialect.

Of course with voice-over work, typecasting doesn't apply, since your physical features do not matter. You can alter your voice to portray either sex, or any age or ethnic group. Voice-over artists and many comedians (stand-up, improv, and skit comedy) expand their talent by developing a number of believable dialects. These artists often need to be able to flip easily from one accent to another. Robin Williams won our admiration for just such ability.

Don't wait until you're cast in a dialect play to learn accents. Learn a number of them now, as an ongoing part of your training. Have them ready in your arsenal, so that you'll be able to do a cold reading or improvisation *tomorrow* for an audition. Then, when you're cast in a show, you can perfect a specific one.

How should my acting resumé list the dialects I can do?

Only list the dialects you feel so comfortable doing that you could ad-lib or cold-read in them when asked. As with the listing of foreign languages, first name those dialects you can do fluently, and then mention those you are somewhat proficient in. But don't be surprised if you get a sudden call to do a Polish accent, when you've only listed British, Southern, and German. Often, when actors list *any* dialects at all on their resumé, agents and casting directors assume they can do *all* dialects. This goes back to the average person's mistaken belief: that either people can do accents or they can't.

Are certain accents easier to learn than others?

In my experience teaching dialects, I've found that my clients were able to pick up the American Southern and Brooklyn accents the most easily. These dialects seem to be ones most American actors can mimic without a lot of drilling, if they can relax and get the feel of the character. Standard British seems easy at first, since it doesn't have many vowel and consonant changes. But the British accent has an ease in articulation and a smooth, melodic delivery that is so different from the middle-class American speech that it doesn't always come easily. The British manner of movement also takes some practice, particularly that of the educated upper class. Their posture and head carriage show a dignity and poise that reflect their proud history and breeding. They move their hands and feet with economy of effort. Most Americans move unreservedly and slouch comfortably!

The easiest foreign (non–English-based) accent to develop is Italian, due to its pure vowels and definitive dental placement (the tone is focused against the back of the upper teeth, making a word like "this" become "dees"). Italian is also an expressive, demonstrative accent that actors can more easily throw themselves into than they can the more restrained ones (like Asian or Russian). French and German are two of the toughest to master because they have so many vowel and consonant substitutions, as well as that unusual uvular "r" (done with the back of the tongue).

I have a natural regionalism. Will that hinder my dialect work?

If you have a strong regionalism or foreign accent, it may be perceptible through any accent you attempt to learn, depending on how much flexibility and control you have over your vocal instrument. Consider how your natural rhythm contrasts with the accent you're learning. Analyze how your overall mouth shape contrasts with the new accent.

For example, if you have a Puerto Rican accent, it's possible that you speak in a quick, staccato rhythm and use a narrow mouth opening, and you may leave off the ends of some words. If so, you'd have to learn a new manner of phrasing and of enunciating your final consonants in order to do most of the continental U.S. and European accents. If you have a strong Southern dialect, and you're attempting an Italian accent, for example, your vowels may be overly drawled out to form diphthongs when they should be pure vowels.

Did you know that "General American" is considered a dialect—one that actors who naturally speak with a regionalism or accent can learn? It's one that every actor should be able to flip into when the role demands it. General American (also called "neutral American" or "nonregional American" or "career speech") sounds as if you have no dialect at all, because it does not label you as being from any particular locale. It is perceived by many people to sound college educated and middle class to upper middle class. It is the type of speech generally expected of spokespersons, corporate executives, and other white-collar professionals. If you have a regionalism, Neutral American is the first dialect you should learn. If you do a nonregional American accent well, you can even list it on your resumé, along with the other dialects in which you are proficient. Learning it can only broaden your range as an actor.

The standard for good speech is much debated—and so is its terminology. "Standard American" is a term referring to a nonregional dialect that is considered more elevated than General American. Standard American is appropriate for upscale, English-speaking American characters. It is often called for when doing classical pieces in the U.S., such as the plays of Shakespeare, Moliere, or of the ancient Greeks, in cases when the director does not want the actors to sound British. Many modern speech and phonetic trainers have abandoned the term "Standard American" in favor of "American Stage Speech," and consider it to be a dialect that all actors should learn. Some refer to it as "Classical Stage Speech" or "Theatre Speech." It is taught by Edith Skinner in her text *Speak With Distinction*, and by Robert L. Hobbs in his book *Teach Yourself Transatlantic*.

Several stars have had to learn an American accent for film roles. Nicole Kidman has been praised for how she was able to drop her Australian accent for her role in *Batman Forever* and most of her recent roles. Many British actors, including Anthony Hopkins and Albert Finney (in *Erin Brockavich*), can do very fine American accents. British-born Kenneth Branagh developed both an American and a German accent for his two characters in *Dead Again*. Bob Hoskins was convincing as a New Yorker in *Who Framed Roger Rabbit*. You may be surprised to hear that his natural accent is closer to the Cockney he used in *Michael* and in *Hook*. American actors with thick Southern accents, too, have worked with a coach on a neutral American accent, like Holly Hunter did to prepare for her role in *Always*.

It's interesting to note that British speakers often find it easier to do a Brooklyn or an American Southern accent than to do a straight General American one. This is mainly because the American "r" is difficult to reproduce. Since Brooklyn and Deep South speakers drop the final "r," just as the British do, the sound doesn't pose a problem to speakers of British English. Kenneth Branagh played a perfect "Southern Gentleman Dixie soldier" character in *Wild, Wild West* opposite Will Smith. The hard "r" of the Texan accent is also fairly easy for them to reproduce, since it is such an exaggerated sound. And with both the New Yorker and Texan accents, the outspoken energy and strong stress patterns of the dialects provide British speakers with a noticeable contrast to their own country's customary reserve in manner. British speakers seem to be able to do a

Texan or Brooklyn character more easily, since they are able to exaggerate the character's typical vocal and nonverbal traits.

So, for American roles, to "lose an accent" is actually to learn the General American accent, and all American (as well as non-American) actors would be well advised to study this dialect. In the same way, actors in other nations who have regionalisms should learn the standard, educated speech of their own country. Arnold Schwarzenegger worked for months and months with a dialect coach to lose his Austrian accent before he began filming *Twins*. For him, to learn an American accent would have been silly, because he was already known for his continental mystique. Instead, Schwarzenegger learned a High German dialect, which is perceived as more educated, stronger, and clearer than the Austrian one.

You may have to standardize your speech before learning certain dialects that contrast radically from your own speech pattern. There are a number of speech trainers who teach accent reduction, if you need private sessions that go beyond what a regular voice and diction course would cover. I have developed a 3-CD set with book, *Accent Reduction Workshop for Professional American Speech*, that can help you to practice your nonregional American speech. See the final page of this book for more information.

Once you've addressed your own regionalism, you can begin to build the skills you need in order to do believable dialects, and do them well. This book will introduce a well-tested method of dialect acquisition—a method that really *works*—so you don't have to depend solely on "knack" to master a character voice. You will be certain that your dialect is consistent, accurate, and utterly convincing.

CHAPTER 2

AUDITION PREPARATION
FOR A DIALECT PLAY

How should I begin to prepare for an audition in dialect?

To prepare for a dialect play, first obtain accurate audition information. Find out from a *reliable* source (such as the director or his assistant) if the play is, in fact, going to be done in dialect. Don't make assumptions. Just because a theatre company has Joe Orton's *Loot* or Noel Coward's *Blithe Spirit* in its season line-up, this doesn't mean the director will necessarily choose to use a British dialect in the production. He may want to move the piece to an American locale. Or he may go without a dialect due to time constraints or available talent. If any of these are the case, *hopefully* that particular script adapts well without losing anything. Certain phrases and place names may have to be edited out or reworded. Relocating the setting of a play is no easy task, at least for most realistic pieces. If a story is an historic or cultural piece, it would likely lose much of its impact if done in American accents. But some directors feel that if they don't have the time or resources to ensure that the accents are done perfectly, they'd be better off not trying them at all. The best policy is to check before you invest energy in learning a dialect for an audition.

If you do find out that the play will be done in dialect, ask the director if a dialect will be *preferred* or *required* for the audition. Some directors find attempts at dialects distracting, while others want to hear a light attempt. Still others expect them to be fully polished. You may also run into a director who doesn't care one way or another, or who has made no decision on the matter because he assumes the actors who are cast will learn the dialect on their own and magically have it perfected by opening night.

Most directors would certainly be impressed when someone comes into an audition with a good dialect. Why? Because an actor reading in the appropriate dialect is more likely to seem like a natural "fit" for the role. I've observed many auditions for shows I was preparing to coach, and I've noticed this: actors auditioning in dialect often land the role, even over a more "talented" actor who couldn't do the dialect. Don't make the director "imagine" you as the Russian character—*be* the Russian character. Have a consistent, clear dialect that is light enough to allow your character to shine through. This will show that you are professional, disciplined, and ultimately trainable. The director will be able to see this even if your audition accent is more of a general standard rather than the specific accent of the play's city, era, or style. If you're uncertain about what the director is looking for in the accent, it's okay to ask him if you're going in the right direction with your character's speech.

Another important question to ask the director concerns the *format* of the audition. If he asks for a prepared monologue or a reading from selected scenes, you could learn the dialect sound by sound, just for those pieces. But if the format requires improvisation or cold reading, you'll need to be quite adept with the dialect, able to ad-lib with ease.

Finally, find out if the director has hired a dialect coach as part of the production team, who will be available to help you learn and polish the dialect through rehearsals. If he hasn't hired a coach, perhaps he could recommend one with whom you could train privately. Ideally, you would have a few dialect sessions with the coach well before the audition.

What do I do regarding my dialect at callbacks?

If you are invited to a callback audition, a good rule of thumb is not to completely change your dialect (unless directed to do so), but to show some improvement. That will further impress the casting director as to your seriousness about the role and your craft. If possible, before your callback ask the director what improvements he is looking for in terms of your speech and dialect.

Are there dialect CDs and texts I can study, in order to learn an accent on my own?

There are a number of texts and tapes or CDs available that provide instruction on how to do specific accents. Some of the methods, like David Alan Stern's *Acting with an Accent* tape series and Jerry Blunt's *Stage Dialects,* have been well known for years. And there are new resources out on CDs, and even on the web. You can locate these by looking in the Bibliography of this text, which includes publication information for all of the available programs, as well as ordering information and web sites. The books, tapes and CDs can be ordered online, purchased in bookstores, or possibly borrowed from the library. In terms of choosing which ones to buy, be aware that each instructional method has its own strengths and weaknesses. The best advice is to study and compare what each program has to say about the dialect you're currently learning.

The following section is an overview of the prominent dialect acquisition texts and CDs. I will compare and contrast them, and offer practical tips on how to use them along with this book. As you prepare a particular dialect, I recommend you study as many of the methods I'm outlining here as you can find, and compare for yourself what they have to offer.

David Alan Stern's *Acting with an Accent*

David Alan Stern's method for dialect acquisition has become prominent in the last decade because of how he approaches the sounds of a dialect through its "tone focus." His series of one-hour tapes with texts are called *Acting with an Accent*. His revised editions are all on CD. Lessons for individual dialects can be purchased separately, through his web site, or directly from his company, Dialect Specialists, Inc. Many large libraries carry the entire set. Stern's lessons begin with a clear explanation and drills on the resonance. He explains how to use a "kinesthetic trick" to trigger the correct point of focus in the mouth. For example, for Cockney, he created this kinesthetic trick: "Try pretending that the sound is an insect and that you are an animal gulping at that bug. Your goal is to catch and swallow the sound in one movement."[1]

Following the resonance drills, Stern demonstrates the lilt and stress patterns peculiar to that accent, with related pronunciation changes. The phoneme changes (vowel and consonant substitutions) are introduced next, using the IPA (International Phonetic Alphabet, an international system of transcribing human sounds), as well as the symbols created by Arthur Lessac. (Lessac's symbols for the "structural vowels" are explained in his well-known book on vocal production, *The Use and Training of the Human Voice*.) If you haven't been drilled in the use of these symbol systems in a vocal course, it can be a bit confusing at first. But you can refer to Stern's chart at the beginning of his text.

Stern leads the self-taught dialect student through coached drills of words, then sentences, then passages, leaving space on the CD for the actor to mimic. He speaks in the accent almost the entire time. He shares tips on how to achieve the lightest flavor of the accent, and how to strengthen it all the way to stereotypical proportions for comic effect.

He does offer isolated changes and a few variations in the dialect to differentiate among various regions from which different characters might come. But he does not speak directly about the character of the dialect's native speakers. This is unfortunate, because this kind of information could give the actor insights into the reasons for the particular resonance and melody he suggests. Stern concludes by reciting a passage, usually from a famous poem or song, marked for the dialect in IPA.

Other dialect trainers tend to agree that the only disadvantage to this series is that Stern has recorded all the dialect tapes himself, with no sample cuts of primary-source (authentic) speakers, and he tends to bring a flavor of his own New York accent to his dialect work.[2] Stern does not suggest the importance of finding primary sources. But his method is revolutionary and extremely helpful and clear. So, if you use his tapes, be sure to also listen to native speakers.

Jerry Blunt's *Stage Dialects* and *More Stage Dialects*

Another very well-known dialect acquisition method is Jerry Blunt's *Stage Dialects*, though now considered somewhat dated, as he collected the clips in the 1970s. His textbook with its accompanying audiocassettes includes instruction for Japanese, Brooklynese, American Southern, Standard British, Cockney, Irish, Scots, French, Italian, German, and Russian dialects. In each case, following a very brief introduction about the dialect, he focuses on its vowel and consonant substitutions. (Substitutions means consistent changes of specific vowel and consonant sounds). He drills the actor on words, then phrases, then fluency in sentences, using an approach that is similar to Stern's format, leaving a space on the tape for you to mimic each exercise.

Blunt does not address the lilt and placement, as David Alan Stern does. Yet, he does give several examples of authentic dialects on his tapes. You're not told, however, when the example is a secondary source (a scene or reading done in dialect by a non-native speaker, such as himself or another actor). He uses IPA notations, which he teaches in an opening chapter. But his passages are not notated in IPA, as in the Stern text.

Especially helpful is Blunt's list of special pronunciations of proper names, idioms, and common expressions. (I think it's also important to know the fiery slang and curse words of a particular dialect, but so far none of the instructional methods have dared to teach these!) For example, many Italians speaking English as a second language incorporate a lot of Italian phrases into their English speech. Blunt drills the correct pronunciation of common phrases like "Buon giorno," "Ciao," "Prego," and "Bene, grazie." This is important, because sometimes we think we're pronouncing these foreign phrases and place names correctly when we're not. You could possibly use some of the slang and common expressions that Blunt suggests to salt and pepper your speech with, when improvising in your accent.

With Blunt's method, be aware that each dialect he teaches is a "standard" (generic) one for the stage—he doesn't distinguish between the rural or urban, northern or southern speech of any of them. For example, Blunt teaches an Irish accent without differentiating it from that of Northern Ireland. His American Southern is the Plantation Southern (with the dropped "r," as spoken by Scarlett O'Hara, Blanche DuBois, "Golden Girls" actress Rue McClanahan, and Tom Hanks in *Forrest Gump*). No mention is made of the other variation of American Southern, with its hard "r's," which is the dialect spoken in many of the cowboy films. Possibly the reason Blunt doesn't offer the regional variations within a country is because his book is an older one, originally compiled in 1967—an era when learning a generic stage standard was adequate. The text has been rereleased for a new publication and is now in paperback.

In 1980, Jerry Blunt produced *More Stage Dialects*, with over fifty transcribed samples of dialects from a wide selection of locales. With few exceptions, all of the passages are conversational, which is ideal for hearing the natural rhythms, inflections, and idioms of running speech. In the text, each dialect sample is preceded by a very brief paragraph of introduction. This book includes maps of each region, which is an invaluable resource to your studies.

Professor Blunt is no longer with us, but in 1994 the Blunt family released the rights to go into a second edition. You might be able to find the Blunt books in the reference section of a library. They've been commonly used as course textbooks, so you may be able to borrow them from a generous teacher or former dialect student. The *Stage Dialect* text without the tapes could still be somewhat helpful if you listen to other resources. The *More Stage Dialects* text, however, would be fairly worthless without the tapes.

Gillian Lane-Plescia's *Dialects and Accents for Actors*

Especially for learning the British-based dialects, Gillian Lane-Plescia has produced the most current set of tapes. The author, a native of England, speaks in a lovely British accent. She has tapes with small, handy booklets on Standard British, Cockney,

Scots, Irish, South African, Australian, Welsh, Liverpool, and the North Country (northern England), each sold separately. Using IPA, her method launches immediately into the vowel and consonant substitutions, followed by a very brief discussion of the lilt. The substitutions are kept to a minimum, which makes the dialects easy to grasp.

The most outstanding feature of Lane-Plescia's method is that she has collected a variety of excellent authentic sources. She is careful to tell the listener exactly what region each speaker is from, as well as their occupation, which suggests their class. She has two or three different speakers read a word list and colorful practice sentences. Then Lane-Plescia presents her recordings of the conversational speech of male and female natives from various regions, vocations, and personality types. All of these people speak clearly enough to be appropriate for the stage (though sometimes their energy level is low, making the melody flatter than an actor should use on the stage).

The other significant feature of Lane-Plescia's format is her list of a few other primary sources to investigate, such as current films and PBS programs. The author has recently completed a series of additional tapes on American Southern dialects, the major European accents, Accents for Black Actors, and new varieties of Standard British. You can also purchase individual tapes on various other dialects through her "Personalized British-based Dialect Service" by contacting her directly. Check the Bibliography of this text for her web address.

Paul Meier's *IDEA and Accents and Dialects for Stage and Screen*

Paul Meier, professor of Theatre and Film at the University of Kansas and one of today's most prominent dialect experts, has created the first on-line archive of primary source recordings, called IDEA (International Dialects of English Archives), with assistance by Shawn Muller. Added to daily, this fabulous compilation has over 400 recordings of native speakers, in both English language dialects and accents of other languages. The speakers read test passages, like "Comma Gets a Cure," as well as speak spontaneously. These recordings are the most current resources available of contemporary speakers, which is an invaluable tool for your research.

Professor Meier also published *Accents and Dialects for Stage and Screen*. This is an 8-CD set with a 174-page instructional book, with IPA transcriptions to help you learn the dialects. Paul Meier has many services and resources to offer on his web page at www.paulmeier.com.

Lewis and Marguerite Herman's *American Dialects* and *Foreign Dialects*

The Hermans wrote two popular texts back in the '40s and '50s which have been recently updated for a second publication by Routledge/Theatre Arts Books. Though these texts have no tapes accompanying them, I still recommend them as a valuable resource. The Herman books confirm what is presented in this book: that many of the speech characteristics of a dialect can be directly attributed to facets of a nation's cultural character. Each chapter offers a short but wonderfully pithy discussion of that nation or region's character, and how it affects the manner of speech of its people. Definitely try to find the Herman texts, if just for this section alone. In the *American Dialects* book, each chapter even has a map to clarify the region in the U.S. where the particular dialect is spoken.

The Hermans' section on lilt and stress shows a few phrases notated as musical notes on a scale—a good idea, but without any demonstration this may be clear only to actors who sight-read music. Then the vowel and consonant changes are introduced. The authors don't use IPA, but their own "phonetic respelling," which is fairly easy to understand once you get used to it. I find that most actors are not as proficient in IPA as they should be, unless they've just graduated from a conservatory or university theatre program where it was taught. Here are a few examples of the Hermans' phonetic respelling for the Tidewater (or Plantation) Southern accent. The word "there" is respelled "THAuh," "temper" is respelled "timPUH," "dog" is "dAW-OHg," and "man" is "MAin."[3]

The drawback to this method is the huge number of vowel and consonant changes they cover. They give so many substitutions and exceptions that an actor is likely to give up. The substitutions for the Mountain dialect of Kentucky and Tennessee go on for twenty-two pages. David Alan Stern and Gillian Lane-Plescia do a better job of helping an actor figure out which are the *major* vowel and consonant changes for an accent. If you know the most *important* substitutions, you will be able to grasp the dialect more quickly and be able to adjust it to its lightest form when necessary.

The grammar changes in the Hermans' books are priceless, because they really give you insights into your character's manner of speech. This could be of more importance to writers than to actors. (In fact, the text is subtitled *A Manual for Actors, Directors, and Writers*.) But if you were ad-libbing or were adapting your role to a dialect that was different from the one that was originally intended, the grammar changes and unique pronunciations would be a boon. When it comes to certain foreign accents that are rich in broken English or slang, the grammar is vital to the flavor of the speech. Here's an example of a few grammar changes for the Southern dialect: "How come you ain't never growed corn?" for "Why haven't you ever grown corn?" and "I'm fixin' to go that-a-way" for "I'm preparing to go that way."[4] (Do remember, as you study any of these books I'm mentioning, that the material may be dated. Slang and grammar change over the years, and the modern-day Cockney, for example, may have little use for the Cockney rhyming slang that spiced up the speech of his ancestors. If you pick up the older Herman text from 1947, its chapter on "The Negro Dialect" would certainly be considered politically incorrect today, and has been changed in the updated publication.)

The Hermans close each chapter with a few monologues from plays. These are fun to read, since they are written in dialect, or "eye dialect," as they call it. The monologues in *Foreign Dialects* are also rewritten in phonetic respelling. These would be valuable to have on tape, but at the time of these books' publication, tape recorders were not commonplace, being the cumbersome reel-to-reel models. These monologues do, however, give an excellent (if somewhat stereotypical) picture of their particular cultures, because the characters speak about their own attitudes and lifestyles. Especially since no tapes are available to support this work, I found it surprising that the Hermans do not suggest where (or even *if*) their readers should go to listen to dialects being spoken. Still, it should be remembered that in the Hermans' era, dialect students had far fewer source materials available to them. Films on video and DVD (which provide today's most convenient examples of spoken dialects) were unavailable to the Hermans' original readers.

Evangeline Machlin's *Dialects for the Stage*

Evangeline Machlin has devoted her life to studying and collecting recordings of dialects from people all over the globe. She put together a set of tapes and a manual called *Dialects for the Stage* in 1975, employing a "play it and say it" technique of imitation. She covers over twenty of the most commonly used American and foreign dialects. You should still be able to order or find *Dialects for the Stage* in bookstores.

The manual contains transcripts of conversational speeches, with some pronunciation guidelines. Rather than using IPA, she created a type of phonetic respelling, which is even easier to follow than the one used in the Hermans' text. For example, "please" would be spelled "plEEz," and "save" would be spelled "sAYv." Every speech is phonetically respelled, so that you can follow along as you listen. On one cut per accent, she leaves a space for you to mimic, line by line. One dialectician critiqued it this way:

> "Tapes are of uneven quality; some are quite good, while others are either difficult to understand or seem to have been made by capable students rather than native speakers. A chief value of the tapes is that they include multiple examples of each dialect."[5]

She generally clarifies the class, occupation, and energy level of the tapes' speakers, but we're not always sure if a particular cut is a primary or secondary source. At the end of each chapter, she lists several plays in which characters speak in dialect, and a few recordings for study.

Machlin emphasizes a vital point: that melody (or lilt) is the key to the aural impression of most dialects. Look for her vocal production book, *Speech for the Stage*. It has an excellent chapter on dialect acquisition in which she notates on a musical scale phrases from several accents, using dots of differing sizes to give you an idea of how long to hold out stress words. This seems a little less daunting than the Hermans' method of using actual musical notes. Machlin gives wise advice when she says that the actor must eat, sleep, and breathe in the new dialect until it becomes natural.

J. C. Wells's *Accents of English*

Wells collected some great samples of twenty different accents, all of which are English-based dialects. He briefly introduces each cut, telling you a little about the speaker and what sounds and special pronunciations to listen for. There are several samples of each dialect, which is useful for comparison of neighboring regions. You can refer to the brief booklets included, which list the dominant vowel and consonant changes. All of the samples are excellent, with the exception of the American ones, which don't really sound strong enough to be recognizable as Southern, New Yorker, or Canadian. See the Bibliography for a list of the accents he covers.

Donald Molin's *Actor's Encyclopedia of Dialects*

The *Actor's Encyclopedia of Dialects*, by Donald Molin, originally came out in 1991 to teach foreign accents. The American dialects are not covered. Sometimes bookstores or reference sections of libraries carry the text, but many seem to have either lost or never ordered the accompanying tape. Molin introduces the derivation of each dialect, then explains its vowel and consonant changes. He uses a rather confusing set of his own phonetic transcription. The charts of sounds for different regionalisms within a country are quite difficult to understand, but could prove to be very helpful for finding just the right speech pattern for a particular city, and a character's social class, formality, sex and age. Some of the charts show stronger vowel and consonant substitutions than I would recommend for the best clarity on stage. Music, rhythm, and pace are discussed. Molin makes suggestions for movies in which one can hear the dialects he discusses. Unfortunately the films aren't very current, nor are they the very best examples of the accents. Molin's is the only dialect text with photos, which is a wonderful idea. The photos are of actors in his suggested films, which can help you sense the essence of the people who speak in that dialect.

Hughes and Trudgill's *English Accents and Dialects*

A valuable resource that is perhaps less well known in this country (and is thus difficult to find in stores or libraries) is *English Accents and Dialects* by Arthur Hughes and Peter Trudgill. The tape is an excellent opportunity to hear primary sources tell stories about their lives. Personality, expression, and melody ring out, with all the realistic fillers, coughs, and sniffs. You feel as if you are sitting right there in the speaker's living room having a conversation. This is one of the best instructional tapes available for you to listen to in order to perceive the organic *feel* of different dialects. Ten different regions in the British Isles are covered in this method.

Just one thing to take note of about the tapings: since each person is speaking casually, unaware of a need for good diction, sometimes it's hard to catch what they're saying. An actor on stage would have to be clearer than these examples. Hughes and Trudgill do write out each person's entire speech in their text, so that you can follow along. The speeches are not transcribed into IPA.

The text is short but very detailed, and not an easy study for actors, even if they know the IPA. It seems to be aimed at the academic dialectician, since the authors use all kinds of phonetic terms that actors may not be familiar with, like "affrication," "velarization," and "post alveolar frictionless continuant."

Trudgill and Hannah's *International English*

Peter Trudgill teamed up with Jean Hannah to create a guide to the many varieties of English that are spoken around the world. The taped examples are good demonstrations of the vowel and consonant substitutions. But the drawback to *International English* is that each person on the tape does a reading rather than spontaneous speaking, which does not give the true flavor of the music, grammar, or personality of their speech. Some people with wonderful accents just happen to be dull readers. Hannah and Trudgill introduce RP (Received Pronunciation, which is Standard British; also called Oxford or BBC British), and then samples from Australia, South Africa, Wales, Canada, the U.S., Scotland, Ireland, the West Indies, West Africa, and India. The IPA symbols are used in the list of vowel and consonant pronunciations. However, the passages being read in the text are not transcribed, which would have been helpful.

This text gives a detailed examination of grammar and vocabulary which is difficult to sift through, but is certainly worth the effort. In the grammar section on Scottish, the authors list such changes as: "How are you keeping?" for "How are you doing?" and "That's me away" for "I'm going now," and "It's the back of nine o'clock" for "It's soon after nine o'clock."[6]

Should I get a dialect coach?

If the production team has not hired a dialect coach or vocal director, it certainly would be to your advantage to get someone to tutor you in the accent. An experienced dialect coach can teach it, demonstrate it, and adapt it to suit the particular role you're up for. They can show you how strong to make it, assessing how much you can realistically learn in the time frame you have before the audition. I've had actors frantically call me the day before a television or film audition that they just found out about. I've even given coaching over the phone in such situations, if they already have some grasp of the dialect. I hate to admit it, but I've helped many actors "fake their way through the audition" by giving them quick tips on how to achieve the lightest flavor of the dialect, by discussing the character and the overall feel, placement, and rhythm of the region's speech. I'm not recommending you allow yourself to get stuck in this difficult position. But last-minute notice for auditions seems to be the nature of the film and television business, so you need to be prepared with quick ways to get to a realistic accent. This book was written to share just such secrets with you.

Where do I find a coach?

Call acting schools and university theatre programs to see if they have a dialect specialist on their faculty, or if they can recommend someone who is freelance. Call equity and community theatres and ask the directors if they know a coach, and ask other local actors who they go to. Dialect coaches probably advertise in local trade papers or theatre publications.

Be sure to find someone who specializes in dialects for the stage, since not all vocal coaches are dialect trainers. There are a number of competent speech coaches who can teach you how to soften or lose your regionalism, but they may not be proficient in stage dialects. And, although you may find natives who speak in the accent you need, they do not necessarily know how to teach it. More about what to expect when working on a production with a dialect coach is included in Chapters 7 and 8.

Can you suggest an OUTLINE I can fill out for the dialect I'm learning?

On the following pages is the Dialect Acquisition Form I designed for my students. As you study the dialect texts and tapes/CDs described in this chapter (and/or work with a coach), and as you continue your research about the culture and speech of your character, you can take notes on the areas that are outlined on the form. I encourage you to make a copy of it for each of the dialects you learn in the future.

The order of the points on the form is especially important: notice that you learn about the dialect's people and their culture first, and the vowel and consonant substitutions last. Notice that the initial key word for each of the vowels make sentences, i.e., "Lee will let Ann pass," "Turn over the cup," "Sue would call on father," "Go pay my boy now, beautiful." Memorize these. If sometime you don't have the chart with you and are listening to a dialect for which you want to transcribe the substitutions, you can write these sentences down the page, and jot down what they change to. Then you will know you've included every one of the vowel sounds.

All of the elements on this Dialect Acquisition outline will be clarified as we go along. To help you envision an application of the process laid out in this book, Chapter 9 includes an example of this outline filled out completely for a specific Irish role from *Dancing at Lughnasa*.

DIALECT ACQUISITION
for _____

STEPS:

1. CULTURAL CHARACTERISTICS: Research/discuss with the director the character of the people and their land (social class, economic level, education, culture, etc.)

2. YOUR CHARACTER: Now consider, in light of this cultural environment, how your individual character expresses himself/herself vocally and physically (how his/her voice and movement is a reflection of energy level, drive, self esteem, occupation, health, education, personality traits, parentage and other biographical information)

3. TONE FOCUS / Placement:

   Kinesthetic trigger:

   Manner of articulation:

(From *The Dialect Handbook* by Ginny Kopf)

4. VOCAL PATTERNS / describe the "music" of the speech:

     Inflection patterns:

     Rhythm and phrasing:

     Tempo/speed:

     Stress patterns:

     Volume/intensity:

5. BODY LANGUAGE OF THE CULTURE / movement and manners, typical dress:

6. List SPECIAL PRONUNCIATIONS, unusual phrases, idioms, slang, expletives, grammar changes:

7. VOWEL SUBSTITUTIONS:

IPA	Dictionary	Key words	Substitutions
[i]	ē	Lee, need, seal	=
[ɪ]	ĭ	will, is, window	=
[ɛ]	ĕ	let, end, step	=
[æ]	ă or a	Ann, can, pat	=
[a]	ȧ or a	pass, ask, dance	=
[ɝ]	ur, ûr, or ur	turn, early, certain	=
[ɚ]	ər	over, mother, actor	=
[ə]	ə	the, honest, above	=
[ʌ]	ŭ or u	cup, luck, love	=
[u]	o͞o	Sue, noon, school	=
[ʊ]	o͝o	would, look, put	=
[ɔ]	ô, o, or aw	call, Paul, law	=
[ɒ]	ŏ	on, honest, long	=
[ɑ]	ä or ŏ	father, drama, large	=

DIPHTHONGS:

IPA	Dictionary	Key words	Substitutions
[o] or [oʊ]	ō	go, own, most	=
[e] or [eɪ]	ā	pay, ache, save	=
[aɪ]	ī	my, I, nice	=
[ɔɪ]	oi	boy, oil, royal	=
[aʊ]	ou or au	now, pound, around	=
[ju]	ū or yoo	beautiful, music, few,	=

R-COLORING: key sentence

ur   ər   o͞or   ōr   ĭr   īr   ĕr   ăr   är

Fern's father is sure the four fearful fires barely carried far.

8. CONSONANT SUBSTITUTIONS:

IPA	Dictionary	Key words		Substitutions
[p]	p	pop, hope, appeal	=	
[b]	b	bob, grab, fabulous	=	
[t]	t	taught, great, fated	=	
[d]	d	dad, food, radical	=	
[k]	k	kick, cake, exclude	=	
[g]	g	gag, dig, argue	=	
[m]	m	mom, same, summer	=	
[n]	n	none, seen, sentence	=	
[ŋ]	ng	sing, ringing, having	=	
[f]	f	fife, safe, fifty, phone	=	
[v]	v	very, live, every	=	
[s]	s	sister, pass, face	=	
[z]	z	zones, buzz, loses	=	
[θ]	th	thin, bath, method	=	
[ð]	th	this, bathe, mother	=	
[ʃ]	sh	show, fish, direction	=	
[ʒ]	zh	pleasure, treasure, beige	=	
[h]	h	how, hello, inhale	=	
[r]	r	roar, rear, foreign	=	
[l]	l	lily, still, follow	=	
[hw]	wh	where, why, what	=	
[w]	w	wow, win, growl	=	
[j]	y	yes, yellow, you	=	
[tʃ]	ch	church, picture, question	=	
[dʒ]	dg or j	judge, manage, region	=	

ADDITIONAL CHANGES:

CHAPTER 3

SCRIPT ANALYSIS
FOR A DIALECT PLAY

When I first read the play, what am I looking for?

The very first time you read the play, don't get caught up in the technical details of how you're going to do the dialect. Remember that the play is a story that will move people, not a showcase for your dialect. Read it straight through for your initial gut-level responses to the play as a whole—its story, mood, characters, and images, and how the playwright communicates her ideas through the language. Read the play several times, writing down your early impressions. Try to catch the *spirit* of the play and its characters. This is very important because the feel of the dialect, the very *root* of the dialect, is right in the text—in its rhythm, melody, tone, and manner of articulation.

Keep in mind that the author wrote the play to be performed in dialect. That's how she heard it in her head. The dialect wasn't tacked on as an afterthought like a last-minute costume piece: it happens to be the way the people of that world she created express themselves. So let the feel of the characters and how they express themselves *wash over you* as you read the play. Use your imaginative right brain, rather than your analytical left brain.

Once I'm cast, what kind of script analysis do I do? Is it different than the one I'd do for a straight play?

Script analysis for a dialect role is the same kind of analysis that you've already learned for straight plays, as outlined in one of your acting textbooks. (Frances Hodge's *Play Direction* outlines a clear character analysis, as does Barton's *Acting, Onstage and Off.*) However, a dialect play will definitely demand more work than a straight play. You'll find the workload similar to that of being in a period play, where you research the era, or of being in a musical, where you learn songs and dances in separate rehearsals. When cast in a dialect show, you will do daily drills and cultural research, in addition to your regular character analysis and line-learning. The remainder of this book will lead you through the process, step by step, all the way through your closing night.

What kind of notes should I be taking as I study the script?

You've already read the play, noting your first emotional impressions. On subsequent readings you can become more technical in taking notes on the given circumstances—the who, what, when, where, why, and how. Get specific about the "where" (the country, the region, the city). Look it up on a map—don't guess. Find out what countries and regions surround it. This will be important to your overall grasp of the dialect, because the speech of a border city usually takes on the qualities of both of its neighbors. Here are some examples. Once you look on a map and see where Liverpool is in England, it makes sense that it sounds somewhat Cockney, but with the upward lilt of the Northern Irish dialect. It is right across the channel from Belfast, Ireland. Many of the northern English and northern Irish towns have that upward inflection that many people recognize as Scottish: Scotland is the closest neighbor. Now locate Wales on the map. The Welsh dialect has sounds that are a cross between British and Irish. Knowing a little bit about the speech of bordering countries will help you learn the region's accent.

If your play is set in an imaginary city, ask the director about her vision for the play's locale and how you should carry out your research. Brian Friel's notes about his Irish play *Dancing at Lughnasa* place it in County Donegal, in a small, rural town he calls Balleybeg. Even though Ballybeg is a fictitious town, Denise Gillman (the director for the Central Florida premiere) showed her cast exactly where in that northwestern Irish county she envisioned Ballybeg. This was important because she knew that the dialect needed to be absolutely realistic. In fact, any dramatic work which is set in an exotic, fictitious locale (*The Mouse That Roared*, for example) needs to have a consistent dialect—though not necessarily a geographically accurate one.

You may be called upon to invent an accent if your character is from a fictitious locale. You may remember comic actor Bronson Pinchot's character, Balki, in the '80s TV series "Perfect Strangers." He claimed he was from an exotic country in the Far East that viewers had never heard of. Pinchot created an entertaining and unusual dialect that sounded like a cross between five different foreign accents, to give his character an eccentric charm. In the TV series "Taxi," Andy Kaufman (as the "foreign-born" Latke) and his wife (played by Carol Kane) spoke not only in a charming new dialect but invented a whole language. Actors depicting characters from other planets often must come up with "otherwordly" accents. Peter Jurasik, in playing Londo, the first Centauri in "Babylon 5" (the "Star Trek" spin-off) used an accent that mixed the speech he remembered from his Czech grandmother, a character in *Clockwork Orange*, and an Irish guy he knew. And the speech pattern of Jar Jar Binks, the babbling amphibian Gungan who helps the heroes in *Star Wars, Episode I: The Phantom Menace*, was created by George Lucas and written out phonetically for the voice actor to learn.

Though most dialect texts and tapes teach a "standard" accent for each country, we know that there are actually many dialects within a country. In France there are dozens of different regionalisms, though the Parisian version is the one most commonly chosen for an educated French character. In Scotland, the further north you go, the stronger the dialect gets. Afrikaans is a very specific South African dialect, and sounds different from Black South African. We remember the character of Henry Higgins, the dialectologist in the musical *My Fair Lady*, who can recognize English dialects that vary practically from one street to the next.

In Germany, one's dialect is not so much an indicator of class as it is of locale. As in France, there are numerous regional variations, though for stage, people usually choose to do a Berliner accent. This "High German" is the standard written and spoken form in Germany today. It was originally spoken in the southern and central uplands (hence its name). "Low German" was spoken in the northern plains, and is still heard in most farm areas. In classy, metropolitan Hamburg, High German is the standard. Berlin is in the east, with an even more exact High German. Frankfurt is in the west, and the speech is quick, colorful, and more run together (like the Bavarian dialect), reflecting the region's less formal, less competitive reputation. It's interesting how German speech patterns tend to mirror the patterns in popular German folk music. Northern music is march-like and heavily stressed; the further south one travels, the more melodic, playful, and loosely structured the music becomes.

A challenging dialect role is one in which your character needs to have a mix of two or more accents. For example, if your character was raised in one country but has picked up qualities of another. The role of Lady in Tennessee Williams' *Orpheus Descending* requires the mixed speech of a native Italian transplanted to Mississippi. In the play, *Candide*, the Old Woman speaks with a blend of Polish, Spanish, Russian and a number of other accents she's assimilated in her travels. Or what if the character is "putting on" an accent to impress or fool someone? In *Rock Star*, the lead tries to fake an English accent when he gets a gig with a rock band. Val Kilmer puts on a number of accents as *The Saint*, a freelance thief, to fool his worthy adversaries. If cast in these types of roles, you would have to carefully sort out if the accent needs to be intentionally bad or intentionally well done, and whether it should come across comical or dramatic. Get a dialect coach to help you score out which sounds to choose from both accents, and how to make it believable.

As you continue to analyze your play, other important things to note, besides locale, are any other character details that might affect the character's speech. What is their socioeconomic level, their education, the extent of their travel, their role models, personality, health, energy, jobs, activities? The character of Rose in *Dancing at Lughnasa* is emotionally disturbed, and the actress playing her must discover a manner of speech that sounds like a two-year-old in an adult's body. Her tone and rhythms could be more erratic than the traditional Irish lilt of her sisters. In contrast, the speech of the sensible eldest sister, Kate, could be more steady and precise than her sisters, to reflect that she is an educated schoolteacher who feels overly responsible for the welfare of her family. Chapter 4 delves further into how your character analysis will help you develop the right speech patterns for your role.

How does the director's concept affect my script and character analysis?

If the director's concept is not clear to you as rehearsals begin, ask questions of the director to try to get a grasp of her vision for the play in terms of style and mood. It's especially important to know how she sees your character in comparison to the other characters. Work to clarify to yourself the choices she's made, so that you know in what direction to begin research, keeping in mind that she (or you) may change directions later.

The director may choose to make your character a different nationality than the one the script calls for, or a different energy type. For example, Sergeant Match in Joe Orton's *What the Butler Saw* was played well as a laid-back Jamaican in one production that I dialect coached, and as an intense Irishman in another. One director decided to make Nick the bellboy Liverpudlian instead of the usual Cockney. This brought interest to his character because it is such a curious accent. It actually heightened the character's comic potential, since the slow rhythm and loose diction of the Liverpudlian bellboy contrasted with the rapid-fire delivery of the educated London characters. The next time I coached that play, Nick played it in Standard British, which had the surprising result of accentuating his persuasiveness and sensuality.

The director may give you freedom to improv or ad-lib. If so, you'd have to be so fluent in the dialect that you could not only sightread in dialect but be able to ad-lib in dialect without inconsistencies. Professional improv performers need to develop skills to switch dialects effortlessly.

How do cuts or additions in the text affect the dialect?

If the director has made any cuts or additions to the script, it could affect the rhythm and flow of your character's speech. Hopefully, the cuts or additions were done with extreme care and with insight into the native speech of the culture represented in the play. It is much more difficult to cut or add to a dialect play than to a straight American play. I recommend getting the advice of a dialectician before attempting to make such changes.

How can I verify correct pronunciations of obscure words in the text?

During another private reading of the play, make a list of words for which you'll need to find the pronunciation and definitions. Do not guess, and do not expect your director to do this work for you. It will save time in rehearsals if you don't have to stop to ask about a word. Many larger dictionaries include foreign words and phrases. If your own dictionary proves inadequate, you can simply call the reference department of a major library and they can look up the words for you. There are a number of foreign dictionaries listed in this text's Dialect Directory under the "Books" section of resources for each country.

How reliable are scripts that are written somewhat phonetically "in dialect"?

Several plays have been written which attempt to indicate in their *spelling* the variations in the accents of the characters. This is known as "eye dialect." Here is a selection from an older play, *Pietro the Foolish*, showing how playwright L. K. Deighton suggested the speech of the Italian character, Pietro.

But, Caterina, I ask-a heem for sure! I say, "Meester, ees thees alla the right?" And he say, "Sure teeng!" Then he tella me again how hees wife she ees dead and how he mus' go queeck far away, how hees wife's folks they don' like-a heem, how from heem they want-a the bambino and how he pay us the mon to take-a the care of the bambino, one, mebbe two, three year, and each year more mon.[7]

Some plays written in eye dialect are very well done, particularly the Irish plays. But don't blindly trust that a playwright's phonetic notations are accurate throughout the text. Consider it as just one of your resources, but don't base your accent on how the author wrote it down. Remember, the playwright is not a dialectician, so these phonetic spellings may not always be perfectly accurate or consistent. You may misinterpret their spelling. And some sounds are difficult to write phonetically using the standard alphabet.

Anne Nichols wrote her play *Abie's Irish Rose* somewhat in dialect for the Yiddish characters, and it would take some knowledge of the Yiddish sounds to avoid mispronunciations. For example, the last phrase in Solomon's line, "Don'd think of it, Mrs. Cohen. Forged it!"[8] is "Forget it," rather than the one-syllable word it looks like. Watch for different ways that authors represent a glottal stop. Some type it as an apostrophe. For example, "little bottle" would be "li'le bo'le" for Cockney. Another mispronunciation may occur if an actor is unaware of the guttural sound for the Scottish expletive "ogh" or "och." It shouldn't be pronounced as written; it's more of a throaty "kh" sound. When reading a German dialect script, you'd need to know that "ja" (meaning "yes") was pronounced as if spelled "ya," rather than with a "j" sound, as written.

How can I begin to identify my research homework?

Start a list of elements that will require research, particularly aspects of the culture and era your character lives in. Your director may also give you specific research assignments (films to see, books or articles to read, actual places or people to visit locally). The director of our cast of *Alice in Wonderland* assigned the cast several specific tasks: studying the original book, reading a few other books by the same author, seeing the full-length cartoon together, and visiting a local British pub to listen to several of the native Londoners working there. These homework assignments definitely helped the cast and production team. However, your director may or may not be an avid researcher, so again, don't expect her to have all the answers.

CHAPTER 4

PRE-REHEARSAL RESEARCH

Why do I have to do research on the culture of the region?

Along with your regular script analysis, your research for a dialect play will include researching the character's culture to discover *why* the people speak the way they do. The way a person expresses himself (rhythms, melody, tone, manner of articulation, pace) is shaped over time by numerous cultural and environmental influences. Even the mouth shapes used for diction will make more sense to you once you study the people and their land. In addition, this research helps you understand how your character moves, so that you *look* believable in terms of that culture's nonverbal mannerisms. Meryl Streep did an intensive study of the Australian culture along with her dialect studies in preparation for her role in *A Cry in the Dark*. The actress was totally convincing because she sounded, moved, and responded like an Australian rather than an American. If you saw Meryl Streep's portrayal of an Italian American in *The Bridges of Madison County*, I'm sure you'd agree that the character's nationality had a lot to do with defining who she was.

The national cultural characteristics of a people involve their personality tendencies and their attitudes. A region's people have attitudes about their language, their land (the visual setting, the textures, smells, sounds), family relationships, and the country's social, moral, political, cultural, and religious environments. Of course, the era also shapes these attitudes. The physical environment, and even the climate, affect a people's mood and manner of communication. Accepted modes of fashion and mannerisms affect movement, gesture, and freedom of expression. This kind of information can be gleaned from feature films, documentaries, books, audio, and interviews of native speakers.

The film *A Fish Called Wanda* provides a vivid example of how culture shapes character. I often recommend the film to my students, because it marvelously points up the contrasts between "Yanks" and "Brits." John Cleese plays a very proper

British parliament member, trying desperately to let go of his personal and cultural inhibitions long enough to enjoy a wild affair. The object of his desire is a liberated, playful American woman, played by Jamie Lee Curtis. She displays the speech, movements, and mannerisms of everything he finds attractive in a "typical" American—freedom of self-expression, openness, energy, and ambition. She finds his reserve and propriety charming. He has a wonderful comic monologue where he mocks himself for being so "typically British."

> ARCHIE: Wanda, do you have any idea what it's like being English? Being so correct all the time, being so stifled by this dread of doing the wrong thing, of saying to someone 'Are you married?' and hearing 'My wife left me this morning,' or saying 'Do you have any children?' and being told 'They all burned to death on Wednesday.' You see, Wanda, we're all terrified of *embarrassment*. That's why we're so . . . *dead*. Most of my friends are dead, you know. We have these piles of corpses to dinner. But you're alive, God bless you. And I want to be. I'm so fed up with all this . . . I want to make love to you, Wanda."9

Shouldn't I avoid stereotyping nationalities?

While it's wise to be aware of the problem of stereotyping individuals, don't worry that you are stereotyping a culture by looking for its general national characteristics. Different cultures do have their own personality traits and attitudes, qualities which natives themselves will admit to. People of particular vocations and socioeconomic levels have distinctive gestures, slang, and pronunciations, and they are often quite proud of them. Find out what is considered the cultural "norm" for the people you are studying, and how your character veers from or follows that norm.

Think of it as trying to find an "archetype" of that nation. In the Dialect Directory, I provide a list of film resources of such archetypes. For example, Maurice Chevalier and Leslie Caron give us an archetype for the French, and Crocodile Dundee for men from the Australian Outback. Though opinions will differ (often heatedly) about what the archetype is for a nation, use this simply as a starting place from which to build your very unique character.

Here is a good example. In several sources, Irish writers describe themselves as people who are rooted to the land, who find strength and dignity in owning land. The Irish describe themselves as headstrong fighters, individualists with fiery tempers and a quick wit. In the Irish film *Far and Away*, the lead characters (played by Tom Cruise and Nicole Kidman) demonstrated just how far they would go to get the land they wanted. She broke the strong tradition of her era and her people by braving the difficult trip to America. The dialogue sizzled with quick tempers and dry wit. The Irish are survivors of horrifying ordeals throughout their history. This film, as well as many other films portraying the Irish, shows us this overriding spirit of survival.

Another example is the Italians, whose national characteristics include energetic expressiveness, family devotion, and a vibrant interest in romance. Italians give music and food a social importance, and they honor their parents and traditions. These traits are evident in many works, from *Moonstruck* to "The Sopranos." Characters in these stories who break from their cultural norms become the heroes—or the victims. This was the theme of the romantic films, *Fiddler on the Roof* and *My Big Fat Greek Wedding*. You can see how incorporating the cultural characteristics both complements and intensifies the intrinsic drama of each of these films.

The two Scottish films *Braveheart* and *Rob Roy* would not have been so moving if they had been done without authentic accents. In these films, the historic figures come alive for us, and the character of the Scottish people is the fire that illuminates their motivations. The Scots are characterized in their literature as being vital, independent, and courageous in the face of oppression (a recurrent theme in Scottish history). They are a sturdy, hard-working people, in spite of land that is difficult to farm. They are fiercely loyal to kin and country, and have a proud ancestry as warrior-hunters. You may have noticed how dramatically the Scots contrasted with their English enemies in these movies.

How does the physical environment affect a character's speech?

The physical environment in which your character lives plays a definite part in shaping and altering your character's speech. Consider the New Yorker dialect, and more specifically, the Brooklynese. Brooklyn's environment can be described as a large, busy metropolis, moving at an aggressive pace. Its people are mostly from the working class (in transportation, foods, merchandise, etc.), and are fiercely proud of their city in spite of the noise, exhaust, and dirty conditions to be found there. This competitive, over-crowded environment nurtures an independent spirit, a vitality, and a desire for individuality that is almost childlike in its insistence to be heard. Interestingly enough, overcrowded conditions seem to have the opposite effect on Japan's largest cities, where the result is increased conformity, reserve, and respect for authority.

We can hear the echo of the New York environment in its residents' speech—it can be loud, fast, and direct. Blue collar New Yorkers command attention with physical expression and heavy stressing of words, rather than with melodic inflection. They tend to underline or punch every word in a monotone, then jump dramatically to another pitch for the next phrase. Unlike the British, New Yorkers embrace such a freedom of expression that they don't feel they have to control their tone quality to sound "pretty." And, because many working-class people do not have time to make education, culture, and refinement priorities, they can be unconcerned about precision in diction. David Alan Stern suggests a kinesthetic trick for learning the New Yorker dialect that ties in with their cultural image. He says to speak as if you're chewing gum (creating the correct placement of an exaggerated arch of the tongue, with a lazy tip).

In contrast to Brooklyn, a slower-paced, spread-out, rural environment often produces slower, more relaxed speech. We can hear this in some of the American Southern regions and in the Australian Outback.

The lilting melody that characterizes Northern Irish speech is reflective of the region's environment. Rolling green hills and fields of wildflowers stretch as far as the eye can see. Counties in the rural northwest, such as Donegal, have wild, undeveloped mountainous territory and a dramatic coastline. The land's thousands of acres of unproductive grass, heather, and peat bog are fit only for grazing sheep. Given this difficult environment, the strong upward lilt of the Northern Irish dialect seems to express tenacity to face frustration and hardship head-on with an "irrepressible gaiety."[10] It has often been said of the Irish that "the land and the people are one."[11] The elements that have molded their land and their culture have molded the character of the people. This is true of all cultures, so I encourage you to research how the physical environment may possibly affect the inflection, tone quality, volume, stress patterns, and rhythms of your character's speech.

How does climate affect a person's speech?

Climate can affect a culture's overall mood and manner. The rain and fog of Britain certainly seem to have a sobering and dampening effect on her people. In Ireland, the weather is as unpredictable as the Irish themselves. If it is not raining, it is threatening to rain. Sheets of mist cause lack of definition that can shroud things, and make a person feel cut off from the world. In regions where the people protect themselves against inclement weather (snow, wind, rain), it is not uncommon to find that the mouth is also more closed off, creating a dialect that has a smaller mouth opening. (Of course, a smaller mouth opening could also be the result of cultural factors, such as a history of repression or hardship.)

In contrast to the effects of colder regions, the bright warm sunshine of the Southern Californian and South American cultures invigorates and frees them socially. For the South American, this can result in quick, "hot," expressive speech. But for the Los Angeles sun worshipper, the result seems to be a laid-back spirit. The *humid* heat in Mexico and parts of the Deep South could very well contribute to the slower, drawled speech.

Although these are generalities, I believe it is worthwhile (and interesting) to consider the possible effects of climate on a culture.

What kinds of cultural characteristics am I looking for?

Here is a list that will help you identify elements of your character's culture. The remainder of the chapter will direct you to sources of information about these elements. As you study, try to figure out the overriding norm, the cultural tendencies—though you will most certainly encounter paradoxes and exceptions. You will probably find that attitudes and manners vary within a culture's different age groups, due to a "generation gap." And (as in any play analysis) you'll find that the story's *era* plays a significant role in shaping your character's world.

SURVEY OF YOUR CHARACTER'S PEOPLE AND THEIR CULTURE:

1. What is their attitude about their LAND (the physical environment—the sights, sounds, smells, textures)? Is it urban or rural? Isolated, insular communities? Or interdependent?
2. Describe the CLIMATE. How might this affect mood or manner of communication?
3. What is their attitude about their NATION? Are they nationalistic? Proud of their country? Or do they identify more with their region, or family unit?
4. What are the NEIGHBORING NATIONS? How are the people influenced by these neighbors? Are the people well-traveled?
5. What is their attitude about their LANGUAGE? Are they proud of their native language or accent? Or are they embarrassed by sounding "different"? Where and how do they learn English? Do they learn other languages? Is being well-spoken or articulate important in their culture? What about the use of SLANG?
6. What is their attitude about EDUCATION?
7. Attitude about POLITICS?
8. Attitude about THE ARTS? In particular, what kind of MUSIC is popular?

9. Attitude about SPORTS?

10. Attitude about RELIGION?

11. Attitude about FAMILY? What is the family hierarchy (patriarchal, matriarchal)?

12. Attitude about SOCIAL INTERACTION (marriage, courtship, sex, morality, sex roles, femininity/masculinity)?

13. What is their overall ENERGY level and DRIVE? Their work ethic? Are they considered ambitious?

14. Is there a recognizable CLASS SYSTEM? Who has the power? Who are the outcasts?

15. List important HISTORIC EVENTS that seem to affect attitudes and mannerisms.

16. List important TRADITIONS (cultural, religious, family). Are the people considered traditional, or non-traditional? Independent individualists, or conformers?

17. Is there a "generation gap"?

18. List their overriding PERSONALITY TRAITS.

19. Describe their SENSE OF HUMOR.

20. What is their attitude about CLOTHES? What types of clothing are worn by different classes, occupations, ages?

21. Describe their MANNERISMS AND GESTURES. How do they tend to sit, stand, walk, handle props? Do they have freedom in expression, or restriction? Why?

22. What is their sense of appropriate PROXIMITY? What is the accepted norm for a polite distance between two strangers? Two friends? Two lovers? How do they show affection? What are some typical greetings?

23. What seems to be VALUED above all? What are they most proud of?

The following is an example of the kinds of notes you can take in answering the questions above. This is a summary of my research notes on the Irish, in preparation for a production of *Dancing at Lughnasa*. This description was collected from many sources, most of which were written by natives of Ireland. (Sources are included in the Dialect Directory.)

The way the Irish people speak mirrors the physical aspects of their land and their attitudes toward it. Their speech is also a result of Ireland's sorrowful, tempestuous history, and of her people's attitudes about their traditions, language, family relationships, religion, education, and politics, and of her place in the world.

The lilting melody that characterizes the Irish speech is reflective of the greenery of Ireland's rural past. Legends of leprechauns and elves, and tales of love and adventure, mystery and wonder, have been passed down generation to generation. The Irish people's romantic land is lush with rolling green hills and fields of wildflowers. The lilt of their accent could also come from the warmth and friendliness of the people. "God has made the Irish gregarious, loquacious, and addicted to celebration."[12] Fairs and festivals date back two thousand years in their country. The Irish are world renowned for their hospitality. "The tradition of kindness and cordiality of Irish country people was, and is, one of the crowning glories of the Irish nature."[13] Author Richard O'Connor calls Ireland the "land of the open door."[14]

These people are not worriers. They "hang loose" with no illusions. They jeer at fate with an "insane optimism."[15] By the same token, they are prone to melancholy, introversion, and wistfulness. Their land has dealt them harsh blows, returning their brutal toil with famine and poverty. Their farmland produces rich crops only after the rocks are hand-picked out of the ground, one by one. Irish history has been an ongoing agony. Leon Uris calls Ireland a "lovely, but sorrowed island"[16] in his book *Ireland: A Terrible Beauty.* He says, "Ireland has been cruelly and stupidly administered and her people shamefully persecuted with every sort of indignity brought to bear."[17] Invasions, exile, brutality, and bloody wars born of greed are etched into the character of her people. Is it any wonder that the Irish, a people who had no forceful means with which to protect themselves, had to find ways to regain their dignity?

One way they could regain their dignity was through the power of words. The Irish have a long tradition of loving wit and wordplay. They are verbal fencers, and are known the world over for paddy-wackery (exaggerating on exaggerations), the indirect compliment, and leg-pulling. If the receiver of a put-down takes it as a sincere compliment, they've won. Irish people are notorious for being self-critical, almost to the point of making it an art form. Yet they are defensive about criticism from others, especially outsiders. But they can also laugh at themselves. This love of wit and words expresses itself in an articulate manner of speech, as if they are spitting the words out, with a quick delivery. An American actor doing the Irish accent must develop this "love affair with words,"[18] in order to give the right "zing" to the witty line. Many quips should be wry and underplayed rather than overt and loud, the way many American comedians deliver jokes.

It is important to note that during the mid-1800s, the Irish went through a rough and painful transition from speaking the Irish-Gaelic language to speaking English. The Reformation had made illiteracy virtually universal, so without written words, people had to develop sharp wits. They became expert storytellers. In the 1800s, when English became the imposed language, the Irish made it their own by embellishing it, creating new phrases, and giving it a new melody. Later, writing became the weapon they defended themselves with. Irish playwrights, poets, and prose writers continue to be among the most prolific in the world.

Another way that the Irish rose above their ancient woes was by direct attack. They are fighters who are accustomed to facing hardship head-on. Leon Uris named the first chapter of his book on Ireland "An Unconquerable Spirit Endures Through a Tragic History."[19] This spirit tends to make them strong indi-vidualists, rather than team players. Part of this is because Ireland is an island, isolated and surrounded by her ancient enemies and the vast sea. The Irish are ferocious in sports, especially known for their boxing prowess, because they tend to be never-say-die fighters. They refuse to be shamed. An outburst of fiery emo-tion can surface out of nowhere. What they become most passionate about is their land and their own Irishness. They also have a strong protection of family. The unpredictable rhythms of their speech, the wide, emotional inflection, and the manner in which they "sit on" or stretch out stressed syllables can be linked to their fiery temperament.

When the Irish do not choose to face a problem head-on, they are good at repressing their emotions. They can hold in the pain behind silence and a tough exterior. This is evident in their rigid alignment and held jaw. This rigid exterior can also be attributed to their resistance to change. They hold on to the traditions and superstitions of the past. A people who have been beaten back down for centuries do not tend to become risk-takers. A past of poverty leads them to be economical, even to the extreme. They simply cope, knowing it will all work out in the end.

Strict traditional Catholicism has stifled many natural impulses, including sex and displays of affection. The Irish bachelor is common, with marriage often considered anticlimactic and burdensome. The Irish boys' doting mothers waited on them, making leaving the nest unappealing. Women are traditionally thought to be interfering, though this has been changing since the 1970s.

The rural north, where Donegal lies, is still old-fashioned due to the isolation caused by Ireland's political divisions. Neighbors and kin in isolated regions such as Donegal tend to develop powerful bonds. There is an "emotional tie to a patch of ground,"[20] a sense of the land being "yours." The people of Donegal are known for their love of conversation and gossip.[21] The region is also known for its fishing villages, its quarries, and its hand-woven tweed and knitwear. County Donegal has a rugged, dramatic coastline. The mountains and the sea can be seen from any farmhouse, and the area's lakes (or lochs) are considered mysterious by many. As in much of Ireland, thousands of acres of Donegal's land are unproductive peat bog, heather, and coarse grass. In such conditions, it is no wonder that frustration and apathy challenges the human spirit. Yet the Irish are still considered a dauntless and tenacious people.

As you research a culture, you can jot down brief notes in list form about the people and their land. Here is a list I made when I was researching the Australians prior to dialect coaching the play *The Sum of Us*, written by David Stevens. These are rough notes taken from my study of a number of books and tapes written by Australians, sources which are listed in my Dialect Directory under "Australian."

Australian (male) character tendencies
cheerful, pleasure-loving
willing to help the individual; no one is just a statistic
dry sense of humor
rough and ready, like the land
sane and energetic
practical
"too smart to be romantic"[22]
independent; tends to dislike authority, especially police and military
skeptical about the value of religious, intellectual, and cultural pursuits
dislikes affectation
his heroes are in sports
loyal to his mates, even if they may be wrong
tends to be tolerant because his country was first settled by the Brits as a penal
      colony
taciturn rather than talkative, yet enjoys social contact in town
loves the land, first and foremost (75% of Australia is the Outback, very spread
      out)

loves horses and gambling

"Make no waves and keep your head down"[23]

"Do your own thing, and don't let any other sod know you're doing it or he may
      want some action too!"[24]

great improviser, willing to "have a go" at anything[25]

From studying these notes, the "Aussie" manner of speech and movement begins to
make sense. The Australian dialect has many of the sounds of Cockney (because of its
early settlers), but the two cultures are very different. So you can't just "do the Cockney
accent with a little more nasality," as I hear some people suggest. The Cockney's ancestors were primarily the poor urban factory workers in the heart of busy London. In
contrast, the Australian's ancestors were the rural cowboys, taming a wild land that was
very isolated. They had to be practical and tough, as they vigorously embraced their own
independent style. This is reflected in speech and movements which are more practical
than flowery. They demonstrate their high regard for egalitarianism and self-reliance in a
confident, relaxed manner. Their rate of speech tends to be slower than that which is
heard in busy London. The Australian's melodic inflection displays a playfulness, a
rough push of energy, and a dry sense of humor.

The defining physical movement in any culture is head carriage. You'll begin to
look and sound Australian if you pull your head back slightly, with a bit of a tilt. It makes
you feel stronger and tougher, and gives the voice just the right kind of nasal quality.
Americans tend to be very expressive with the head, and physically free with their faces,
shoulders, and arms. The lower-class Cockneys feel freer to be more expressive than the
more understated upper-class British do. Australians typically hold their arms in close
to the body. Facial expression is all in their eyes. In fact, their speech seems as if it is
done with a wink. See Chapter 6 for a more detailed examination of how your character's
body language affects your dialect choices.

How can I best use the DIALECT DIRECTORY in my research?

The Dialect Directory offers a selection of hundreds of current resources to use in
order to hear and observe the dialect of the specific culture you're studying. You'll find
suggestions of feature films, television programs, documentaries, audiotapes, CDs, and
books for studying the most commonly used stage dialects. I also list which dialect tapes
and texts teach a particular accent. Sources are categorized alphabetically for over thirty
different dialects, including African, Asian, Australian, British, Cockney, French,
German, Irish, Italian, Russian, Scottish, Spanish, several American Southerns, New
Yorker, and more.

Do turn to real-life, authentic speakers as your best resource. Use the resources
listed in the Dialect Directory to confirm and illuminate your research on any dialect.

Can't I go right to the source and interview real people?

Whenever possible, seek out primary sources to listen to. "Primary sources,"
remember, are native speakers of that accent. "Secondary sources" are actors or speakers
who are putting on the accent. Visiting the region you're studying would be ideal, granted.
But if you can't travel, perhaps there is an Irish pub owned by a Dubliner in your city, a
family-owned Middle Eastern restaurant, a Spanish shop, or a Japanese grocery store.

Donald Molin suggests in his *Actor's Encyclopedia of Dialects* that you seek out locales in your city where you can hear authentic dialects. He says to look for ethnic centers, churches, and folk-dance centers. Large cities have an International Cultural Center that you can call to get the name of the contact person for a specific ethnic center. Colleges often have a foreign student association or international student center, where you can meet people from many different cultures. Also check with the ESL (English as a Second Language) Department for leads.

The best primary source would be someone who lived most of his or her life in the region you're researching. If they have been away from their native land for too long, their dialect, pronunciations, and mannerisms may be a mixture of too many influences. Try to find primary speakers who are somewhat similar in energy, personality, age, and social class to the character you are going to play.

Once you've found a locale with authentic speakers, be discreet and just observe. You may pick up a gesture or a common phrase that you can use. Or you may be direct and ask for a brief interview. Tell the person that you are studying their culture and their dialect; this approach may prove more successful than a direct explanation, since some people might feel intimidated if you were to tell them you are an actor who is going to portray a character of their nationality. Overall, though, you'll probably find that people *love* to talk about home. Ask them about where they grew up, about holiday celebrations and traditions they hold dear, about a special event in their life. Ask them what local sights they like to recommend to visitors. Ask about their hobbies and their family. They will probably be more than willing to talk about such things, with an energy and a naturalness that will be far more helpful to you than if you were to ask yes-and-no questions. You might ask your interview subjects if you may record the conversation. However, they may or may not feel comfortable with this, so definitely ask first.

If you really want to do it right, you need to interview the native speaker about how they learned English. Here is a list of possible questions.

INTERVIEW QUESTIONS FOR NATIVE SPEAKERS:

1. Where were you born, and where have you lived throughout your life?
2. What is your age, occupation, and level of education?
3. When and how did you learn English?
4. Were you trained by someone with a Standard American accent (or even someone with an American regionalism)? Or was it by a British teacher, or someone from your own country?
5. What language or dialect did your parents or major caretakers speak? And what was your parents' upbringing, occupation, and education?
6. Do you speak predominantly English at home, or in your native tongue?
7. Do you speak any other languages? How does this seem to affect your dialect when speaking English?
8. How do you feel about your speech overall (comparing how you speak English with how you sound in your native language)?

Carefully choosing primary sources by finding out the answers to the above questions will give you clues as to how well your interview subject speaks American English, and how they handle English grammar, slang, and proper pronunciation.

Which library resources will aid my research?

Your county library should have a section of books about any country or American region you need. Look on the web by "subject," under headings related to your character's native region—"Ireland" or "Irish," "Italy" or "Italians," for example. Then look under that subject's subcategories (such as "Description and Travel," "Social Life and Customs," or "Culture"). The best finds are books with titles something like *The Italians*, or *Portrait of the Irish People*, or *The Land and People of China*. These books may be too long to read in full at this time, but their opening chapters, or a select few, will offer a wonderful summary of the character of the people you are researching. Select those chapters that seem to apply to your character in the play. For example, if you're playing an Irish priest, read the section on religious customs. If you're playing a British member of Parliament, read the section on politics. If your character is planning a wedding, read the chapter on marriage and family.

The books listed in the Dialect Directory will be a good head start for you. The best (and least biased) ones are written by natives about their own people. Find one from my list, and you'll see others sitting next to it on the library shelf that may also be useful to your research.

What about the web?

Of course, you can search the internet under the city or country you're studying. You can look under Yahoo or Amazon.com or a Google.com. The travel site often will have video and RealAudio clips. There are obviously endless possible searches to aid your research. But I do warn and encourage you to not solely depend on web searches for your research. Don't be lazy. Get away from your computer and actually seek out all the primary sources you can, right in your city, and go to the beautiful visual sources in books. Plus, realize that anyone can write an article for the web, so always check the validity of the source. In my dialect courses, I limit internet sources to no more than three entries, to encourage them to "put feet to their research."

Why are travel books and videos essential resources?

Travel books are indispensable. The information they contain will help you make sense of your character's motivations as you reread and rehearse your part. The books generally have a beautiful, brief overview of the country and its people, with short chapters called "The People," "The Land," "History," "Education," "Natural Resources," "Sports," "Music," and so on. Some travel books describe the culture's attitudes and habits as a help to the American traveler, so that the travelers learn the acceptable customs of a particular country. Thus, you'd find out that the British are not friendly and talkative to strangers while in their subways (in the Underground) because they are respecting others' privacy. You'd find out why the Germans are so dependably on time for meetings, and why Mexicans have more of an elastic sense of time, and would not feel that it was rude to show up minutes past an agreed-upon meeting time. Hand gestures in the U.S. that are perfectly harmless, such as our "okay" sign or our "peace" sign, are considered vulgar in several countries. When Europeans count on their fingers, "one" is indicated with the thumb rather than the second finger. And when Europeans knock on the door, they often knock with their palms facing their faces, in contrast to the American way. You can begin to incorporate some of the new gestures into your performance: a proper British handshake, a Japanese bow, an Italian wave, a Continental kiss on both cheeks. the coquettish French pout.

Peruse the pictorial books especially, and just let the images come alive for you. These are the things your character sees when he walks down the street in his own country. Imagine the smells, sounds, and textures of the land. Take some time studying the pictures of people. The soul of a people can be captured in still photos. A typical cock of the head, a clutch of the hand, a body posture, a leg position while sitting can give you insights, both conscious and subconscious. The *eyes* say a lot about the character of a people. Study the raise of an eyebrow of a British gentleman, the fiery gleam in an Irishman's eye, the weariness in the eyes of an older Russian woman, the knowing wit in an Aussie sailor's eyes.

Travelogue videos from your library or video store are also a perfect overview of a country or an American state. Often the video is narrated by a clear-speaking native, who shows you points of interest and briefly tells you about that region's history and culture. These travelogues usually include interviews with individuals who were born and raised in that region, so that you have the opportunity to listen to natives from several different walks of life.

What other audio materials are useful?

Cultural documentaries, instructional audio material, and books on tape or CD, narrated by native speakers, allow you to experience the appropriate speech cadences while learning about the region's culture. One such book on tape is Robert Louis Stevenson's *Kidnapped*, read marvelously by Bill Simpson. Simpson does all of the different characters' voices, some of which are lower-class Scottish, others upper-class Scottish. If you are learning a German accent, there are a number of World War II documentaries. Historic events are often chronicled in documentaries and political speeches by world leaders. I've suggested a number of documentaries in the Dialect Directory.

Check your library for popular play performances put on tape, CD or video. Through the years, the Royal Shakespeare Company, The National Theatre in London, The Abbey Theatre in Ireland, and other professional theatre companies have gone into studios to record their best performances. Check for cassette tapes and CDs of current live performances of classic plays.

For studying foreign accents, I encourage you to obtain the language learning tapes. You'll be able to really focus on the "music" of the language—its inflection and stress patterns, its energy, its possible mouth shapes. Foreign films, too, are a fabulous way to study the soul of a particular people and the texture of their raw speech.

Why not just rent the movie?

Carefully selected feature films, documentaries, and television programs provide an excellent opportunity to both hear the dialect you're studying and to watch movement, carriage, mannerisms, facial expressions, and typical dress. Watch the characters dance, play sports, woo a lover, do chores, and take on other daily activities. We too often take for granted the way we do things in America, so observe well. Try to find films that are set in the same era as your play's. Good video store employees know their collection and could lead you to just the right film. They can help you find foreign films, which are listed by country in their catalogue. Check under "E!Online" on the web for any subject, film, TV show, or actor's name. If you know of a star with a good native accent, you can look up their name for a list of all of the movies they were in. For example, if you could look up "Gèrard Depardieu" for a great example of clear-speaking French. Also try your county library or university interlibrary loan department if your video store doesn't carry an older film that you want.

Watching films should not replace your search for real-life primary sources. Because films are so accessible, it becomes a temptation for actors who are looking for shortcuts to rely on films as their only resource. If you want to be believable, seek the real thing.

How will I know if these films are reliable sources for the accent?

When it comes to assessing the authenticity of a dialect that you hear in a feature film or television show, you would most likely need the advice of a good dialect coach. The Dialect Directory will be a good start for you. It lists a number of reliable films you could use in your research, with notes on which characters to especially listen to. In several cases, I even note which sources are *not* that reliable. When listening to any authentic-sounding speaker, you have to take into account that he or she may have a mixed dialect. (For example, the person may have been born in Mexico City, but learned English at an early age in Cuba, and learned to mimic the speech of his Jamaican nanny before moving to the Bronx.)

When listening to dialects in films, it is important to be able to distinguish the socioeconomic class of the speaker. A rural dialect differs from a city dialect. In a range moving from middle class to lower class, accents tend to become progressively less controlled in tone quality, inflection, and rhythm. Vowel substitutions possibly get heavier and more predominant, and articulation less precise, in comparison to the sounds of the upper class. Grammar becomes less formal and slang pervades. In other words, the speaker usually loosens up and allows his sounds to be less exact. When in doubt about reliability of a source, you may need the advise of a qualified dialect trainer.

How do I focus my research?

Once you begin researching, you may very well get carried away. It will most likely fascinate you. Although a broad understanding of the history of your character's culture is important, you should eventually focus your research on resources that reflect the approximate time period of the play you're working on. By focusing your study on that era, you'll be able to comprehend how and why your character developed his attitudes about certain things. Here's another example from the play *Dancing at Lughnasa*. It is very significant that the play is placed in the summer of 1936, a time when the effects of the Industrial Revolution are beginning to be felt in northwest Ireland. The handicrafts done by country people like the Mundy family in Balleybeg will become obsolete as the factories rise in influence. The culture's repression of sexuality due to strong religious tradition also has significance to these sisters living in the 1930s. Their attitudes are further molded by the fact that there is no father figure in their home, something that was much more of a stigma in the '30s than it is today.

For each source you find, do take into consideration its date of publication or production. Obviously, the most current sources are the best ones to use. Though traditions die hard in many countries, some works that were written twenty years prior to the time period you're researching may reflect cultural attitudes and practices that have since been abandoned.

CHAPTER 5

ADAPTING THE DIALECT
FOR THE STAGE

Why would I need to adapt the dialect? Can't I just listen to an authentic speaker and mimic what I hear?

The realistic accent of a person, the one you might hear on the street, has to be adapted for the stage. If you try to exactly mimic a primary-source speaker, your dialect may pose a clarity problem for your audience. We Americans tend to slur in casual conversation, and foreign visitors who learned English as a second language may have trouble understanding us. In the same way, realistic "street" dialects tend to be slurred because the people speaking them are not on stage, and aren't overly concerned with clarity. The bottom line is, if your audience can't understand you, that perfectly accurate accent is worthless.

The standard stage dialects you learn from a dialect text must also be adapted, because they are too generic. They are not specific enough to locale or to character. These dialects also can be dated. Several of the most prominent dialect texts were written well over ten years ago. Language, mannerisms, and slang evolve, and you have to keep up with the times.

Keeping clarity in mind above all, you need to adapt a dialect for the stage or screen according to:

    (1) your audience,

    (2) your play's locale,

    (3) your character choices,

    (4) your director's concept, and

    (5) your individual capabilities.

We'll discuss each one, to help you make the wisest choices for your particular play and character. An experienced dialect coach can be a great help in making these very important and sometimes difficult decisions in adapting a dialect.

Why would I need to adapt the dialect for my audience?

Fortunately, modern film and television have familiarized our audiences with many clear, natural-sounding dialects and accents. Audiences hear British, German, Russian, Italian, French, Australian, African, and Jamaican, to name just a few. Big box office hits of the '90s featured excellent Scottish and Irish accents. Even so, it has only been in the last decade that we have seen a trend moving from clichéd stage dialects toward ones that were more realistic, consistent, and specific to locale.

Because our audiences are becoming more sophisticated through exposure to realistic dialects in film and television, it is imperative that we give them realistic ones on the stage. If a play is set in Dallas, it has to be a Dallas accent, not a generic Southern accent, as was acceptable years ago. If the play is set in Houston, or in Fort Worth, it will have a slightly different sound and style than if the setting is in Dallas, though the accent will sound Texan overall. Though all are Southern, the dialects of Louisiana, Alabama, Tennessee, and North Florida are different, and audiences know it. Less than twenty years ago, audiences seem to have been less fussy. Watching several old classic films and TV series from the '40s or '50s would convince one of this.

Years ago, speaking roles were not commonly given to actors whose ethnic background matched that of their characters. This often resulted in sad, clichéd portrayals of minorities. Since the early '80s, more care seems to have been taken in casting ethnic characters for film and television, and in the portrayal of accurate dialects. Credit must be given here to Meryl Streep, whose integrity in learning realistic, seemingly flawless accents for such films as *Sophie's Choice* (Polish), *A Cry in the Dark* (Australian), *and The Bridges of Madison County* (Italian-American) has paved the way for a higher standard of accuracy for today's stage dialects.

Our modern audiences demand realism in dialects, just as they demand detailed realism in set pieces, costumes, and action stunts. Hollywood may never let Kevin Costner rest about his inaccurate British accent in *Robin Hood*, nor Julia Roberts for her Irish in *Mary Reilly*. Yet film-goers continue to praise the dialects of certain actors. Meryl Streep's abilities with dialects are legendary. The brilliant Peter Sellers was known for his many dialect characters. Kevin Kline and Robin Williams have played a dozen different dialect roles. Holly Hunter, known for her thick Georgia dialect, learned a Scottish accent for *The Piano*. Tom Cruise and Nicole Kidman did convincing Irish accents for *Far and Away*. Michelle Pfeiffer's Russian accent for *Russia House* was admirable. Mary McDonnell proved herself beautifully proficient doing a Native American dialect in *Dances with Wolves*, a British one in *Sneakers*, and a Swedish one in *O, Pioneers!* All of these professional actors spent arduous hours learning and rehearsing the proper dialect, most of them using the help of a dialect coach. Elizabeth Smith is a prominent "dialect coach to the stars," credited with teaching the accents for the film *Rob Roy*. Another is Julie Adams, Jodie Foster's trainer for *Sommersby*. Adams's mentor is the legendary dialect coach, Robert Easton.

Our theatre audiences also demand clarity, since they are used to being able to hear effortlessly in movie theaters and at home in front of their TVs (where they have control of the volume button on the remote). These audience members will get distracted, or even annoyed, if they can't understand you.

There are amusing exceptions to the rule for "clarity above all," and that is when the character is being unintelligible as an actual character trait. In "King of the Hill," the animated series set in Arlen, Texas, Boomhauer has a mountain dialect that trails off into incoherent mumbling with hilarious results. Brad Pitt's Irish dialect in *Snatch* was so incoherent that two British characters later in the film commented how they didn't understand a word he said. I must admit that, before this comment was spoken, I was struggling so much to understand Pitt during this film that I thought he just didn't have a handle on the accent (recalling his uneven Irish brogue in *The Devil's Own*.)

How do I adapt it for MY AUDIENCE?

Though you've committed to researching the common speech of a specific city, you must adapt this speech to what will best communicate on the stage for the play's particular audience. This could mean softening the dialect by using a weaker form of the vowel and consonant substitutions. Or it could mean choosing a smaller number of vowel and consonant changes, selecting the major sounds that give just a flavor of the accent. You may also need to slightly lighten your acquired dialect during the first few minutes of the play, and to be especially clear and articulate. This will give the audience's ears a chance to adjust to listening to a new dialect.

You have to be able to empathetically anticipate how your particular audience is going to receive the sounds they hear. Audiences are different in every city. Ask yourself, "What do they *expect* to hear?" Here are some examples.

And a Nightingale Sang is a play by C. P. Taylor set in Newcastle, in the North Country of England. Because the play deals with specific historical events of that region, the Newcastle accent absolutely should be used, as opposed to a Standard British or Cockney. But the accent is a hard one for actors to learn, since it sounds like a cross between Cockney and Irish. This accent also tends to distract audiences because it is far less familiar than British or Cockney. Even when it is done exceptionally well, audiences may think the actor is flipping back and forth between Irish and Cockney. In most American cities, you must admit that only audience members who are from the North Country would probably be able to tell if the accent was accurate to Newcastle. Sometimes you have to "cheat" and do a lighter or more generic accent if you think your audience would have trouble easily accepting the true one.

Robert Schenkkan's *The Kentucky Cycle* is a good example of a play which demands an accent that is accurate to the locale. In the production I coached, I taught the actors the very specific Kentucky accent, rather than let them do what I call their Southern "dialect du jour." However, I advised them to be somewhat more articulate and a little less throaty than an authentic Kentucky backwoods native might be, because clarity was posing a problem.

Audience's expectations sometimes fall into stereotypes, and sometimes the best choice is to give them what they want. Stereotypical accents work better for high comedy than for drama. Audiences expect to see a proper English butler, a Cockney maid, or a French maid. They accept a British nanny, a Swedish chef, a German psychologist, a street-smart Brooklynese secretary, a tough New Yorker cop, or taxi driver. Another stereotype is the Irish policeman or gardener. In the case of Irish, modern audiences are becoming more familiar with the Northern Irish lilt than with the Southern Irish, because of a number of recent films set in the north. In the British farce *Move Over Mrs. Marcum*, the housekeeper is written as German, but the character could be adapted to Swedish. In one college production I saw, an energetic Puerto Rican actress played the role, which worked quite well.

The character of Uncle Jack, in Brian Friel's Irish play *Dancing at Lughnasa*, was born in County Donegal in the same (fictional) town as the rest of the play's family. At the start of the play, he has just returned home after spending the last twenty-five years serving as a missionary in Uganda, Africa. There he spoke Swahili almost exclusively. The audience may question: how much of his Northern Irish accent would he have retained? And would he regain more of his original Irish accent the longer he is home? Would he have developed, perhaps, the strong rhythms of the Swahili speech to some extent? A wise choice would be a a "mixed dialect"—a slight Irish accent (mostly just a trace of hard "r's") and the more evenly-accented syllables of the Swahili language. And, since a month passes in the course of the play, perhaps his Irish lilt would get just a bit stronger by Act Two.

Here are some other examples from film, demonstrating how audience expectations affected decisions about the final dialect used. Dennis Quaid played a New Orleans cop in *The Big Easy*, attempting the difficult Cajun accent. But it was generally hard to accept that well-known actor as a Cajun character. An audience's tendency would be to listen to his unusual accent rather than truly buy into the character.

In *Out of Africa*, Meryl Streep learned an accurate Danish accent months before the shooting of the film. Robert Redford's character, described as an Englishman, did not end up with an English accent, though he'd originally learned one for the part. A decision was made that American audiences would not be able to accept such a big star using a strange accent. Perhaps we could accept Meryl Streep's speech because she had established herself as a performer who could do dialect roles well. So Redford used his own voice. However, audiences were perceptive enough to wonder why he did not attempt an accent. Many of the film reviews mentioned it. Perhaps the filmwriter could have changed a line or two to make his character hail from America, if it would not alter the plot too significantly. (However, since *Out of Africa* was based on real people and events, this may have been inappropriate.) Audiences are not accustomed to hearing any dialects from Harrison Ford, so it was distracting to hear him attempt a light Russian accent as the submarine captain in *K-19: The Widowmaker*. Liam Neeson and all the co-stars were coached to speak in the accent. In reality, the entire crew would have spoken Russian, not English, but an American-made movie with all subtitles would not have worked either. These are tough decisions for the director and a difficult task for the dialect coach of that film.

The choice made for Lee Marvin's character in the film *Gorky Park* was admirable. In the book by Martin Cruz Smith, Lee Marvin's character was a Russian trapper. For the film, a line was changed to make him an American trapper visiting Russia. Whether the director felt audiences could not accept Lee Marvin as a Russian, or whether Marvin could not do a convincing Russian accent, the result was an adaptation that worked.

Arnold Schwarzenegger has a recognizable Austrian accent that audiences could accept well enough as Russian in the film *Red Heat*, probably because it sounds exotic enough to be foreign—or possibly just because it's Arnold Schwarzenegger.

Ultimately, whether to adapt your dialect for your audience should be a decision left up to the director, with advice from the dialect coach. The author may even have provided you with notes. In the case of Uncle Jack in *Dancing at Lughnasa*, playwright Brian Friel introduces Jack by saying he has "scarcely any trace of an Irish accent."[26]

How do I adapt the dialect according to the PLAY'S LOCALE?

In the research section in Chapter 3, we talked about how important it is to pinpoint the accurate dialect for a specific locale. I believe that realistic plays and films should be done in dialect, especially if their focus is on the historic aspect of a people, or on their culture. Plays that focus on action or storyline could possibly be done in General American if nothing would be lost. This decision is left to your director.

A Texas character study, like *Greater Tuna*, or a Tennessee Williams play set in the Deep South, would suffer if the accents were not consistent to the locale. British farces that are played without the British accent tend to lose their sparkle.

The family members in *Steel Magnolias* should have accents that reflect the fact that they were born and raised in the same town. The actors need to listen to one another and agree on speaking the same northwestern Louisiana accent. It's possible that a character like Clairee could have a contrasting Southern accent, as she could have moved to Louisiana from her home in Alabama. Yet in the 1989 film, as well as in several productions I've seen, the uncoached actors chose to do whatever generic Southern accents they were used to doing. The result was a mixture of well-done and poorly done, accurate and inaccurate accents for that play's locale.

How do I adapt the dialect according to my CHARACTER CHOICES?

Once you've learned the generic, "standard" dialect and understand what your character's particular nationality considers the norm in terms of attitudes and speech, you can move on to fine-tuning your dialect. You accomplish this by answering several questions about your character:

1. Does your character follow the traditional personality and attitudes of his people, or does he veer from what is considered the norm? Be specific about identifying the areas in which your character could be considered "typical" or "traditional" for people of that region, and which "atypical." Keep this question in mind as you consider the following areas.
2. What does your character value? What does he want? What does he dislike?
3. What strategies will he use to get what he wants? (What is his drive or will)?
4. Has he spent his entire life in his hometown? Has he traveled or lived elsewhere for any length of time, and has therefore been influenced by other cultures or lifestyles?
5. What is his parentage? What is his parents' background?
6. What is his age? (This is important because it may shape his attitudes, speech, and movements, due to a "generation gap." For example, a twenty-year-old in the 1960s would think, move, dress and speak differently than a sixty-five-year-old in 1960.)
7. What does he do all day, for work and for play? How might this influence him physically and vocally?
8. How does he express himself physically and vocally? What are his mannerisms?
9. What is his level of self-esteem?
10. What is his energy level? His health?
11. Who does he spend time with socially?
12. What personality traits does he have? Are any of these seemingly inherited, or do any seem to be learned?
13. What kind of education does he have? What is his intelligence level?
14. What does he like to eat?
15. How would you describe his sense of humor?
16. What kind of music does he like?
17. How does he dress? Who influenced the way he dresses?   (cont.)

18. Where and how did he learn English? How does he feel about his accent—
    is he proud of his accent, unaware of it, or ashamed of it?
19. What is his attitude toward "outsiders"?
20. What is his attitude toward politics? Religion? Education? Marriage and
family, and any other institutions his culture values?

Chances are, the main action of your script revolves around the fact that certain characters in the play are rebels against the norm, or trailblazers. That's what makes for drama. Do you see why it is so important to study the culture of a people? To play this "rebellion against the norm" requires that actors understand what the norm *is*.

An important thing you need to consider about a character you're researching is how he feels about his accent in relation to others. Is your character proud of his heritage and thus using the uniqueness of his dialect to his advantage? For example, a Frenchman who becomes aware that his foreign accent is perceived as sexy and romantic by an American girl may play up the exotic features of his speech to win her. Or is your character ashamed of his accent because he perceives that it sets him apart as "different"? Perhaps he is constantly being misundersood. This embarrassment may cause him to demonstrate a shyness abroad that he does not have when he is with his own people. Or he may try to hide or minimize his accent because he feels people are pigeonholing him into a stereotype. If your character is from a foreign country, does she speak predominantly in her native language, or in English? Is your character upwardly aspiring, and quite pleased with herself that she's learned how to upscale her dialect when speaking English? Does her newly acquired "upscale" dialect slip when she is excited, or tired, or not around people she has to impress? You may even have a character who flaunts her accent in spite of the fact that it has been deemed socially unacceptable by her associates.

Something else to take into consideration is that the accents of native speakers naturally get stronger when they are excited or angry. You'll hear Herbert Lom's Czech accent become stronger and stronger in the film *The Pink Panther Strikes Again,* as Klousseau slowly drives the Chief Inspector insane with his antics. When *Sophie's Choice* came out, Meryl Streep was critiqued by reviewers as being inconsistent with her Polish accent, but actually, she appropriately exaggerated her accent in scenes of highest emotion, and then lightened it when her character regained composure.

How do I adapt the dialect according to the DIRECTOR'S INTENT?

Your director may or may not have strong opinions about your character's accent. She may be a purist, demanding accuracy and long coaching sessions. She may not think about dialects at all. But in the early stages of rehearsal, hopefully you will get some idea of the theatrical style the director is aiming for. It is the degree of strength of the dialects that can help determine (or can actually destroy) the intended style of the play.

A good rule of thumb is that the dialects should be quite realistic with most theatrical styles, with the exception of broad comedy, satire, or farce. If comic style is the aim, your accents may possibly be exaggerations. A choice to do *What the Butler Saw* by Joe Orton in a farcical style, for example, could mean exaggerations in the comic High British nasality and widest inflection for the snobby upper-class characters, and a stereotypical Cockney whine for the lower-class characters. The bellboy could be Liverpudlian, since that dialect has distinctively comic potential. An Italian accent, if exaggerated, tends to sound quite comic, as it did with two early "Saturday Night Live" characters, Father Guido Sarducci and Rosanne Rosanna Danna.

Many other accents become comical when stretched to the cliché. A Mexican accent can remind one of Cheech and Chong or Speedy Gonzales, German of the buffoons in the TV series "Hogan's Heroes." Certain Cockney dialects remind us of sassy Monty Python caricatures.

How do I adapt the dialect according to MY ABILITIES? What if I'm having trouble?

Each actor comes into the rehearsal process with a different aptitude for learning an accent. They may have preconceived ideas of how the accent should sound, depending on where and if they've heard it before. Plus, they may have preconceptions about how one should approach learning a dialect. They may have blocks to learning something new, or blocks to making the adjustments for this show on an accent they have learned previously from another instructor. Be honest with yourself, so that you can adapt the dialect according to your own abilities. Be patient with how others in the cast approach the learning process.

Certain actors seem to have a better aptitude for learning dialects than others. Actors who are singers or musicians tend to be able to more easily pick up and understand the rhythms, stress, and melodic patterns of dialects. Dancers and devoted athletes also tend to have a better aptitude, because they have already developed discipline in muscle control, a skill that is needed in dialect acquisition. Plus, these performers are used to critique on every aspect of their technique, and they realize that even the smallest adjustment can make all the difference in the quality of the end product.

Your vocal and physical technique also comes into play when learning a dialect. Your strengths can work to your advantage in your dialect acquisition, just as your weaknesses could potentially hinder the final outcome. For example, if you have a naturally nasal resonance, you may find it easy to capture the correct nasality of an Australian dialect. If you have less than adequate articulation, you'll need extra work to pull off the ease of the crisp High British diction. Can you roll your tongue? No? You may not sound convincing in such dialects as Scottish or Russian, which demand a rolled "r." Maybe a vocal coach can help you.

Does your posture trap you? Actors with a naturally erect, poised carriage would more easily be able to adopt the movements associated with certain accents, such as British, Irish, Middle Eastern, or Indian. In contrast, an actor accustomed to slouching and punctuating stress words with a head bob would need coaching to develop the new habits necessary for such roles.

Know that your natural strengths and weaknesses will shine through whatever dialect you do. But be directable, flexible, and adaptable.

CHAPTER 6

THE REHEARSAL PROCESS: POLISHING THE DIALECT

How do I begin to polish my dialect during the first few weeks of rehearsals?

With all the many performance elements you have to juggle as an actor—lines, blocking, character development, costumes, props, cues—a dialect becomes yet another element that demands your attention. It can be overwhelming. But discipline yourself early in the rehearsal process to drill the dialect, and your hard work will pay off.

You must drill the vowels, consonants, placement, and flow of the dialect as part of your daily homework. The instructional dialect texts and tapes that are listed in my Bibliography, such as those of Gillian Lane-Plescia and David Alan Stern, have many pages of drills. Listen to these tapes or CDs and mimic the drill sentences for ten or fifteen minutes every day, twice a day. According to scientific studies regarding how we learn, several short daily sessions are more effective than practicing for two hours, but only once a week. Through this discipline of drilling, you'll learn the mechanics of the dialect, memorizing the mouth shapes for the vowel and consonant substitutions until they are second nature. Do this very early on in the rehearsal process, preferably in the first two weeks.

Make a concise list in the front of your script of the vowel and consonant substitutions you'll need to incorporate into your speech. This is just a quick chart to refer to when you begin marking your lines for the dialect. Ask yourself, "What are the *major* vowel and consonant changes for my accent?" Your list can look something like the following for the major changes for the Cockney accent:

ā = ī   r̸ (dropped at end of syllables)
ē = uh-ee   r (linked to open vowels, i.e., "care if")
ī = oy   h̸ (dropped at beginning of words)
ō = ă-oo   t̸t̸ (glottal stop on medial and some final "t"s)
o͞o = uh-oo   -ing̸ (dropped "g")
ă = almost ah
ŏ = aw (very forward)
ow = ă-uh-oo

Should I make phonetic notes right in my script?

Mark your text for the dialect. From your list of vowel and consonant substitutions for this dialect, see if you can locate those sounds in your lines. If you've never been exposed to phonetics, you may find this difficult. But you'll find it gets easier the more you work with it, so keep trying. A voice/speech trainer can help you. Circle vowels that change, and underline consonants that need to be pronounced crisply. Write the word phonetically above the line in your script. Or jot down a word that rhymes with it, to help you remember a pronunciation. You can use phonetic respelling, IPA transcription, or whatever notation system you've learned or want to create. It doesn't matter, as long as it's consistent. For Standard British, cross out every "r" at the end of syllables, and put a linking line after "r's" occurring at the end of words that are followed by an open vowel (i.e., "pair‿of shoes" and "tear‿open"). Cross off the silent "h's" and the "t's" that become glottal stops, if you're doing Cockney (i.e., "h̸ello H̸enry" and "litt̸le spot̸ of tea"). Put a little slash above "r's" that have a trip or a tap, as in Italian or Spanish dialects, like this: (r̸).

To help you visualize it, here's a paragraph from George Bernard Shaw's *Pygmalion*, with an actor's notations for the Cockney dialect. First I'll show it with phonetic notations:

oy   uh-ee   ī   ă-uh   aw   aw   aw
I want to be a lady in a flower̸ shop stead of selling̸ at the corner̸‿of Tottenh̸am

aw   ă-oo   ī   ă-oo ī   uh-ee   oy   aw   uh-ee uh-ee   uh-ee
Court̸ Road. But they won't take me unless I can talk more̸ genteel. H̸e said h̸e

uh-ee uh-ee   oy   ī   aw ah   ī
could teach me. Well, h̸ere‿I am ready to pay h̸im—not asking̸ any favor̸—and

uh-ee uh-ee   uh-ee   oy
H̸e treats me as if I was dir̸t.[27]

And here's the same passage using IPA:

ɔɪ   əi   ɪə   ɑ: ɒ   ɔ: ɔ:

I want to be a lady in a flower shop stead of selling at the corner of Tottenham

ɔ: æʊ   ɑɪ æʊ   əi   ɔɪ   ɔ   ɔ: əi əi   əi

Court Road. But they won't take me unless I can talk more genteel. He said he

əi   əi   ɔɪ   ɑɪ   ɒ ɑ: ɑɪ

could teach me. Well, here I am ready to pay him—not asking any favor—and

əi əi əi   ɔɪ

he treats me as if I was dirt.

Double-check your work. It's easy to miss a sound. Say the lines aloud as you mark them, so that you learn to hear when you're correct and when you're incorrect.

Remember to underline unusual phrases, slang, idioms, and expletives (explosive expressions, like swear words) in your script, being sure you know what they mean. Proper names need to be clarified too. Practice saying these lines clearly so that your audience will understand you. You may have to say these unusual phrases more slowly, and possibly with a slightly lighter accent to allow your audience to catch it.

Do I have to mark every single one of my lines?

Yes, take the time to mark every line. Then, as you're memorizing your lines (always aloud), all the notations are there, and you'll memorize that line in a consistent dialect. Eventually you may get to the point where you can sight-read anything in the dialect without needing any notations. But for this important project, when even one inconsistent line could rob your character of believability, why chance it?

It's inconvenient that play scripts are not double-spaced. Phonetic markings can get messy, squished between your single-spaced lines of dialogue. If your lines are few, or if you have the time, you'd be better off retyping them with sufficient space between lines. Actually, writing out your lines in longhand is a great line-learning technique, so this could help both your dialect and your memorization.

Marking phonetics in your script is the boring, technical part of dialect acquisition. But the dialect will really sink in if you do it, because you'll be using all of your feedback systems for learning a skill. You'll be using your hearing as you say your lines aloud, your sight as you see the markings, and your kinesthetic sense as you feel the muscles of the lips, tongue, and face create proper placement. The physical act of writing notes is also a way of using your kinesthetic sense, because writing things out imprints it into your brain. Imagery further impacts how you learn. If you don't mark your text, you're only trusting your ear in learning a dialect.

You'll be tempted to put this homework off. You'll say, "I'll work on my dialect after I learn my lines." Or you'll say, "After I get my character, the dialect will be easy to add." Putting off polishing your dialect is a trap I've seen too many actors fall into. If you procrastinate, it will never happen, because later on you'll just get tied up with all the other production elements.

You need to memorize your lines in dialect, with the understanding that your character and the dialect are one. Even though you are trying to create the illusion of "naturalness" and spontaneity in playing your character, you must work hard on the technical aspect of becoming proficient in your dialect.

What are diacritical markings?

Diacritical markings are symbols used in dictionaries and phonetic books to indicate such things as which syllable is stressed, lengths of sounds, and specific placement of vowels and consonants. It is not standardized; there are many discrepancies among diacritical marking systems (DMS's) used by different dictionaries. Some speech and dialect trainers use diacritical marks along with their IPA notations, and will provide you with a list of symbols so that you can understand their vocal notes.

Below is a partial list of diacritical symbols that you may run across in dialect books. More detailed explanations and applications of these symbols can be found in Louis Colaianni's book *The Joy of Phonetics and Dialects*, pp. 69-72. Colaianni prefers to call them "nuance markings" since "they detail the nuance of how someone speaks."[28] You'll also find a catalogue of diacritical markings in *The Phonetic Symbol Guide* by Geoffrey K. Pullum and William A. Ladusaw, and in the back of Edith Skinner's *Speak With Distinction*.

:   sound is lengthened, for example [ɑ:] is longer than [ɑ] and [ɑ::] is even longer

ɾ   r is tapped, as in the Spanish or Italian [ɾ]; also notated as [ɾ], which is an alveolar (upper gum ridge) tap

rʳ   r is rolled or trilled, as in Scottish and Russian [rʳ]

ʔ   glottal attack or stop, such as used to indicate a dropped [t] in the Cockney word "little," and the dropped [h] in "hello"

~   nasal, "ny" sound, as in the Spanish sound [ñ] in "piñata"

ʰ   aspirated, as in the plosive consonant [pʰ]

..   extra breathy, as in [a̤]

"   lips rounded, as in [ɒ"]; other sources mark lip rounding as [˓] as in [nǫ]

"   lips spread, as in [ɒ"]; other sources mark lip spreading as [˓] as in [hị]

꞊   tongue arch is lower, as in [a̞]

˔   tongue arch is higher or raised, as in [a̝]

_   tongue is further back, as in [a̠]

+   tongue is further forward, as in [a̟]

◾   dentalized sound, as in [t̪], such as in the Latin dialects

.   syllabic consonant, for example when an [l], [n] or [m] is used as a con-
         sonant, as in [lIt l̩] for the word "little"

˯   the unvoiced consonant is voiced, for example [t̬], making it sound more
         like a [d]

x   the throaty "kh" or "ch" sound, as in the Scottish word "loch" and the
         Russian initial [h]

ß   a cross between [b] and [v], such as in Spanish and Japanese dialects

Will I have the accent once I've written out all the phonetics?

Remember that you can't produce a believable dialect solely by following the phonetic markings. Even IPA transcription, which is more exact than phonetic respelling, can't breathe life into a dialect. It is very difficult to be definitive about putting human sounds into writing, thus there are some discrepancies in how different dialecticians write out the vowel and consonant substitutions for accents. That is why I didn't attempt to give you phonetic charts for all of the dialects I mention in this book. Learning accents is, unfortunately, not as simple as memorizing phonetic changes. Throughout this book you've been instructed to first consider the culture of the people and the "music" of their speech—their common inflection patterns, stress patterns, and rhythms. This also includes *tone*. As you do all of the substitutions, you should keep in mind the tone focus, or placement, as introduced in David Alan Stern's method. It would be a good idea to include a few notes to yourself about the tone focus and vocal patterns in the front of your script in the same place where you have all the little cheat-sheet notes of the vowel and consonant changes.

Tone focus will make all the difference in how you approach dialects. As I've suggested, no realistic dialect is produced simply by vowel and consonant substitutions. David Alan Stern spends nearly half of each of his one-hour tapes on drilling the proper tone focus for the accent he's introducing. I've often heard actors who seem to be doing everything *technically* right for the Standard British in terms of vowels, consonants, inflection, rhythm, and stress patterns, but it just doesn't quite sound *real* until they think the tone forward in front of the lips. Stern suggests a "kinesthetic trick" for each accent—an imaginary point of focus to get actors to have the proper mouth shape and tongue placement. With the help of an illustration, he demonstrates that the tone focus for Standard British is way out in front of the lips.[29] Stern helps us to grasp the feeling by contrasting the forward British tone focus with the Standard American, which is in the center of the mouth. Tone focus has to be explored. Don't be concerned if you don't feel it at first. That's why he drills it. Your sensitivity will grow.

What I'm asking you to add to Stern's method is this: the importance of the cultural study. He does not always give an image for each dialect he teaches. In my own training, I try to suggest one that makes sense according to the specific culture. Some of them may seem silly at first, but they work. For French, my kinesthetic trick (or trigger) is "spitting up grape seeds," tying in with their country's grape harvest. Many of the French sounds are way back in the throat, but many are also on the tip of the tongue. So, when you do that guttural spitting of a grape seed, you feel the right placement for the uvular "r," for example. You'll also feel the dental placement for consonants like "th," "t," and "d" (i.e., "this" and "that" sounds more like "zees" and "zat").

I've had a lot of success teaching the Irish accent once I've introduced my image for the tone focus: hold the jaw (slightly apart, not clenched) and say "Grrrr." This echoes the Irish attitude of tenacity amidst trials, as if the character is saying, "Grrrrr! I dare ya, punch me in the jaw! I can stand there and take it." This basically unmoving jaw position makes all the vowel formations happen naturally, and reinforces the placement for the hard "r's."

If you tend to learn by kinesthetics, by the way things physically feel, you can actually put your fingers up and hold your jaw steady for the Irish accent (index finger lightly on the upper jaw, middle finger on the lower jaw). For German, pinch back the sides of your lips with your fingers as you speak, and it creates the small slit you need in your mouth opening. Then when you get used to the feel of it, you can drop your fingers and try speaking. Put your fingers under your chin to feel the base of the tongue pulled down for a throaty accent like Russian. Literally using your hands to feel what the muscles are doing is often the very trigger to get you into an accent.

To get you started in the right direction, I've provided you with a kinesthetic trigger and some notes about lilt, placement and diction for each of the dialects listed in the "Dialect Directory" in the back of this book. Do read my introduction about the "Dialect Directory" before you use this valuable section of the book.

Would recording myself help?

A tape recorder is an excellent learning tool. Say your lines into a tape player or CD recorder and play them back. With practice, you will get better and better at being able to hear if you are doing it right.

If you have a dialect coach, or know an actor who is proficient in this dialect, this mentor can coach and correct you as you read your lines. Tape-record your sessions with your coach.

What other refinements do I need to make outside of rehearsals?

Go back to your marked text every few days, after you've memorized your lines, just to review your dialect. Many actors never refer back to their script again once they've memorized it. But for a dialect show, you absolutely need to. If your show has a dialect coach, expect to get notes about any vocal problems you are having. You should definitely mark your script when you get these notes, highlighting the specific words or phrases that you pronounced incorrectly. Put a big circle around these phrases, so you can find them and drill them at home. Refer to your text each day as you go over your lines, so that you won't make the same mistakes twice.

How often should I practice my dialect?

You need to get to a point where you not only can do your own character's lines in dialect but can read in dialect anything you pick up. Read letters from Mom, soup can labels, cereal boxes, other plays by the same author. See if you can be consistent without actually marking the vowels and consonants. Visualize the phonetic markings in your mind's eye.

As you're driving, a great way for you to practice is to read road signs. The phrases are short enough that you'd be able to figure out each sign's pronunciation in dialect and then drill it a few times.

Your next step is to become comfortable speaking spontaneously in dialect. Only then will you know you've really got it. If you can ad-lib, you are beginning to equate the dialect with the character. Eat, sleep, breathe, make dinner, and do your chores ad-libbing in dialect. Several of my students say it starts to drive their roommates crazy, but they keep practicing! Listen to the music of the culture you're studying. Keep researching its people by watching films and travelogues, and looking at picture books.

It's only when you start *thinking* in dialect that you know that it is truly becoming natural. You may even get to the point where, when someone is talking to you outside of rehearsals, you spontaneously answer them in dialect, using foreign expressions and phrases as your character would. You are *becoming* the character.

Do I need to do a dialect warm-up before every rehearsal?

It's important (and fun) to do all of your regular vocal warm-ups and tongue twisters in dialect. The tongue twisters are crucial for creating the flexibility you'll need for foreign accents. Standard British definitely requires more articulate speech than that of most American actors. Plus, the British accent has an overall feel of *ease* in its fluency, something that cannot be achieved without technically drilling, using lots of tongue twisters.

On the way to rehearsal every day, use the time to drill and warm up by reading road signs in dialect, as I just suggested. Say them five times, as fast as your mouth will go. Run through your lines. Talk to yourself. Or sing along with your car radio—only do it in dialect.

Here's another idea. When I dialect coach a play, I make a pact with the actors that the minute they arrive at rehearsal, they speak in dialect. Ask your director to help support this discipline. Even when you stop to ask for a line or to ask a question, try to maintain your dialect, never "breaking character." It's a creative way to get more practice in ad-libbing in the dialect.

You need to warm up your dialect before you speak your first lines on stage. When I watch a play, I can tell if the actors didn't warm up, because their dialects are shaky for the first few minutes. And that opening scene is critical in establishing whether are not you are going to be believable to your audience. Be careful, too, that you don't abandon your warm-up once your performances start. With all the commotion of opening a show, it's easy to forget.

What can I do if I keep losing the dialect?

You need to have a "trigger" for it. This is anything that helps to initiate or trigger the right feel for the dialect at any moment of the day. It can be a song, a representative phrase, or even an image of someone speaking in that dialect. Many actors I know sing "Wouldn't It Be Loverly," from *My Fair Lady*, to trigger the Cockney accent. Or they pace through a few lines of "I'd Do Anything," from *Oliver*. "O, Danny Boy" or "My Wild Irish

Rose" are good ones for Irish. Mimicking Maurice Chevalier singing, "Thank heavens for little girls. . ." may help trigger the French.

Even an overblown cliché can work. It's okay to use a "Lucky Charms" or "Irish Spring" commercial as your trigger. You're not basing the whole accent on that cliché. Mel Blanc's cartoon character of Speedy Gonzales at least gets me started in the right direction for a Mexican accent. You'll come up with your own ideas.

It helps me to picture someone speaking in the accent I'm working with, someone who easily and vividly comes to mind. It can be someone you've met, or an actor saying a few famous lines. For the Plantation Southern, I tell people to picture and then mimic Blanche DuBois from *A Streetcar Named Desire* saying, "I've always depended on the kindness of strangers."[30] How about Foghorn Leghorn from the Looney Toons cartoon saying, "Son, I say—I say, don't *do* that!"

In David Alan Stern's method, he advises using the tone focus exercise of counting to ten as a trigger. Even a monologue you learned in a certain dialect, one you marked phonetically and know perfectly, can become a trigger you can go back to years later when you need to resurrect that dialect.

Actors always admit that it's harder to be consistent with their accent when their character is excited or angry. As you listen to authentic speakers, you'll probably notice that their accent tends to get heavier with intense emotion. They express this emotion through exaggerated melody, extensions of vowels, emphasis of consonants, and through peculiar phrases. When they are self-controlled, they may be able to speak very clearly, with just a light flavor of their accent, but when they are out of control, the accent's full strength is released. However, the opposite happens when actors begin to develop a dialect: they tend to forget to do the dialect substitutions when their character is upset. So be sure you've drilled your dialect to the point where *it* will intensify as your *character* gets more and more intense.

When my scene partners speak in a different accent than mine, how do I avoid picking up their accent?

It is especially difficult to maintain your consistency when a fellow actor in your scene is doing a different accent. It's a challenge to be cast in a play where all of the characters speak in different dialects, as in some of those Agatha Christie murder mysteries. When you're cast as an educated British character, and are playing opposite a Cockney, it is difficult, but you must maintain your own dialect. Otherwise, you'll seem to jump back and forth from one class to another.

The answer is to drill your lines until you have the accent down cold. It's really a matter of staying in character, isn't it? If you've equated your character with the dialect from the very beginning, and have memorized your lines in dialect, you should be able to maintain your character, and thus his or her manner of speech throughout your performance.

It's true, certain accents are infectious. I'm sure you've all been around a Southerner, or maybe someone from England, and you've found yourself easily picking up his or her dialect. I noticed this in Richard Gere's Lancelot in *First Knight*. He used his own American accent for the film, but he picked up a few British "o's" and dropped "r's" in one scene with his British co-star. Gere was the only one without a British accent in the entire movie, and I thought he would attempt a light Standard British. The prologue introduced Lancelot as a "Wanderer" rather than the French knight of the original Camelot story. (He must have "wandered" over from America. But then again, America had not yet been discovered in King Arthur's time.) Because of the historical inconsistency of his dialect (or lack of one), we had to use a willing suspension of disbelief to accept his character.

Dennis Quaid's accent in *Dragonheart* seemed to change from scene to scene. His guttural American accent sounded Scottish in scenes opposite the dragon (which was voiced by Scottish actor Sean Connery), and then slightly British in the scenes he did with his English co-stars. It's easy to be a chameleon with your dialect, especially in film scenes that are taped weeks apart and out of sequence. So stay "in character" and "in dialect."

How do I handle those foreign phrases and expressions?

Foreign words, slang, expletives, and other idiomatic expressions help to bring the "local color" to your character's reality. But the meaning of these expressions may or may not be clear to an audience. First, make sure you've done your homework and have underlined the phrases you think your audience may not be familiar with. Know exactly what these phrases mean and how to pronounce them. Remember: don't guess or assume.

Brian Friel's play *Philadelphia, Here I Come* is peppered with dozens of expressions common to the Irish. Here are just a few of these idioms (underscored in the following excepts from the script) that you'd probably have to look up in a British-American dictionary:

An' sowl.[31]
By the hokey![32]
Aye, Ben Burton was a right skin.[33]
He's not in the half-penny place with them.[34]
I don't think I'm in form the night, boys.[35]
We'll show them a weed or two, eh?[36]
Out to the sand-banks! Get them in the bloody bent![37]
Bull on regardless! Yaaaaah![38]

You can see how these phrases might be pretty confusing to an audience. I want to show you an amazing passage from Wertenbaker's play *Our Country's Good* that has so much Cockney slang that you'd have to look up nearly every phrase in order to understand it well enough to play it effectively. The character is Liz Morden, a convict in an Australian penal colony in 1787, telling the story of how she got caught.

Liz, he says, why trine for a make, when you can wap for a winne? I'm no dimber mort, I says. Don't ask you to be a swell mollisher, Sister, men want Miss Laycock, don't look at your mug. So I begin to sell my mother of saints. I thinks I'm in luck when I meet the swell cove. He's a bobcull. He says to me, it's not enough to sell your mossie face, Lizzie, it don't bring no shiners no more. Shows me how to spice the swells. So. Swell has me up the wall, flashes a pocket watch, I lifts it. But one time, I stir my stumps too slow, the swell squeaks beef, the snoozie hears, I'm nibbed.[39]

When you study tapes and movies, listen closely to how idiosyncratic expressions and expletives are said, because the playwright won't necessarily write them out the way they are pronounced on the street. One example is the Cockney phrase "go on," which has the same meaning as the American expression, "Oh, come on, you can't be serious." But the Cockneys typically slur "go on" together as they give it that mocking downward inflection, so that it is pronounced "gawwn." You could mark it in your text as "go͡ on." Sometimes authors write it as "garn." The Irish expletive, "Jesus, Mary and Joseph!" typically has a pattern of inflection going from high to low, a pattern you would not necessarily know unless you'd heard it said that way by an Irish person.

Try this: once you've looked up a particular expression, try speaking your line of dialogue, replacing the phrase with its more familiar definition. This will help you figure out how you'd say the unfamiliar phrase in terms of tone of voice. Then see if you can insert the foreign or slang word using that same tone of voice, adding a flavor of expression that will give the audience a clue as to its meaning. Maybe a gesture or facial expression will help get the meaning across. Don't rush or mumble the phrase. Articulate it and stretch it out a bit. This goes for proper names and place names too. Practice saying all cultural idioms until the way you say them remains clearly articulated, yet seems to be the natural way that your character would say them. Although it seems obvious, you've got to remember that your audience hasn't heard these lines every day the way you have. It will frustrate audience members if they keep hearing mushy words they don't understand, and at a certain point they'll subconsciously give up trying to follow you.

Can I paraphrase some of my character's lines?

A paraphrase or simple inversion could affect the author's intent in terms of the flow of the dialect. Each dialect has its own distinctive rhythm and stress pattern that contrasts with your own American speech. Wording and phrasing are other elements that make a culture's speech distinctive. So you're best advised to memorize your lines word for word. Otherwise, it's sort of like trying to ad-lib a flubbed line of Shakespeare's poetry: the rhythm gets thrown off.

How do I find the "music" of the dialect?

During the rehearsal process, when we are learning the mechanics of a dialect and getting caught up in the placement and accuracy of each vowel and consonant, often the "music" of the language is lost. Go back and listen to your primary sources. Forget about listening to the diction and just let the music of the speech wash over you. Get a refreshed sense of the predominant patterns in the melody, the rhythms, the beat of stress. Return to the root of the speech, to its rawest form. If you're doing a foreign accent, listen to foreign language tapes to hear the original tongue, and watch foreign films with subtitles.

What specifically should you be listening for? Try to discover the phrasing and rhythm of the speech. Does the speaker tend to speak in long, flowing phrases, or in short, syncopated beats? Would you consider the speech smooth or choppy? What's the speed and tempo? What patterns are in the volume? Is it loud or soft overall? Does it build in intensity, or fade away at the ends of sentences?

If you have trouble with this, know that your "ear" can be developed through exploration. Some of the dialect teaching methods will answer these questions for you, or you can seek a dialect coach's help. Louis Colaianni's book, *The Joy of Phonetics and*

Dialects, can get you started in learning how to listen to the sounds and rhythms of dialects.

I have found that listening to the traditional music of the culture is indispensable to understanding the music of the culture's speech. The correlations are astounding. The Yiddish dialect has a distinctive sing-song lilt that is historically derived from the melodies of the songs and chants of traditional Jewish temple services. During several workshops for the casts of *My Children, My Africa!* and *Blood Knot*, both by Athol Fugard, I played some traditional black South African music and we explored how the distinctive strong rhythmic beats are echoed in African speech.

The folk music of Italy, its romantic ballads, and even its opera songs express that nation's energy and freedom in wide pitch range, passionate surges, and easily flowing melodies. The Italian manner of speech has the same qualities, wouldn't you agree? Contrast this music with the dark, rich tones and heavier underlying beat that is found in Russian folk music. The restrained, fragile melodies of many Asian folk ballads give clues to the restraint that can be heard in the speech of East Asians. Comparing a culture's slow, sad ballads with its spirited dance music will give you insights about how that culture celebrates and releases stress.

I always play tapes of music during my dialect workshops. If time allows, I piece together several tunes from different countries so that the actors can begin to hear how the songs contrast in mood and rhythm. For example, I might play cuts from a country-western song, a Jamaican reggae tune, a German polka, and a French folk song, and then contrast them with a Scottish jig.

I often record a collection of songs for every cast member of a production I'm coaching. They are encouraged to play the tapes in their car or at home to just let the music become a part of them. If you are doing a Southern play, you might try tuning into a country-western station every day as you drive to work. There are no rules—just listen and see what happens. Besides, it's part of your character study to figure out what kind of music your character likes to listen to in her leisure time (popular, classical, folk, etc.). Her taste in music is, of course, influenced by her class and generation. You may think that you don't like your character's musical preferences at first, but if you listen to the music every day, you'll most likely develop a taste for it, just as your character has.

I'm not sure if other dialect trainers have found the study of a culture's music and dance to be significant. The subject is not referred to in any of the other dialect books I've seen. But I can testify that the more I work with music while coaching shows, the more I am amazed by the discoveries I make. So I invite you to make the music of your character's culture a part of your research. If you are an actor who is also a dancer or musician, this may very well be the key that unlocks your understanding of dialects.

What does DANCE have to do with dialect work?

Dance has a lot to do with dialects. Once I started incorporating a study of the culture's traditional dance forms into my dialect work, I got incredible results. As with listening to a culture's music, researching its dance traditions gives vital clues to the culture's native speech patterns. And you don't have to be a professional dancer to pick up on these clues. I first discovered this when I coached *Dancing at Lughnasa*. The action of this play includes a number of dance sequences which are important to the understanding of the characters' development. Our production had a choreographer (Paula Gale of Orlando) who had studied Irish dance in Ireland. I attended a number of her dance sessions just to observe. The things she said to the actor-dancers as she coached them exactly paralleled what I had been telling them about their speech in my workshops. The structure and style of the dances reflected what the actors were learning regarding breath, rhythms, rate, stress patterns, posture, tension and relaxation.

What follows are the notes from the research I did on traditional Irish music in preparation for *Dancing at Lughnasa*, and the inferences I made regarding the speech and movement of the play's characters. Then I'll show you the notes I took at the dance rehearsals, which absolutely confirmed much of what I had researched about the Irish culture.

The taped music used for the production was primarily from four albums by the Chieftans, as selected by the director. I gave the cast an hour of taped selections, and instructed them to listen to the tapes often. I asked them to listen for elements that would evoke the following moods, rhythms, images, and movements.

The melody and rhythms suggest a jauntiness, with an impudent head carriage; perhaps even a quick toss of the head. The erect torso is held in staunchly for security, resistance, and personal dignity, and indicates a readiness to defend oneself. Eyes flash. Below the erect torso, the feet stay close to the earth they love, but cannot resist a jig from the hips down. These moves are a reflection of the solid baseline of the music (often a drone with bagpipes or drums) underlying the playful, happy melody up on top. This is the Irish paradox of being restricted (by their past struggles and their own traditional attitudes), yet overcoming it all with a spirit of joy. The melodies are as unpredictable as the people. The music seems both free and restricted at once, with patternless, narrow melody, no predominant downbeat, no wide pitch jumps. Endings of songs are simplistic and often abrupt, without flourishes, like the Irish themselves. Or the ending may be a sad fade of the bagpipe.

Breath seems to emanate from high in the chest, as felt in the tones and driving baselines of the music. The gut is tight and the chest heaves with a pride, an exuberance, and a sense of pushing down the pain right below the throat.

Some pieces reflect the lovely simplicity of the rural land, of fields and flowers. Others are contemplative airs, with pipes and flutes, giving a sense of isolation, loneliness, and longing. One can almost see the mist.

Dance pieces often begin with expectant moderation and work up to a frenzied release, which the Irish so long for.

I observed three dance rehearsals. Here are several of the phrases used by dance instructor Paula Gale to lead the actors in the traditional Irish dances and stage movements that were used in the production. See if they don't confirm and augment my notes above.

- Maintain balance; equal weight, even for shuffles.
- Posture aligned, ninety degrees to the earth. Head held tall, up proudly through the ceiling, with a straight high back, pulling up sternum.
- Broad, wide back as one walks; straighten spine from the bottom up like a zipper, as if taking wrinkles out of your shirt. Restraint and support.
- Suck it in (literally and figuratively). Take it. Never let defenses down. Always up, never down.

•Use little head shake.
•Ears in line with the shoulders. Head not jutting forward like Americans.
•Never curve. Keep back straight, even when bending over to the ground to work.
•Slides are low and close to the earth.
•Hands on hips or very stiff, straight at sides. Not feminine hands, hands used to work. Energy through hands, even in stillness.
•Joyful hops, light defiant stomps, and pendulum swings are from hips down, while torso stays tall and proud.

The film *Strictly Ballroom* features marvelous flamenco dancing in a number of scenes. The body language of the Latin people, as well as their dance, leads with a high chest. The speech, too, seems to emanate passionately from above the heart. There is a scene in which the older Spanish woman is teaching the young Australian dancer (the romantic lead) how to feel the beat of the music. She beats it out on his chest, trying to get him to feel the dignity and pride of her people in a raw, organic way. Then, as he proceeds to dance, he displays that high, proud carriage of the chest. As it does in this example, the raw energy of your character's speech and movement emanates from somewhere within your body. Find out where.

This aspect of the relationship between a people's dance and their speech needs more exploration. But the next time you see live cultural dance, or a foreign film where a dance is shown, think about these things:

– overall attitude (proud? sexy? restrained? exuberant?)
– overall silhouette
– spine shape and tension/relaxation
– head carriage
– freedom or rigidity in the torso, affecting breath (how deep the breath seems to go, and whether the breath release is unrestricted)
– arm carriage and movement
– leg movement
– where the energy seems to emanate from, and what "leads" (the head? pelvis? chest? legs? toes?)
– large movements or small?
– use of space (large area or small? linear or curved? patterned or unpatterned?)
– type of rhythm (syncopated? smooth? staccato?)
– rate (fast or slow? rushing or relaxed? steady or unpredictable?)

Such ponderings may lead you to a better understanding of your character's speech and movement patterns in the dialect. Even just a little knowledge is a powerful thing. So your grasp of the dialect will deepen the more you know about the culture.

How important are my nonverbal expressions in creating a believable dialect?

It is not enough just to sound convincing—you've got to *look* convincing as well. Since our nonverbal expressions are said to contribute more than 80% of our message, it should be no surprise that they are a very important part of your dialect characterization. As you work on the blocking, gestures, movements, and bits of business for your role, be mindful of those things you learned from your cultural research in Chapter 4 concerning body language.

It is not politically incorrect to say that there are definitely some distinctive nonverbals associated with different cultures. These gesture and movement tendencies emerge from a region's historic and cultural influences. A people's attitudes about their self-image and their world are often translated into physical expressions. Their social class, education, and age help determine their body language too. As has been described previously, you should research to find out what the culture's acceptable "norm" is, in terms of mannerisms and movements. Then consider how your individual character fits into this traditional or typical role model of their people.

Once your show is blocked, review the notes you took when you researched the culture (see the list on p. 40) and your character (see the list on p. 53). See what you can now *apply* to your blocking and movements. None of the other stage dialect texts and tapes that are currently on the market cover the body language that should accompany specific dialects, so I'm pleased to introduce this important element to readers of this book.

Nonverbal communication not only includes the physical, but the voiced expressions. This includes mouth sounds and wordless utterances used in moments of anger, excitement, exhaustion, despair, hesitation, and contentment. The sounds may be a cultural habit, or an individual character habit. Each dialect has a manner in which they produce a vocalized pause, or "uh." They may have a distinct way that they express an "Oh" for specific emotions. You'll pick up on these mouth sounds by listening to authentic sources.

How do my carriage and gestures contribute to my dialect work?

Chapter 3 suggested that the most telling thing about a person is his head carriage, as well as how he holds his hands and feet. An American will stick out of a crowd in a foreign country without opening his mouth, even if he is dressed as a native. The "typical" middle-class American tends to move his head and shoulders a lot, use facial expressions openly, and sit, walk, and stand with comfort in mind (even if that means slouching). Contrast this with the upper-class British, who tend to be erect with a dignity that was passed down through the centuries. "Dignity" is not always the first term that people from other cultures use to describe exuberant Americans! We carry ourselves with far less nationalistic pride than most other countries. This is largely due to how young a nation we are. Even our oldest traditions, many of which are borrowed, are no more than two hundred years old.

The British economize on extraneous, fidgety movements. They would feel very comfortable sitting with quiet hands and feet, where Americans show their nervous energy with fingers fussing and toes tapping. Did you know that it's considered to be quite "American" for males to cross their legs by putting one ankle on the opposite knee? British males tend to sit with legs crossed at the knees, which is considered a more feminine posture to Americans. We've been teased by the British about our tendency to smile too much and laugh robustly, whereas they've learned to control their emotions behind straight faces. They admire our gregariousness as much as we admire their poise.

I had a dialect student who studied in Australia for two years, and one of the things she noticed about Australian body language was how the Australians kept their arms close to their bodies, instead of flailing them around freely like Americans. One reason for this may be that they are respecting each other's personal space. Or perhaps their attitude and lifestyle are too practical for the fussiness of showy gestures. You'll also notice more confined gestures in cultures that have been beaten down by centuries of repression and hardship.

Contrast these examples with the often wildly expressive gestures of the Italians. Perhaps you've heard your Italian American friends mock themselves by saying, "If you tied my hands, I wouldn't be able to talk!"

Remember that weather can influence body posture. Cold weather and ever-threatening rain make people bundle up and close in, whereas heat can make people sprawl loosely. Climbing temperatures can also put emotions (and expressiveness) on the surface.

There are hundreds of symbolic gestures that are known to the people of certain regions. Take nothing for granted merely because it is familiar to you. Our American "okay" sign, with the forefinger and thumb making a circle, is considered vulgar in Brazil and Germany. "The gesture is also considered impolite in Greece and Russia, while in Japan, it signifies 'money' and in southern France, 'zero' or 'worthless'."[40] Americans who absentmindedly stroke their cheek should realize that it means "attractive" in Greece, Italy, and Spain. In Yugoslavia it means "success," and elsewhere it can mean "ill" or "thin." Fingers crossed means "good luck" or "protection" to Americans and Europeans. But in Paraguay, the gesture could be offensive.

The meaning attached to the act of waving varies throughout the world. Americans wave a hand to mean "good-bye," but in Peru, the gesture means "come here." In Greece, a hand wave, especially one close to the other person's face, is a serious threat. We teach our kids to wave "bye-bye" with palms turned out and all of the fingers wagging up and down together, where many Italians learn to wag the fingers with palms in, because showing the open palm is considered to be pretty brazen.[41]

There are a few books that discuss international body language. One that is really fun to read is *Do's and Taboos Around the World*, edited by Roger E. Axtell, written to help the business traveler avoid misunderstandings when dealing with foreign clients. It gives you tips on the proper etiquette for handshakes, greetimgs, eating, gestures, use of slang, and all kinds of other do's and don'ts. Another fabulous resource is *Kiss, Bow or Shake Hands: Doing Business in Sixty Countries*, which not only shares the gestures and body language of different cultures but gives a social, historical, and cultural overview of the people, and even how they organize and process information, and their value systems that determine behavior. See the Bibliography for several other sources that provide tips for business travelers abroad.

What about facial expressions and eye contact?

I've mentioned how important it is to watch facial expression in films and in still photos of the people you are studying. Lower classes often have more freedom of facial expression than upper classes do. For example, Cockneys are freer than the upper-class British because they aren't as concerned about preserving appearances. Working-class Southerners and New Yorkers use a lot of facial expression. The high-class British and French express distaste with a lift of the eyebrows, as if to say, "Well! I never!"

Eye contact has its own language. Unless they're especially shy, Americans are bolder with eye contact when meeting new acquaintances than are the people of many other nations, though our focus is pretty scattered when we chat with someone we know. We consider staring at a stranger to be rude, where it is a compliment in certain countries. Many Asians learn to lower their eyes in respect, at just the appropriate moment. Find out what the tradition is for eye contact for the country you're researching.

What is proximity?

On your national characteristics checklist (p. 40), I told you to note acceptable standards for *proximity*, or physical nearness. How near can people from the culture you're studying stand to someone to whom they've just been introduced, without feeling uncomfortable? Does the distance change considerably once they become friends? Do they like to get into the other person's space through touch? (Italians, for example, often find a way to touch your arm when they are making a point.) How close do they stand when arguing? Is it nose to nose, as the French are known to do? How do they show affection in public? Is it different in private? I've noticed when traveling in Mexico, and also when observing Latin American visitors, that it's not uncommon for friends of the same sex to link arms as they walk, sometimes three or four people across. Americans are less likely to hold hands or link arms with same-sex friends as they walk. Yet we are fairly open with lovers in public, and we feel free to hug friends as a greeting.

You'll see Spanish and Latin American young people walk arm in arm with their parents, even when they are teenagers or older. In the United States, it seems that even pre-teens begin to feel they don't want to be caught dead walking close to their folks! The British have a larger comfort zone than Americans do. They tend to keep a respectful distance from acquaintances and are more conservative about public shows of affection. The American comfort zone, even with a new acquaintance, is a little closer—about the distance of a bent arm. Don't be offended when Middle Easterners seem to crowd you in conversation. It is polite in their society to be able to come into your breathing space.

This aspect of proximity will affect your blocking and business when it comes to your physical relationship with the other characters in the play. It will affect how you greet people, whether they are a stranger, friend, family, new love, or old love. It will affect how you shake hands, bow, sit, stand, and walk. If you've ever been in a period play, I'm sure you've had to learn and apply the physical movements and manners of that distinctive era. The work you'll do on your dialect role is similar in that you have to make adjustments that will be believable for that culture. Use wisdom and sensitivity though, because it is possible your director will give you blocking and business that conflict with what you've studied and observed. The director may have you standing or sitting closer to your scene partner than would be appropriate for that nationality, or grabbing someone's hand when linking arms would be the more traditional show of affection.

Always defer to the director's wishes. If you're in a situation in which you can show and discuss your findings with the director, do it privately, after rehearsal. If your production has a dialect coach, you can discuss the issue with him or her. Ideally, the director can consult the dialect coach about the accuracy of the body language being used for a dialect role.

My dialect won't stay consistent during the stop-and-go rehearsals!

That's to be expected. The dialect's melody and rhythms get off track with so many stops and starts. Run-throughs of scenes are the best times to feel the flow of your speech. So just keep running your lines in dialect at home, tape-recording yourself, and correcting your mistakes.

At this point in your rehearsal process, you're probably feeling more confident with the consistency of the vowel and consonant substitutions. The things to check yourself on as you run your lines at home are correct placement (tone focus), and the proper flow of the music of the dialect.

There is going to be another time in the rehearsal process where you'll feel like your proficiency in the dialect takes a big step backward. This will be when you're first getting "off book." That rehearsal where lines are expected to be "cold" is a rough one, so your director needs to realize that the clarity, consistency, and flow of your dialect are probably going to be less than perfect. Don't get frustrated if you can't keep all the things you're juggling up in the air during these first off-book sessions. If you've been drilling all along, it will all come together eventually. Remember though, what I advised earlier—if you've waited to get off book before beginning to learn your dialect, chances are it will be very difficult to incorporate it now.

Do you want me to ACT, or do the dialect perfectly?!

As a dialect coach, I hear every actor say this at least once. It's hard to get into the emotions and actions of your role and also have the dialect down perfectly. You feel pulled apart. You'll want to tell your dialect coach or director, "Hey, I'm trying to act here! Don't pick apart my sounds!" You'll resent anyone giving you dialect notes.

When you feel self-conscious about your speech because someone is analyzing every word, how can you be expected to act? The rehearsal process was designed to be just that—a process. Until you can "marry the technique and the talent," you need to expect some ups and downs. You'll probably get worse before you get better, during certain steps of the process.

It's normal to feel vulnerable and a little defensive about how your accent is sounding. My actors know I'm only there to help them, yet they often verbally respond to one of my notes with, "I know! The second it came out, I knew it was wrong. You didn't have to tell me!" As a coach, I don't take that personally, nor do I back down on giving the note. I'm actually encouraged, because it means the actor is learning how to listen to himself, and is catching himself mid-stream as he makes mistakes.

The goal of a good dialect coach is to teach the actor to monitor himself. I hope you do have a dialect coach for your show, and I hope he is relentless about correcting you. After all, he just wants you to sound wonderful. We all need an outside ear to critique us. I also hope there is a mutual trust built between cast and coach, and that you have the assurance that the critique is coming from someone who respects you and cares about your feelings. Most dialect coaches have a strong acting background and fully understand what you're going through in creating your role. In Chapter 8, I'll give you more insights about what to expect when working on a production with a dialect coach.

CHAPTER 7
RUN-THROUGHS, DRESS REHEARSALS, OPENING NIGHT, AND BEYOND

Please don't give me any more to think about!

If you started working on your dialect early on, as my book suggests, by the time you move into run-throughs of your play you will really begin to feel that the character and the dialect are one. It will seem so natural for your character to speak in dialect that you can concentrate on all the other pressing and exciting aspects of opening your show. You need to feel confident and comfortable in your overall performance—the blocking, lines, characterization, rhythms, and builds.

I want you to be able to "relax into the dialect." This can only happen if you aren't struggling with it, and when you don't feel you need to push it in order to be accepted as believable. I was impressed by Kevin Kline's French character in the film *French Kiss* (co-starring Meg Ryan). I think Mr. Kline had become so comfortable with the French accent that he relaxed into it. He wasn't pushing it or acting it. He believed he *was* that character—a character who happened to be French.

Let me give you one more word of advice as the final polish to your mastery of the dialect: speak like you know what you're talking about. This is an interesting phenomenon—I'll be listening to a monologue of a student of mine who has the technical mastery of the dialect, as well as an understanding of the character and the culture, and the monologue will sound satisfactory. Then I'll tell him simply, "Now, say it like you know what you're talking about," and he'll instantly do it with much more conviction of character. The dialect rings true, and I believe him. And that's the whole point.

How do I keep the dialect consistent through all the pressures of dress rehearsal?

During this stage of the rehearsal process, your nerves may affect your consistency and fluency with the accent. As you would for any performance, with or without a dialect, channel your adrenaline, focus on your character's thoughts and actions, and *trust yourself*. Trust that all your hard work of drilling and rehearsing will result in a believable performance. As a coach, I've come to expect that actors' dialects may not be perfect at dress rehearsals. Forgive yourself and do better tomorrow. You have a lot of new things to think about. A last-minute costume piece or added prop might throw you off at first. A fake beard, teeth, or other make-up design might impede articulation in a way you didn't anticipate. A costume may constrict breathing needed for proper projection.

I've mentioned in every chapter that clarity is the most important thing. The dialect is nothing if you simply aren't being heard. Since more and more of the technical elements of your show are in place at this point, you should notice how set pieces, sound effects, even light cues affect acoustics. In many theaters, the sound is more muffled when an actor faces sideview or upstage to deliver lines. So, you'll need to articulate more and possibly be louder, if you are blocked to face upstage. A sound effect, musical bridge, or noise on stage may compete with the actors' voices. The volume of the orchestra or a sound effect may have to be negotiated with the director, or the actors may have to compensate with more projection.

If you're doing an offstage voice, not only do you need to be heard, but your voice needs to have the appropriate acoustic properties. For example, you may need to sound as if you are yelling from across an open field, when in reality you are squashed up between one of the set's flats and the theater's back wall. Or you may need to sound like you're calling from a locked closet, when you are really just standing in the open wings. Some experimenting with your body placement offstage (facing different directions, different walls, or the open flies, for example) can achieve just the right acoustic sound to be believable. Get help from someone listening from the audience—the vocal coach, the director, or an assistant with a good ear.

The presence of an audience has an impact beyond what it does to your nerves. Audiences impact audibility. They move slightly and make noise, even when attentive. Their clothing muffles sounds coming from on stage, whereas a theater of empty chairs does not. Your director should help you anticipate this difference in audibility by asking the cast for raised volume in rehearsals.

During these final run-throughs, the strengths and weaknesses of your overall vocal technique will be glaringly obvious to the director. That's why the more vocal control you have, the better. The dialect will not hide your weaknesses. It's probably too late to bring in a vocal coach to "fix" problems with projection, articulation, or tone. Of course, some dialects naturally tend to be louder than others, such as New Yorker or Italian. Some, like Brooklynese and the Mountain dialects, tend to strain the actor's voice, because they constrict the throat. So you may have to compensate in order to be heard, and also to stay healthy vocally throughout the run—you may need to open your mouth more, articulate more instead of straining, or lighten up on the vowel and consonant substitutions. All I'm saying is, be open to adjustments for the sake of my adage: "Clarity above all."

It's SHOWTIME, and I think I'm ready.

It's opening night, or the first day of your shoot. Congratulations! Do your warm-ups—in dialect—just as you have during each rehearsal. Often, I see warm-ups abandoned on opening night amidst all the hurry and flurry. Get into character before the performance by ad-libbing in dialect as you put on your costume and make-up. Play the taped music you've found of your character's culture and let the images it invokes ignite and warm you. Every day, you should review the dialect troublespots you've marked in your script before you arrive at the theater or studio. Keep eating, sleeping, and breathing in the dialect.

How am I going to keep the dialect fresh throughout the run?

Sometimes, as the rhythms and characters develop through the show's run, the dialects start to dissipate or go in a wrong direction. Certain dialects even start to get heavier and heavier. Cockney and French are two accents that actors seem to enjoy so much that they get carried away with them. Bad habits creep in, even with the best of us. Just be aware that this could happen to you. When I coach a show, I return several times during the run (or during the months of taping) to give notes on what may be slipping. The actors always welcome such feedback. I want my actors to feel confident in their dialect roles, but also to feel challenged, to realize that they simply "gotta keep on practicin'."

How does this kind of dialect work apply to film and television shoots?

Everything I've talked about concerning dialect acquisition applies to preparing for a film or television role, except that in such cases the actor is leading up to weeks of shooting rather than weeks of a run. But I do think it's tougher to be *consistent* in film and television than it is in live theatre productions.

As you know, a storyline in film or in television is seldom shot in sequence. Such work demands careful attention to "continuity" in costume, set pieces, and lighting. And continuity is just as big a consideration with regards to your dialect. Your speech needs to be consistent, scene to scene, day to day, even if the scenes are filmed weeks apart. Unfortunately, what sometimes happens is that the dialect varies too much from scene to scene, because one day the actor warmed up her dialect to do the filming, and another day she didn't. Or perhaps the actor improved on her dialect as the weeks of shooting went on, so that it sounds different on the scenes that are already in the can. Or maybe she got tired by the end of a long day of shooting, and the accent deteriorated. I suppose one advantage to film over theatre is that you may be able to reshoot the scene, or dub it later, if obvious errors have been made in the dialect. But you, your director, or the editor would have to be pretty perceptive about continuity to catch such errors. This is all the more reason to have your accent down cold by the very first day of shooting.

You may have a situation in which the character's accent is supposed to get lighter, or alter in some way, as the story goes along. A good example of this would be how Eliza Doolittle's speech in *My Fair Lady* slowly evolves from lower-class Cockney to elegant, upper-class British. You hear a similar transformation from Cockney to Standard British in *Chaplin*, a film about Charlie Chaplin, that stars Robert Downey, Jr. There is even a scene in the film where the character is practicing saying "bottle" instead of "bo'le," because he's become embarrassingly aware that his speech makes him seem lowborn. Melanie Griffith's character in *Working Girl* is shown in a few scenes using a tape recorder, to work on diminishing her brash, working-class New York twang, because she hopes to sound more like a classy executive for her important board presentation at the end of the movie. In *Moscow on the Hudson*, Robin Williams's Russian accent gets lighter and lighter the longer he lives in America. How would you make such a transformation in the course of a typical film shoot, when your script is not shot in sequence? You'd need to "score" your script by making notes about the strength of the dialect, from scene to scene, and then refer to those notes right before the shooting of each one.

Dialects in play productions may need to be even more articulate than they might for film work, so as to be clearly understood on a large stage without amplification. On the other hand, dialects in films may need to be more subtle, and also more perfectly accurate to withstand audience's scrutiny under the microscope of close shots.

One more difference between theatre acting and acting in film and television: with TV and film work, it's not uncommon to get last-minute script changes. Be able to quickly mark your script for the vowel and consonant changes and, better yet, come to the shoot prepared to ad-lib in the dialect.

Does it get any easier NEXT time?

Yes, it gets easier. The approach to dialect work outlined in this book is a process, and, because you will be integrating techniques and information that will be new to you, your first dialect role will probably seem pretty complicated. After all, I've opened up a lot of avenues for research and study that you may not have considered before. But your prep for subsequent roles will get easier and will happen more quickly as you get more comfortable with the process.

Performing in a dialect will always delight and terrify you. Hopefully the delight will lead you to explore with utter fascination the way other cultures speak. And I hope you feel just enough terror to persuade you to seize the challenge of perfecting your dialect, knowing it takes both discipline and concentration.

I won't deny it, being believable in a dialect role takes hard work. But that's the mystery and paradox of our craft as actors: we work hard at making it look as if we never even rehearsed.

CHAPTER 8

TO THE DIALECT COACH
(Directors, read this too!)

What does it take to be a dialect coach?

A good dialect coach must have:
– an extraordinary ear (for both speech and music)
– expertise in understanding and speaking dialects, so as to be the best example possible to students
– a thorough knowledge of phonetics
– an ability to communicate well with actors, as a coach and a teacher
– a solid working relationship with the director
– acting experience and/or an ability to relate to the actor's process of creating a dialect role
– strong and efficient skills in script and character analysis, and
– the ability to focus in on the minute details of an actor's technique, yet also to step back and hear the play as if for the first time, as an audience member would.

What does a dialect coach do?

The dialect coach is responsible for helping the actors create and sustain believable, consistent, clear dialects on stage or on screen. She serves the director as well, by being an extra set of ears and eyes, helping to guide the actors as they work to lift the play script off of the page and put it into spoken words that will communicate something to the audience. Whereas the director is concerned with concepts, objectives, motivations, truth in characterization, staging, and composition, the dialect coach can focus on the sound of the spoken word (and in many cases, on the characters' nonverbal communication).

What the dialect coach is NOT

The coach is not hired to make interpretive decisions about lines, but rather to make sure that what was heard by the audience communicated the writer's ideas and the director's intent. Sometimes a director is intimidated by the thought of using a vocal coach or dialect coach, because he doesn't know what a coach does. Maybe he's secretly afraid that the vocal coach will attempt to direct the play, or at least parts of it, since the coach works so closely with the actors as they interpret their lines. If you're wise, you'll always stay in close touch with the director, conferring with him on his intent. Talk often. In your private tutorials with actors, be aware of the line between dialect work and script work. If there's a question of a line having an unclear objective, always question the actor as to the director's intent. An open and honest relationship between the director and yourself must be nurtured early on, so that there is a trust built between you. This trust will grow as you work on a second, third, and fourth production together, as the director sees the fruits of your labor. In other words, he'll see that you are there to help enhance the quality of the production.

In short, the dialectician researches the appropriate dialect, teaches it, demonstrates it, drills it, reinforces it, and ventures forth with the actors and director to discover how to apply it to characterizations that fit the play as a whole. Nan Withers-Wilson put it beautifully in her book, *Vocal Direction for the Theatre*. She describes how the vocal director works collaboratively with the entire production team in making certain that "the consciousness of each of the play's characters is clearly and effectively conveyed by the means of the actors' voices to the ears, hearts, and minds of the audience."[42]

Where can I get information about becoming a dialect coach?

If you want to find out more about being a voice, speech, and dialect coach, there is an organization of strongly committed trainers called VASTA, the Voice and Speech Trainers Association, formed in 1986. I have been a member of the group myself since 1987. Each year, VASTA holds a well-attended summer conference, where members meet to participate in advanced training, to discuss issues, to network, and to offer guidance and information supportive of VASTA's goal of achieving the highest excellence in vocal training. Our international membership includes teachers, actors, and coaches who work in all kinds of performance media—in live theatre, film, television, radio, and public speaking. We teach acting, singing, speech, movement, and speech science to students in all kinds of environments, from academic, to amateur, to professional. The VASTA Mentoring Program offers new voice and speech teachers guidance, encouragement, and opportunities for shadowing and assisting professional trainers. A quarterly newsletter is available to keep members informed about all kinds of voice conferences around the world, about vocal training programs for actors and coaches, and about news pertinent to our specialty. We also put out an annotated VASTA bibliography listing all of the known books and tapes that apply to voice, speech, dialects, singing, movement, and speech science. Check their web site at www.vasta.org for all of the many services and resources they offer.

Are there any books written about vocal coaching?

Nan Withers-Wilson wrote a book that will help you, called *Vocal Direction for the Theatre: From Text Analysis to Opening Night*. Only one brief section deals specifically with dialect coaching a play, but the book is a good source for information about the duties of a vocal coach (or the Vocal Director, as Withers-Wilson prefers to term the position).

Another wonderful summary of the process of dialect coaching is an article called "Preparing a Cast for a Dialect Show," by Bonnie Raphael, who teaches at the American Repertory Theatre in Massachusetts. It is in Volume 33 of the journal, *Communication Education*. Check the Bibliography for where to find both of these resources.

What else can you teach me about dialect coaching?

The first seven chapters of this book trace the process of dialect acquisition primarily from an actor's point of view, providing guidance for actors who must create dialect roles without the benefit of personal dialect instruction. (Obviously, the ideal situation, which is not often the norm, is that the actor always works with a dialect coach.) This chapter is aimed specifically at the dialect coach, although it will also be of interest to the director who is planning to employ one. I don't recommend that directors attempt dialect coaching their own show on top of their directing duties, since they already have enough on their plate. But it is possible to do both, just as it is possible to both direct and star in a production.

In the *ideal* dialect coaching situation, you would be commissioned to work with a production several months before it goes into rehearsals. This would give you time to read and study the play, to research the specific dialects thoroughly, to become an expert on the cultures, and to prepare your workshops and handouts. You should be included in the pre-production meetings as an integral part of the artistic team, along with the stage manager, assistant directors, designers, technical director, musical director, and choreographer.

If you are also a teacher at an academic institution, academy, or repertory theatre company, you're at an advantage, because generally you will know in advance which shows you are going to coach. In this kind of academic situation, you could plan your curriculum to allow you to teach the specified accents before the productions are mounted. I outlined in Chapter 2 how important it is for actors to have a handle on their dialects before auditions.

Unfortunately, what is often the case in the "real world" is that you are asked to coach a show that is already in rehearsals. You (and the actors) are definitely at a disadvantage, because at this point everyone is already caught up in the whirlwind of character development, script analysis, line memorization, and blocking rehearsals.

The worst scenario is when a dialect coach is called in very late in the rehearsal process to "fix" the accents. I'm certainly guilty of agreeing to do this. In some ways, I suppose giving the cast a little help is better than leaving them stranded with none. But I certainly wouldn't want to lead the director to believe that such a practice would be an acceptable one for future productions, as it is an extremely difficult task.

This practice—of putting a sort of band-aid on bad accents that have already been set by weeks of rehearsals—can be avoided. What you need to do is commit yourself to educating the pool of directors you work with. Tell them what you do and how you can best accomplish your goals of teaching and coaching the dialects. (I'll show you how you can educate them in a moment.) You do have a right to refuse a late commission, if the task seems insurmountable. I've gotten calls from directors a week before opening night, with requests like, "Can you lower this actress's voice?" or "Can you make him articulate his British accent more clearly?" or "Can you make him talk and move more like someone from the seventeenth century?" Many problems are coachable, but some just can't be solved in a week, even by the most proficient coach.

As vocal coaches, we must be wise, and we must continue to educate ourselves in this ever-growing field. We must work to promote the integrity of our specialty, giving it dignity by performing our duties with nothing short of excellence. And part of our success will be in how we collaborate with the rest of the production team. We must clearly communicate exactly what we require from the other team members in order to get the job done right.

How can I educate a director about how a dialect coach prepares a cast for performance?

One idea is to let him read this book. He'll be able to see how a coach might work to lead a cast through the entire process of learning a dialect, and he can then discuss with you how the information can apply to his particular show. The other idea is to meet with the director to go over the process.

I recommend that you have several casual meetings alone with each of the directors in your area whose projects would benefit from your coaching. During this consultation, tell these directors how you've worked in the past. Tell them about an ideal situation you worked on, and why you think it was so successful. In each case, make recommendations that suit the director's specific show, and indicate how much work you expect it to take to make their actors' dialects believable. Give them an idea of what could be accomplished with the *maximum* amount of coaching, and what could be accomplished with the *minimum* amount of coaching. You must know what your personal limit is. How much can you do if you have a limited amount of time with the actors? Is it worth your time? Where can you cut corners without sacrificing too much quality? As you become more certain about your skills and about the capabilities of your acting pool, you'll be more confident in presenting your "guesstimations" to the director. Usually, the result of this meeting is a compromise between an absolute ideal use of the coach, and a minimal use of the coach. The important thing is to find a middle ground, one that everyone can realistically live with.

The choice of the play itself will weigh into your guesstimations. Obviously, the process will be easier if the show has a two-person cast and only one dialect, as opposed to a cast of fifty requiring ten different accents. With experience, you'll get to know which accents will take actors longer to perfect, and which ones they tend to pick up the easiest. (See the section in Chapter 1 answering the question, "Are certain dialects easier to learn than others?")

Consider *well* the time frame for rehearsals. Is it a play with a normal five-week rehearsal period? Some professional theatre companies put up a production in a week, requiring their actors to come to the first rehearsal with their lines already memorized. Any dialect workshops and private tutorials would have to be scheduled very early on, and you'd have to attend all the rehearsals.

What are the director's two big considerations? Time and money.

The director, of course, has to consider two big issues before you're employed: (1) scheduling—How much time can we afford to give to the dialect coach's training? and (2) money—How much money can we afford to pay for this coach's time? (And how much is she *worth*? Can we do it without her?)

The money issue is a complicated one, because you have to decide for yourself what is fair to charge for your expertise. Or whether to charge at all. Early in my career, especially in graduate school, I didn't charge. I was building up my experience and my reputation. Now, when asked about my "usual" fee, I weigh a number of issues before giving a price. These issues include such factors as the company's available budget, and whether my schedule permits me to devote my energy to the project at the time I'm needed. As to the theatre's budget, they may not want to divulge it, and you'll have to surmise what they can afford. You can choose to aim for a high fee and hope they will negotiate. You can find out what they've paid contracted specialists in the past, such as choreographers or music directors. They may never have contracted anyone, in which case they won't know what to offer you. But, more often than not, there simply is no budget at all allotted for dialect coaching, especially for small production companies. It may be a number of years before coaching gets its full respect and reward. (Yes, there are a few famous dialect coaches who work with celebrities, but this really isn't the right business for you if you're aiming for vast monetary rewards!)

As you get more experience, you'll get a feel for how to charge fairly for your work. There are a number of factors that will affect how you charge, and at times it can be a tough call. Depending on the circumstances, you may decide to charge by the hour, by the day, or by the project as a whole. I have done coaching for free, for directors whose work I really respected. I've also coached for free as a favor to companies I knew couldn't afford to pay. It all comes back to you anyway, since other people in the business will get word of your fine work, and companies who have budgets for dialect coaching will then hire you for a tidy sum. If you're out there working—and you're very good at it—your reputation will precede you, and directors will seek you out for their projects.

I can only speak from my own experience, but I have found that most play produc-tions that schedule a five-week rehearsal period, allotting 30-40 hours for dialect coaching provides adequate time to do the job well. That time frame includes two dialect workshops, attendance at two to three rehearsals a week, and several individual tutorials as needed.

Can you suggest a written proposal for dialect coaching a production?

On the next pages is a proposal I created for dialect coaching a show. I usually put my proposals in writing for the directors I worked with, to give them an idea of how I choose to work. Individual proposals may vary somewhat, but in general I've found that the outline presented on the next pages provides an ideal use of the dialectician's time and talents, without being at all impractical or intrusive with respect to the director's own rehearsal agenda. You and the director can discuss your proposal's individual points and come to an agreement as to what will work for the current production's particular needs.

There are several ways you can use this sample proposal. It's been printed here on separate pages, so it can be easily photocopied for your production. You may choose to add a contract page, if you decide that you want the agreement to be officially signed. Once you and the director have reached an agreement about the proposal's contents, I recommend giving copies to other members of the production team, such as the stage manager and choreographer (if there is one), so they have an idea of your role in the rehearsal process.

PROPOSAL for Dialect Coaching a Production

1. Dialect coach is available for consultation at audition callbacks to give the director insights as to potential vocal problems or strengths of those individuals considered for casting.

2. Dialect coach is present at first rehearsal, to be introduced by the director to the cast and the other members of the production team. The dialect coach is given ten minutes to briefly state how he/she will work with the cast to help them learn and polish their dialect(s).

3. Dialect coach is present at the first read-through to get a baseline overview of the show aurally (including actors' aptitude for learning the dialect).

4. Coach is also present at rehearsal(s) when directorial concept and style are discussed with the actors, and costume and set designs are shown.

5. Two group dialect workshops will be given about a week apart, lasting one-and-a-half to two hours each, and must be attended by all of the actors who are speaking in the dialect. The first workshop should take place during the first week of rehearsals, if not before. Other workshops or individual sessions can be scheduled that first week, if more than one dialect is to be spoken in the show. The dialect coach prefers the director's presence at these sessions if possible, to impress upon the actors the importance of the coach's work. The director's attendance also helps by giving him/her enough insight into the actor's dialect work to enable him/her to reinforce the coach's teaching in subsequent rehearsals. In addition, the director's presence keeps communication open between all members of the rehearsal process (director, coaches, actors), so that all are viewed as a working partnership. The director should stress to the actors the value of attendance and promptness at the workshops. The workshops are not optional, no matter how well the actors think they know the dialect already, and no matter how small their speaking roles may be.

6. During the second week of rehearsals, the coach may see the need for conducting a drill session with the actors. This session would be between one-half hour to an hour long.

7. Individual tutorials to polish up the dialect will be set up by the coach as needed throughout the rehearsal period. These can be requested by the director or by the actors. One to four tutorials per actor is usually sufficient.

8. The coach sits in on two to three rehearsals per week during a regular five-week rehearsal period and takes notes, which will be given to the individual actors at the end of each rehearsal. The director is welcome to review the notes before they are distributed. Actors are responsible for studying these notes, applying them, and marking the corrections in their script. The director is asked to reinforce the importance of applying the notes that are given.

9. Before the director gives notes at the end of each rehearsal, the dialect coach should be given the opportunity to give dialect notes to the cast vocally if the notes demand demonstration. Most often, the notes can be communicated successfully through written comments, or by pulling aside an actor when he or she is not on stage. The actors will also have a phone number where they can call the coach for clarification. General vocal notes to the entire cast can be communicated by means of a callboard. Actors can initial their notes once they have read them.

10. The coach will communicate with the director before or after each rehearsal about what is needed vocally from the actors, so as not to be giving the actors notes that conflict with the director's (possibly changing) concept for their characters. The coach will give posture and movement notes as well, since an actor's voice and movement affect one another. Overall, communication will be welcomed and sought after, so that the entire production team can work well together.

(This proposal was developed by Ginny Kopf, from her book *The Dialect Handbook*.)

CHAPTER 9

ACTOR'S CHECKLIST

To create a believable dialect role:

1. Do your regular actor's script analysis—the *who, what, when, where, why,* and *how.*

2. Focus on studying the "where"—the locale of your play/film.
   Locate this locale on a map. Know what countries or regions border it.

3. Character analysis—note any character details that might affect your character's speech, i.e.:

*socioeconomic level	*personality	*when and how the
*education	*energy	character learned English
*jobs	*past experiences	*extent of the character's
*daily activities	*role models	travels
*health	*parentage	

   (See p. 53 for character analysis questions to consider)

4. Director's concept—clarify what his/her intent is, including both style and mood of the play.
   Find out how the director envisions your character.
   Consider how cuts, additions, or any alterations in the script will affect your character's speech or movements.

5. Research assignments—start a list of elements that require research, with respect to the play, the locale, and your character, and list possible sources of information, such as:

*films to see (especially those that pertain to the same era and locale of your script)

*local places to visit, or people to interview

*books and articles to read about the culture; plays by the same author; plays dealing with the same culture.

6. Start a list of words from your script that will require research—i.e., foreign phrases and expressions, proper names with uncertain pronunciations, etc.

7. Find and study several different dialect instruction tapes and texts to learn the appropriate standard stage dialect. Do the drills they suggest.

8. Book several private sessions with a dialect coach, whenever possible.

9. Begin filling out the Dialect Acquisition Form (pp. 28-31) using what you've learned from the dialect instruction tapes and the dialect coach, regarding:

    *tone focus   *manner of articulation   *vowel and consonant
    *kinesthetic triggers   *vocal patterns   substitutions

10. Research the culture—find out the national cultural characteristics of the people and their land. (See pp. 40-41 for questions to ponder.)

    See films, TV shows, documentaries, and travelogues; listen to audiotapes/CDs; read books. See the Dialect Directory at the back of this book for resources.

    For additional books on the culture, look in your library's Subject Index under the name of your character's country or region, under the subcategories of "Description and Travel," "Social Life and Customs," and "Culture."

    To fill in step #1 on the Dialect Acquisition Form ("Cultural Characteristics"), take notes on what you find out as you research.

11. Your character—for #2 on the Dialect Acquisition Form, take notes about how your character fits into the overall cultural profile that you've studied. (Refer to your Character Analysis on p. 53.)

12. Listen to traditional music of the country and watch people perform its cultural dances. (See p. 68 for what to watch for.) Consider how these elements affect your dialect.

13. Listen to foreign language tapes and subtitled foreign films to make discoveries about the "music" and body language of the culture's speech.

14. Body language—take notes on what you discovered through your research and through watching films, for #5 on the Dialect Acquisition Form. (See pp. 69-71.) Consider:

    *posture and carriage   *eye contact   *manner of dress
    *gestures   *proximity   *use of hand props

15. Interview real-life primary sources if possible. (See pp. 44-45.)

16. Adapt the dialect—fine-tune your notes for the Dialect Acquisition Form from all you've learned through research, script analysis, character analysis, and rehearsals with the director and dialect coach.

Adapt the standard dialect you learned from the dialect tapes and texts to fit your particular play and character.

Adapt the everyday "street" dialect to what would be the best choices for this stage, this audience, this play, your character, and your own skills. (See Chapter 5.)

17. Keep drilling the dialect—the vocal patterns, resonance, vowels, and consonants.

18. Mark the phonetics for all of your lines directly in your script.

19. Look up any phrases you don't understand, and any words you aren't sure how to pronounce. Drill these until they seem natural and clear when you say them. Jot down "Special Pronunciations" on #6 on your Dialect Acquisition Form.

Be sure to mark proper names and unusual phrases, so that you will remember to clarify them for the audience.

20. Memorize your lines in dialect.

21. Get a dialect coach's help, to polish the dialect. Mark in your script any mistakes you make, and drill them.

22. Ad-lib in dialect.

23. Find a trigger for the dialect.

24. Warm up your dialect for rehearsals every day. Do tongue twisters, read road signs, or run through your lines in the car; do vocal and physical warm-ups in dialect; speak in dialect during the entire rehearsal, even on breaks.

25. Review your troublespots in your script daily. Review any notes given by the dialect coach and director the day before.

26. "Relax into the dialect." "Speak as if you know what you're talking about."
Trust yourself.

27. Keep eating, sleeping, and breathing the dialect.

28. Learn new dialects, filling out new Dialect Acquisition Forms for each one. Periodically brush up those dialects you've learned previously, so they stay fresh for upcoming roles.

APPLICATION
of the process:

Example of the Dialect Acquisition Form
filled out for the role of
Kate
in the Irish play
Dancing at Lughnasa

DIALECT ACQUISITION
for Irish (rural northwestern, County Donegal)

STEPS:

1. CULTURAL CHARACTERISTICS: Research/discuss with the director the character of the people and their land (social class, economic level, education, culture, etc.)

- *rural past, greenery, land hard to farm, heather and bog, rocks, sheep*
- *Donegal is farmland by the sea, wild mountains and coastline, lakes (lochs) considered mysterious, raining or threatening to rain*
- *Donegal known for fishing villages, quarries, hand-woven tweed and knitwear, conversation and gossip*
- *isolated, emotional tie to a patch of ground, family devotion*
- *unpredictable temperament like the weather, hang loose but emotional, spirited*
- *hardworking but slow starters, cautious, economical because of a past of poverty*
- *legends and tales, superstition, oaths and curses, storytellers*
- *tenacious, never-say-die fighters, overcomers; though some apathy in some, due to decades of horrors, injustices, famine, oppression*
- *verbal fencers, wit and wordplay, indirect compliments, put-downs, self-critical but defensive*
- *old-fashioned, traditional, Catholic, elastic sense of time, hospitable, warm*

2. YOUR CHARACTER: Now consider, in light of this cultural environment, how your individual character expresses himself/herself vocally and physically (how his/her voice and movement is a reflection of energy level, drive, self esteem, occupation, health, education, personality traits, parentage and other biographical information)

KATE:

Schoolteacher, only one in family who has a real job, educated, sensible, nurturer, feels overly responsible for siblings because she's the oldest and because there is no father figure, traditional, devout Catholic

She would be more traditional, stiffer, more inflexible, less emotional than her siblings, intelligent, have cleaner articulation and more proper grammar than the others

3. TONE FOCUS / Placement: *out in front of the lips; avoid breathiness in N. Irish*

   Kinesthetic trigger: *Grrrrrrrr snarl and set jaw; can literally hold jaw to practice this*

   Manner of articulation: *rural north isn't as crisp as British, but should be adapted for the stage; hers is clearer than her sisters', as a teacher*

4. VOCAL PATTERNS / the "music" of the speech:

Inflection patterns: *Irish lilt, upward swing in the north like Scottish, wider than American; pitch level tends to be higher than American*

Rhythm and phrasing: *melodic, lyrical, long or short; smooth*

Tempo and speed: *hers is more contained, but Irish tends to be quick*

Stress patterns: *elongated vowels on stress words, higher pitch to emphasize words, as in American*

Volume/intensity patterns: *controlled, but increases in anger; strong at ends of sentences, like throwing a bowling ball up to someone's head*

5. BODY LANGUAGE OF THE CULTURE/ movement and manners, typical dress:

•erect, hold it in, "stuff it," hold the gut down and breathe high in chest
•bend straight over to pick things up
•slow physically, but mentally, a coiled spring
•reserved; movements come from close to the body, outward; economical
•slower head movements than American, as with other British natives
•for Kate: stiffer, inflexible, maybe lead more with the head without bobbing it, less freedom in facial expression, all expression happens in the eyes

6. List SPECIAL PRONUNCIATIONS, unusual phrases, idioms, slang, expletives, grammar changes:

Words to look up from play script:
  eejit, Ryanga, Donegal, aul, whin-bush, scut, turf, loch, Aardstraw, wellingtons, Sligo, Oughterard, Kilkenny, tinker, wastral, Woodbine, bilberries, Armagh, scrabbed, gansey, toff, amn't, notionate, jouking

Other common Irish expressions:

och! = oh!	*bejesus! = by Jesus (swearing)*
wee = small	*you bloody get! (swearing insult)*
doncha know	*cripes! = (swearing)*
da = dad	*Jesus, Mary and Joseph! or*
lad and lass = guy and gal	*Jesus, Mary and J! (swearing)*
me bucko =my friend	*laddie buck = my friend (male)*

(The Irish use hundreds of other phrases common to the British. Other Irish plays use much more slang than Dancing at Lughnasa.)

7. VOWEL SUBSTITUTIONS:

IPA	Dictionary	Key words	Substitutions	
[i]	ē	Lee, need, seal	=	*(no change)*
[ɪ]	ĭ	will, is, window	=	[ə] ə
[ɛ]	ĕ	let, end, step	=	[ɪ] ĭ
[æ]	ă or a	Ann, can, pat	=	[a] ah
[a]	ȧ or a	pass, ask, dance	=	[a] ah
[ɝ]	ur, ûr, or	turn, early, certain	= *retroflex hard* [r]	a<u>rrr</u>
[ɚ]	ər	over, mother, actor	= *retroflex hard* [r]	e<u>rrr</u>
[ə]	ə	the, honest, above	=	*(no change)*
[ʌ]	ŭ or u	cup, luck, love	=	[ʊ] o͞o
[u]	o͞o	Sue, noon, school	=	[ʊ] o͞o
[ʊ]	o͝o	would, look, put	=	[ʊ] o͞o
[ɔ]	ô, o, or aw	call, Paul, law	=	[ɑ:] ă
[ɒ]	ŏ	on, honest, long	=	[ɒ] ă
[ɑ]	ä or ŏ	father, drama, large	=	[ɒ] ă

DIPHTHONGS:

[o] or [oʊ] ō		go, own, most	=	[o:] ō: or aww:
[e] or [eɪ] ā		pay, ache, save	=	[ɛ:] ĕ:
[aɪ] ī		my, I, nice	=	[æɪ] *(squished oy)*
[ɔɪ] oi		boy, oil, royal	=	[aɪ] *(squished ī)*
[aʊ] ou or au		now, pound, around	=	[ɔʊ] *(squished ow)*
[ju] ū or yoo		beautiful, music, few,	=	*(no change)*

8. CONSONANT SUBSTITUTIONS:

[oɚ] = [ɑr:]   or = arrr (form=farm)   hard "r's" and "r" coloring
[aʊɚ] = [ɑr:]   owr = arr (power=par)
[aɪɚ] = [ɑr:]   ir = arrrr (fire=far)

Kate may not drop "-ing" endings, nor might she say the more casual "me" for "my" or "ya" for "you,"
  because of her vocation and personality

Notes

[1]David Alan Stern, *Acting with an Accent: Cockney* (Lyndonville, Vt.: Dialect Accent Specialists, Inc., 1979), p. 13.

[2]Kate Burke and Ginny Kopf, eds., *VASTA Bibliography* (University of Virginia: Voice and Speech Trainer's Association, 1993), p. 29. (The1995 and 1997 Supplements are also in print.)

[3]Lewis Herman and Marguerite Shalett Herman, *American Dialects* (New York: Theatre Arts Books, 1947), pp. 69–91.

[4]Herman, *American Dialects*, pp. 94–97.

[5]Burke and Kopf, eds., *VASTA Bibliography*, p. 28.

[6]Peter Trudgill and Jean Hannah, *International English*, 2d. ed. (London: Edward Arnold, 1985), p. 88.

[7]Louise M. Frankenstein, *Dialect Play Readings* (New York: Samuel French, 1937), p. 41.

[8]Anne Nichols, *Abie's Irish Rose* (New York: Samuel French, 1952), p. 7.

[9]John Cleese, *A Fish Called Wanda* (New York: Applause, 1988), p. 58.

[10]Max Caulfield, *The Irish Mystique* (Englewood Cliffs, N.J.: Prentice-Hall, 1973), p. 5.

[11]Jill Uris and Leon Uris, *Ireland: A Terrible Beauty* (Garden City, N.Y.: Doubleday and Co., 1983), p. 58.

[12]Kathleen Jo Ryan and Bernard Share, eds., *Irish Traditions* (New York: Harry N. Abrams, 1985), p. 181.

[13]Ryan and Share, eds., *Irish Traditions*, p. 45.

[14]Richard O'Conner, *The Irish: Portrait of a People* (New York: G. P. Putnam's Sons,1971), p. 37.

[15]Brian Pell, ed., *Insight Guide: Ireland* (New York: APA Productions, 1986), p. 16.

[16]Uris, *Ireland: A Terrible Beauty*, p. 7.

[17]Uris, *Ireland: A Terrible Beauty*, p. 11.

[18]Uris, *Ireland: A Terrible Beauty*, p. 95.

[19]Uris, *Ireland: A Terrible Beauty*, p. 3.

[20]Ryan and Share, eds., *Irish Traditions*, p. 108.

[21]Ryan and Share, eds., *Irish Traditions*, p. 108.

[22]*Olivia Newton-John Down Under* (music video travelogue), Polygram Videos, 1988.

[23]*Olivia Newton-John Down Under*

[24]*Olivia Newton-John Down Under*

[25]*Olivia Newton-John Down Under*

[26]Brian Friel, *Dancing at Lughnasa* (London: Faber & Faber, 1990), p. 17.

[27]George Bernard Shaw, *Pygmalion*, in *Cavalcade of Comedy*, ed.. Louis Kronenberger (New York: Simon & Schuster, 1953), p. 408.

[28]Louis Colaianni, *The Joy of Phonetics and Dialects* (New York: Drama Book Publishers, 1994), p. 69.

[29]David Alan Stern, *Acting with an Accent: Standard British* (Lyndonville, Vt.: Dialect Accent Specialists, Inc., 1979), p. 13.

[30]Tennessee Williams, *A Streetcar Named Desire*, in *Best American Plays*, ed. John Gassner (New York: Crown Publishers, 1952), p. 93.

[31]Brian Friel, *Philadelphia, Here I Come* (New York: Samuel French, 1965), p. 38.

[32]Friel, *Philadelphia, Here I Come*, p. 40.

[33]Friel, *Philadelphia, Here I Come*, p. 40.

[34]Friel, *Philadelphia, Here I Come*, p. 45.

[35]Friel, *Philadelphia, Here I Come*, p. 57.

[36]Friel, *Philadelphia, Here I Come*, p. 57.

[37]Friel, *Philadelphia, Here I Come*, p. 57.

[38]Friel, *Philadelphia, Here I Come*, p. 57.

[39]Timberlake Wertenbaker, *Our Country's Good* (Woodstock, Ill.: Dramatic Publishing Co., 1988), pp. 66–67.

[40]Roger E. Axtell, *Do's and Taboos Around the World* (New York: John Wiley and Sons, 1990), p. 47.

[41]Axtell, *Do's and Taboos Around the World*, p. 49.

[42]Nan Withers-Wilson, *Vocal Direction for the Theatre* (New York: Drama Book Publishers, 1993), p. 29.

BIBLIOGRAPHY
of Dialect Tapes and Texts

(*Author's note*: I am aware that older sources may use terms that are now considered obsolete or even incorrect; however, to facilitate your ease in locating the proper dialect sample in the instructional texts, I have listed the dialect entries *as the author originally labeled them.* All of these sources can be found through a web search on Yahoo or Amazon.com.)

Allen, Kara B., and Janet Rogers. **Tongues of the North American Project.** Theatre VCU, 922 Park Avenue, Box 842524, Richmond, VA 23284-2524.

This is an ongoing collection of over 40 primary sources of American and Canadian dialects, housed in the Virginia Commonwealth University Cabell Library. If you need a tape (or are willing to tape a primary source from your own region for the collection), you can write Allen or Rogers at the address above.
Dialect tapes are available of 13 Canadian dialects, 5 Chicago dialects, 15 North Carolina dialects, 1 Ohio, 1 Texas, and 3 Virginia dialects.

American Tongues (video #JN233, producer unknown, 1987) and **Communities of Speech** (video #JN225, producer unknown, 1981). Available through Insight Media, 2162 Broadway, New York, NY 10024.

Two videos on American dialects.

Axtell, Roger E., ed. **Do's and Taboos Around the World.** 2nd ed. New York: John Wiley and Sons, 1990.

A very helpful book for learning about the customs, slang, and nonverbal communication of different cultures around the globe. Axtell also wrote *Gestures: The Do's and Taboos of Body Language Around the World, The Do's and Taboos of Using English Around the World,* and *Hosting International Visitors.* See also John Moll's book, *When in Rome,* listed below.

Blumenfeld, Robert. **Accents: A Manual for Actors.** N.Y.: Limelight Editions, 1998.

A thorough instruction book for professional or aspiring actors. He also wrote *Accents of English,* book with CD, of 80 accents of English spoken all over the world. You can view the table of contents of this book on the web by searching under author's name.

Blunt, Jerry. **Stage Dialects.** 2nd ed. Woodstock, Ill.: The Dramatic Publishing Co., 1994. Phone: 1-800-449-7469.

Prominent dialect text with tapes. The set can easily be found in bookstores or can be ordered, as it has a new edition. See my description of this valuable source in Chapter 2.
Dialects taught: Japanese, Brooklynese, American Southern, Standard British, Cockney, Irish, Scots, French, Italian, German, Russian.

Blunt, Jerry. *More Stage Dialects.* Woodstock, Ill.: The Dramatic Publishing Co., 1980. Phone: 1-800-449-7469.

A continuation of *Stage Dialects*, with two audiocassettes, as described in Chapter 2. Dialects included:

Canadian	Down East (New England)
Midwest American	Border States (Appalachia, Tennessee, Ozark, Arkansas)
(Missouri, Nebraska)	Cajun
Southwest	Jewish
Spanish in America (Chicano, Latino)	The Caribbean (Costa Rica, Trinidad, Jamaica)
British Isles (many regions of	Australia and New Zealand
England, Wales, Ireland,	Near East–Saudi Arabia
and Scotland)	Africa (Sudan, Kenya, Nigeria, and Ghana)

Asia (several different regions of China, Vietnam, and India)
Western Europe (Sweden, Norway, Denmark, Netherlands, Austria, Germany, Spain, Portugal, Italy)
Greece and Eastern Europe (Yugoslavia, Hungary, Rumania, Czechoslovakia, Poland, Lithuania)

Brandes, Paul D. and Jeutonne Brewer. *Dialect Clash in America: Issues and Answers.* New Jersey: The Scarecrow Press, 1977.

Essays that may help you understand the origins and growth of certain American dialects. There are chapters on the following "Amerenglish" dialects: Appalachian, Black, Mexican, Yiddish, Big City (New Yorker), and Southern.

British Broadcasting Company Record. *English with a Dialect*. Monaural Record #173.

Produced by the BBC, this recording includes clips of native speakers from a wide range of areas throughout the British Isles. These are wonderfully authentic, informal speeches; however, they may be too thick for stage use without modification. Also note that there are no printed materials, nor are individual bands "announced." Consequently, specific dialects may be difficult to locate on the record. Search for it through BBC's web site to see if it is available on CD. Samples included are:

Birmingham	Devonshire	Manchester	Suffolk	Ireland (Ulster, Eire)
Black Country	Geordie (Durham)	Leicestershire	Sussex	Scotland (Edinburgh,
Buckinghamshire	Newcastle	London (Cockney)	Wiltshire	Glasgow, Inverness,
Cornwall	Hampshire	Norfolk	Worcestershire	Ayrshire)
Cotswolds	Lancashire	Somerset	Yorkshire	Wales (North, South)
Cumberland	Liverpool	Bristol	Isle of Man	

British Broadcasting Company Record. *English with an Accent*. Monaural Record #166.

Similar format to the BBC's *English with a Dialect* (see notes above). Samples are from foreign speakers of British English. Recording includes:

Czech	Italian	Nonregional American	Guyanes
Danish	Polish	Southern American	Indian
Dutch	Russian	Australian	Kenyan
French	Slovak	Canadian	Nigerian
German	Spanish	New Zealand	South African
Hungarian	Afrikaans	Chinese (Hong Kong)	

Bryson, Bill. ***Mother Tongue: English and How it Got That Way.*** Avon Books.

Thorough text, along the lines of Flexner's.

Carroll, David L. ***The Dictionary of Foreign Terms in the English Language.*** Alexandria, Va.: Hawthorne Books, 1973.

Useful for researching foreign phrases in scripts.

Carver, Craig M. ***American Regional Dialects: A Word Geography.*** Ann Arbor: Univ. of Michigan Press, 1997.

Analysis and discovery of the dialect regions of the U.S., and on their historical and cultural origins. It uses fairly complex lexical and morphonological data and maps, but it's a good reference book.

Chreist, F. M. ***Foreign Accent.*** Englewood Cliffs, N.J.: Prentice-Hall, Inc., 1964.

This book, written by a speech pathologist, discusses how to *eliminate* foreign accents (rather than learn them). Still, it may contain some information that could help you understand the specific foreign accent you're studying.

Colaianni, Louis. ***The Joy of Phonetics and Accents.*** New York: Drama Book Publishers, 1994. Phone orders: 1-800-322-0595.

A workbook with exercises and games for learning phonetics, which introduces a fun way to explore sounds by using throwable, soft pillows in the shapes of phonetic symbols. In the section on accents, Colaianni doesn't attempt to teach specific accents, but he does show you how to begin hearing and feeling the sounds and rhythms, so that you will be more attuned to them when you do hear them.

Ehrlich, Eugene, ed. ***The Harper Dictionary of Foreign Terms***. 3rd ed. New York: Harper, 1987.

Useful for looking up foreign words and phrases you encounter in scripts.

Ferry, David. ***Canajun, Eh: Canadian Dialects for Actors.***

With CD, covering Canadian accents from coast to coast.

Flexner, Stuart Berg and Soukhanov, Anne H. ***Speaking Freely: A Guided Tour of American English from Plymouth Rock to Silicon Valley.*** New York: Oxford Univ. Press, 1997.

Traces the origin and history of American words and the changing cultural conditions that produced them.

Foulkes, Paul and Docherty, Gerard, eds. ***Urban Voices: Accent Studies in the British Isles.*** (with tape)

Frankenstein, Louise M. *Dialect Play Readings.* New York: Samuel French, 1937.

Monologues and scenes from dialect plays, written "in dialect" through the playwright's respelling. The compiler admits in her preface that the volume is not intended to be a means of teaching dialects, but rather as a tool for practicing them once one has learned them. Frankenstein includes several selections, listed under: English, Italian, Spanish, French, Irish, Scotch, German, Swedish, Negro, United States, and Jewish. (Please note publication date.) Try your county library to find this.

Hendrickson, Robert. *American Talk: The Words and Ways of American Dialects.* New York: Viking Penguin, 1986.

This book gives the history and development of American dialects in a fun manner. It includes native expressions, definitions, cute poems and anecdotes, and uses loose phonetic pronunciation, to help you understand the rhythms and sense of humor in the dialects. Hendrickson gives specific details about some harder-to-find dialects, like Gullah, Hawaiian, and Northern Maryland.

Herman, Lewis, and Marguerite Shalett Herman. *American Dialects: A Manual for Actors, Directors, and Writers.* New York: Theatre Arts Books, 1947. Phone: 1-800-634-7064.

Prominent dialect teaching method, described in my Chapter 2. There is no audiotape included with this work. A new edition is recently available, published by Routledge/Theatre Arts Books. It can be easily ordered.
Dialects included:
New England
Southern (Dalmarva Peninsula, Tidewater, East Texas)
Louisiana-French (Cajun and New Orleans Creole)
Mountain
Gullah and Virgin Islands
New York City and upper New York State
Pennsylvania Dutch and Philadelphia
Middle Western

Herman, Lewis, and Marguerite Shalett Herman. *Foreign Dialects: A Manual for Actors, Directors, and Writers.* New York: Theatre Arts Books, 1943. Phone: 1-800-634-7064.

Described in Chapter 2. First edition was from 1943, but a new edition is soon to be available. No tape comes with this instructional method. Dialects taught are listed under:

Cockney	German	Japanese	Norwegian
British	French	Chinese	Russian
Australian	Italian	Chinese Pidgin English	Middle European
Bermudan	Spanish	Hawaiian	Polish
Indian (Asian)	Mexican	Beche le Mar	Greek
Irish	Filipino	Australian Pidgin	Yiddish
Scottish	Portuguese	Swedish	

Hughes, Arthur, and Peter Trudgill. ***English Accents and Dialects.*** 3rd ed. London: Edward Arnold, 1983. (41 Bedford Square, London WC1B 3DQ; and in the U.S., 300 North Charles Street, Baltimore, Maryland 21201)

Subtitled *An Introduction to Social and Regional Varieties of British English*, this instructional program comes with an audiotape. Described in my Chapter 2. In Hughes' Varieities of English Around the World, General Series, Vol. 6 covers industrial West Yorkshire.
Dialects covered:
London (Cockney), Norwich, Bristol, S. Wales, Midlands, Bradford, Liverpool, Tyneside, Edinburgh (Scotland), and Belfast (N. Ireland). A new 1996 edition also includes the Devonshire accent.

IDEA   http://www.ukans.edu/~idea/index2.html
International Dialects of English Archives was created by Paul Meier of the University of Kansas, with assistance by Shawn Muller. The first on-line collection of primary sources in English of native speakers, in both English language and accents of other languages. Downloadable and playable on Mac and Windows. Continuously updated.

Karsher, Roger and Stern, David Alan. ***Dialect Monologues.*** Dramaline Publications. Available through Stern's web site at www.DialectAccentSpecialists.com.

Two cassettes (or CDs) with booklet. Dr. Stern (who is American) performs monologues written by playwright Roger Karshner. Volume I includes thirteen of the most popular accents from his *Acting with an Accent* series. On the Volume II tape, he performs and gives instruction for fourteen other accents, including these nine, not found in *Acting with an Accent:*

English S. African	Afrikaans	Cajun
Asian Indian	Welsh	Liverpudlian
Northern Irish	Hebrew	Canadian

Kopf, Ginny. ***Accent Reduction Workshop for Professional American Speech.*** Orlando: Voiceprint Publishing, 2000.

A 3-CD set with 63-page book, to improve the clarity and fluency of your American speech. See the last page of this book for more information. You can get full details about this publication and purchase it through her web site at: www.voiceandspeechtraining.com

Kur, Barry. ***Stage Dialects Studies: A Continuation of the Lessac Approach to Actor Voice and Speech Training.*** Available through the author: 609 W. Fairmount Ave., State College, PA 16801.

This text is a well-organized approach to dialects based on Arthur Lessac's kinesthetic system of phonetics. If you're not familiar with the Lessac system, this book will clearly lead you through it. He provides practice materials for learning the following dialects:

New England	Standard British	Scots	French
New York	Irish	German	Russian
Southern	Cockney	Italian	Spanish

Lane-Plescia, Gillian. ***Dialects and Accents for Actors.***   www.dialectresource.com

> Excellent teaching CDs with booklets, as described in Chapter 2. Individual tapes can be purchased through the author's web site or from major theatre bookstores.   Tapes currently available:
>
> | | |
> |---|---|
> | Standard British | South African (Black, British, and Afrikaner) |
> | Cockney | Australian/New Zealand |
> | Irish (including samples from | North Country British (numerous regions) |
> | North, West, and Belfast) | Welsh |
> | Scots (several regions) | American Southern, Vol. 1 & 2 |
>
> Just developed: Accents for Black Actors (including Jamaican, Trinidadian, Haitian, South African, and several varieties of African-American accents)
>
> New Varieties of Standard British (including a detailed section on the rhythm and melody of British speech)
>
> Major European Accents (French, German, Italian, Russian, and others)

Littell, Joseph F., ed. ***Dialects and Levels of Language.*** Evanston, Ill.: McDougal Littell & Co., 1971.

> Defines American dialects and how they differ, then presents short chapters about the following types of dialects: Yiddish, "Mark Twain" (Missouri), Kentucky, Pennsylvania Dutch, Pidgin English, the Mother Tongue (British), formal talk, and informal slang.

Machlin, Evangeline. ***Dialects for the Stage***. New York: Theatre Arts Books, 1975. Phone:1-800-634-7064.

> Prominent dialect teaching method with tapes, as described in Chapter 2. It can be ordered, and it may be part of some library collections. Dialects included:
>
> | | | | |
> |---|---|---|---|
> | Midwestern | Yiddish | Scottish | Spanish |
> | Southwestern/Texas | Yankee/New England | Irish | General European |
> | Southern | French Canadian | French | Standard Speech (N. American |
> | New York-Brooklynese | Cockney | Italian | and British) |
> | Black American | Welsh | German | |
> | Black African | North British | Russian | |

Machlin, Evangeline. ***Speech for the Stage***. New York: Theatre Arts Books, 1980. Phone: 1-800-634-7064.

> This classic text has only one chapter on dialects, but that chapter is invaluable to dialect acquisition methodology. One of the things Machlin teaches is how to perceive the melody of dialects as notes on a musical staff.

Malmstrom, John, and Annabel Ashley. ***Dialects—USA.*** Champaign, Ill.: Ronald Press Co., 1963.

> This book has an interesting feature: it offers a list of sources from American literature that are written in dialect. The authors discuss how and why certain dialects are distributed across the U.S. You may pick up some useful information about the vocabulary and grammar that are common to a certain region. The authors divide the nation's dialects into the following areas: Pacific Coast, Rocky Mountain, Upper Midwest, Texas, North Central, Inland South, Middle and Southern Atlantic, and New England.

McArthur, Tom. ***The English Languages.*** Cambridge: Cambridge Univ. Press, 1998.

> Fairly recent resource text for the study of English languages, documenting in detail the vast array of versions of English now found throughout the world.

McCrum, Robert, William Cran, and Robert MacNeil. ***The Story of English***. New York: Viking Penguin, 1986. Phone for Penguin Publishers:1-800-227-9604 or 201-385-6521.

This fascinating book and video series gives the history and geographical development of spoken English, from its beginnings to the present time. You'll hear clips of every English-based dialect around the world. You can probably find this in your university or county library.

Meier, Paul. ***Accents and Dialects for Stage and Screen.***   www.paulmeier.com

An 8-CD set with 174-page instructional booklet for 20 different accents and dialects, with IPA transcriptions. Paul Meier Dialect Services also offers over 20 individual booklets with CDS and two compilation books, and can prepare training CDs for other accents and dialect roles you're working on. (See IDEA for other resources produced by Paul Meier and associates or www.ukans.edu/~idea)

Meier, Paul. ***Dialects of the British Isles, Vol. 1***   www.paulmeier.com

A 90-page textbook with 5 CDs.

Molin, Donald H. ***Actor's Encyclopedia of Dialects***. 2nd ed. New York: Sterling Publishers, 1991. Phone: 212-532-7160.

Detailed method for learning several dialects, described in Chapter 2. This source is available at bookstores and libraries, though for some reason it's not always as easy to find the tape that comes with the program.

Dialects taught:

British English	Lithuanian	Australian and New Zealand/Anzoc
American Spanish	Irish	Czechoslovakian
European Spanish	Swedish and Norwegian	Yugoslavia
German and Austrian	Scottish	Hungarian
Italian	French	Finnish
Polish	Cockney	Greek
Yiddish	Indian (Asian)	Portuguese
Russian	British West Indian	

Moll, John, ed. ***When in Rome: A Business Guide to Cultures and Customs in 12 European Nations***. New York: Amacom, 1990.

Formated like Axtell's *Do's and Taboos Around the World*, this will teach you some of the cultural differences of twelve countries from all over the globe, including their nonverbals and slang expressions.

Morrison, Terri, Conaway and Borden. **Kiss, Bow or Shake Hands: How to do Business in Sixty Countries.** Hollbrook, MA: Adams Media Corp, 1994. Available through www.adamsmedia.com.

A must-get resource! Provides invaluable info on each country's cultural orientation, how they organize and process information, negotiation strategies, value systems that determine their behavior, body language, gestures, dress, greetings, protocol.

Oxford Dictionary of Pronunciation for Current English.
Available through Amazon.com

Based on the research of teams from the UK and US, examins Englsih as it is being used in the late 1990s, rather than an idealized RP pronunciation of words. Twice the size of the Jones dictionary and a third larger than the Longman.

Pullum, Geoffrey, and William A. Ladasaw. *The Phonetic Symbol Guide.* Chicago, Ill.: University of Chicago Press, 1986.

Lists and defines numerous phonetic symbols, for use in speech and dialect work.

Raphael, Bonnie N. "Preparing a Cast for a Dialect Show," *Communication Education* 33 (January 1984):43–51.

This is an excellent journal article. It is the only work I've ever found that outlines the process of dialect coaching a play. I've received training from Dr. Raphael in the past and owe much to her in terms of the development of my own methods of vocal training. She can be contacted through VASTA.

Roach, Helen. *Spoken Records.* 3rd ed. Metuchen, N.J.: Scarecrow Press, 1970.

This book contains descriptions and bibliographical information about a large number of speeches, stories, and plays, many of which are good sources for dialects (i.e., Winston Churchill, the Kennedys, Dylan Thomas). Check your library, as the book seems to be out of print.

Schneider, Edgar W., ed. *Englishes Around the World.* Amsterdam: John Benjamins B.V., 1997.

Several volume text. Vol. 1 covers British Isles and North America.

Stern, David Alan. *Acting with an Accent.* Dialect Accent Specialists, Inc., 51 Depot St., P.O. Box 44, Lyndonville, Vt. 05851-0044. Phone orders: 1-800-753-1016, or on-line through DialectAccentSpecialists.com or Amazon.com.

One of the most prominent dialect methods available, as described in my Chapter 2. Order individual CDs with booklets for about $16.95 each, directly from the address above. Stern also offers CDs on how to lose accents (or in other words, how to acquire nonregional American speech).
Dialect CDs available:

New York City	Standard British	French
American Southern	Cockney	German
Texas	British North Country	Russian
Boston	Irish	Yiddish
"Down East" New England	Scottish	Polish
Kennedyesque:: Upper class New England	Australian	Norwegian/Swedish
	Spanish	Arabic
Chicago	Italian	Farsi (Persian)
Midwest Farm/Ranch	West Indian/Black African	

Trudgill, Peter. **Dialects**. New York: Routledge, 1994. Phone: 1-800-634-7064.

A textbook which discusses dialectology, focusing on the British varieties. It invites you to collect data and discover patterns and thinking about general principles related to dialect study. The book also includes a list of sources on dialectology and British dialects.

Trudgill, Peter, and Jean Hannah. **International English.** 2nd ed. London: Edward Arnold, 1985.

This is subtitled *A Guide to Varieties of Standard English* and includes a tape. It is described in my Chapter 2. The program may be difficult to find. Dialects covered: RP (Standard British), Australian, South African, Welsh, Canadian, American, Scottish, Irish, West Indian, West African, and Indian English.

Voorhees, Lillian W., and Jacob F. Foster. "Recordings for Use in Teaching Theatre," **Educational Theatre Journal** 1:1 (January 1949):48–81.

This article is quite dated, but it contains many annotated listings for older recordings on which dialects can be heard.

Wells, J. C. **Accents of English.** London: Cambridge University Press, 1982, 1985. (May be listed as *Accents of the English-speaking World,* or as part of the BBC series *In a Manner of Speaking*.)

Tape with several selections from twenty different regions, with three brief booklets describing vowel and consonant substitutions. It has some great recordings, but is a difficult resource to find. Check your library's audio cassette section. All of the samples are excellent, with the exception of the North American ones, which don't really sound distinct enough to be recognizable as Southern, New Yorker, or Canadian. Check his web site for readable online articles on RP, Welsh phonetics, phonics and accents of English.

Dialect samples from:

RP (Standard British)	Scotland	The West Indies
General American	Ireland	Australia
The North of England	Gen. American revisited	New Zealand
South of England (rural Norfolk)	New York City	South Africa
London (Cockney)	Canada	India
RP revisited (learned)	U.S.: New England	Africa: Nigeria
Wales	U.S.: the South	

Withers-Wilson, Nan. **Vocal Direction for the Theatre: From Script Analysis to Opening Night.** New York: Drama Book Publishers, 1993.

The only book of its kind about vocal coaching, which the author calls "vocal direction." Traces the history of vocal direction; gives advise on how to establish proper relationships with the director and the rest of the production team; outlines the process and responsibilities of vocal coaching a play.

ADDITIONAL INFORMATION:

The American Dialect Society   web site http://www.americandialect.org/
Founded more than a century ago, this society is dedicated to the study of American dialects and dialects across the globe influenced by or influencing it. If you require a dialect that is not covered in any of the sources listed above, or is more specific than those listed here, contact the ADS, and they can put you in touch with a scholastic specialist in the particular dialect you need.

British National Library Sound Archives Listening Service
London, SW 7-2 AS, ENGLAND   To phone from the U.S.: 0-11-441589-6603
29 Exhibition Road   (please verify calling procedure with your long distance company)

When in London, visit the sound archives at the British National Library, where you can listen to dialect tapes at your leisure. The gigantic collection draws from the BBC Sound Archives, including the series on "Dialects of the British Isles." The library is open for your use Monday through Friday, 10 -5 p.m., and is open until 9 p.m. on Thursdays. Please call ahead to have specific materials pulled.

E. L. Easton's English Around the World
Dialect master, Easton, of Hollywood fame has a web site at: http://aleaston.com/world-eng.html

IDEA *(International Dialects of English Archive)*   http://www.ukans.edu/~idea/index2.html
The world's first on-line archive of English language dialects and foreign language accents for theatre and film artists. Added to day by day, a repository of over 440 primary source recordings from all over the globe. Recordings are in English of readings and of unscripted speech. It also has a *Special Collections* which include native speakers pronouncing names, terms and idioms from oft-produced playwrights such as Chekhov and Ibsen. Created by Paul Meier of the University of Kansas, with assistance by Shawn Muller. Downloadable and playable on Mac and Windows. See Paul Meier's web site: www.paulmeier.com

International Society for Intercultural Education   Phone: (202) 466-7883
Call for a member directory if you need an intercultural trainer who can help you understand the mores, behavior, and etiquette of specific foreign countries.

National Public Radio (NPR) archives   web site: www.npr.org
Radio stories with clips of the dialects you're looking for. Often includes helpful biographical information about the speaker. Enter the name of a city or country into the search field.

National Sound Archive of recordings
                    web site: http://bl.uk/collections/sound-archive/accents.html
RealRadio   web site: www.realradio.org
Check the web for radio clips from the region you're studying.

VASTA   (Voice and Speech Trainers Association)   web site: vasta.org
See the web site about this organization, to receive membership information, to receive the newsletter and information about the summer conference, and/or to receive information about receiving the VASTA Bibliography (a compilation of over 350 annotated sorces pertaining to vocal production, speech training, singing, movement, text, and speech science.)
See http://maillists.uci.du/mailman/listinfl/vastavox for VASTAVOX, VASTA's own mailing list, established in 1994 to promote discussion via e-mail of voice, speech and classical text issues for actors, singers, and other professional voice users.

The
DIALECT
DIRECTORY

FILMS, TV SERIES, DIALECT TAPES and CDs, AND OTHER RESOURCES FOR RESEARCHING SPECIFIC CULTURES

INCLUDED IN THE DIRECTORY, ALPHABETICALLY:

Do check the index of this book to help you find resources for dialects not listed here .

(PLEASE NOTE: I've listed sources only for the most commonly used stage dialects; the list is not a comprehensive one for all dialects worldwide. I certainly don't mean to leave anyone out, nor to categorize nationalities together in such a way as to generalize them. Some dialects are categorized together simply for the convenience of locating them. Several regional and social class varieties are represented. For the most part, I have separated dialects according to how the major dialect instructional programs categorize them. I'm listing noticeable dialects, not types of people, to avoid the assumption that all people in that country speak the same way. My apologies if I was unknowingly politically incorrect.)

I've added a feature since the first publication...

Under each dialect heading, I've included some brief notes on what to listen to or watch for overall when studying the films or training tapes. I've given you a possible "trigger" for the accent's placement. I realize these are quite generalized notes and difficult to explain without demonstration, but I hope they get you started in the right direction as you watch the films, listen to training tapes, and listen to many primary sources. I've also created a practice sentence for each accent (written somewhat phonetically in "eye dialect") that attempts to use the major vowel and consonant substitutions for that particular accent. This is simply a fun beginning guide and is in no way claiming to be the replacement to a full study of all the phonetics and sounds and movements of the dialects. Use the practice sentences if you like for your class or personal studies, filling in the proper IPA markings.

Feature films and television shows are listed under each dialect heading. Notes are included recommending which actors to listen to, some of whom are primary sources (native speakers) and some of whom are secondary sources (actors adopting the accent). The popular television programs and miniseries in this list are often available on video. Documentaries are included near the end of each section. Remember to also check for travelogue videos at your video store or library for a wonderfully succinct "tour" of the culture and the land.

I attempted to list the films somewhat according to their value to you in your research. In some instances, a secondary source is so well done that it proves to be a clearer example of the dialect than a primary source that is mixed or unintelligible. Under particular dialect groupings that include multiple variations (for example, East and Central Asia, which includes Japan, China, Korea, Vietnam, and Tibet), I provided notes, to the best of my knowledge, about the specific dialects each film demonstrates. To save you research time, a few notes are given on performers who do poor or inaccurate dialects, although the films themselves may have won critical acclaim. Somewhat stereotypical and exaggerated examples are also included, as you may need to develop characters of this type. Use your own judgment as to which films will be of the most use to you, and which will most accurately reflect the culture and era you're trying to research.

Dialect tapes and texts which teach the particular accent are listed next, in alphabetical order. All of these are detailed in the Bibliography. The category of **"Other tapes"** refers to resources on audiotape, such as narrated books.

Books pertinent to your research about the speech and culture of the region are in the final category. This includes dictionaries of foreign terms.

Check the web for even more sources. The options are endless. Use E!Online (Entertainment Online) or Blockbustermovie.com or imbd.com. When you know of certain actors who have good native accents, you can find a list of all of the films they were in. You'll also be able to find foreign films listed by country to find movies in foreign languages, as a means of studying the music of the speech and the nonverbal expressions of the culture. The web also has RealAudio clips you can browse through for hours of fascinating study.

AFRICAN

(including Afrikaans, which is Dutch-based and has very different vowel and consonant substitutions than Black African)

Listen for: Even rhythm/equally-stressed syllables, grounded chest tone, narrow range, the "r" tap, dental on "th" to a "t" or "d," very open "er" to "uh, so "father thinks" becomes "fah-duh tinks." White S. African sounds almost Australian, but still has the even rhythm and is loose under the lips.

Trigger: Bow head and speak, makes lips loose with space between lips and teeth, think of an African running across the bush and breathing through the mouth.

Practice sentence for Black African: "I am from Africa and that means my responsibilities are whateverI think I should do"="I ahm frrahm Ah'-frri'-kah' ahnd daht means my rre'-spon'-see'-bee'-lee'-tees' ah wah'-teh'-vuh' I tink I shoood doo."

Films and TV series:

Shaka Zulu (television miniseries, available on video)

Cry Freedom (the South African doctor is played by Zakes Mokae)

A Dry White Season (with Zakes Mokae and Janet Sussman, both South Africans)

An African Dream (with John Kani)

The Power of One (some of the minor roles are genuine South Africans)

The Road to Mecca (very good Afrikaans speakers; Kathy Bates accent is okay)

The Fourth Reich (good Afrikanns, all South African cast)

Master Harold and the Boys (starring Zakes Mokae; Matthew Broderick plays the English boy)

Lethal Weapon 2 (the villains speak in South African accents)

East of Kilimanjaro

Dingaka (with Ken Gampu, African film star)

The Gods Must Be Crazy 1 and *2* (starring a genuine South African bushman)

Sarafina (set in South Africa; stars Whoopi Goldberg, but several co-stars are authentic)

Golden Child (comedy; Eddie Murphy plays an African prince who comes to America)

Mandela (about Nelson Mandela, but the stars do not have authentic accents)

The Struggle for South Africa (documentary, perhaps available from WGBH in Boston, includes interviews with Nelson Mandela, President de Klerk, Chief Buthelezi, and Eugene Terreblanche, who speaks thick Afrikaans)

Notes for an African Orestes (documentary about remote villages in Africa)

Paul Bowles in Morocco (documentary portrait of the American composer and author who worked in Tangier)

General Idi Amin Dada (documentary about Idi Amin, dictator of Uganda in South Africa)

(For certain African-American characters, see author's notes and resources listed under "African American," and also "Southern--Deep South" resources)

Dialect tapes and texts:

Blunt's *More Stage Dialects* (Africa—Sudan, Kenya, Nigeria, and Ghana)

British Broadcasting Company Record *English with an Accent* (Afrikaans, Kenyon, Nigerian, and South African)

Lane-Plescia's *South African for Actors*

Machlin's *Dialects for the Stage* (Black African)
Stern's *Acting with an Accent* (West Indian/Black African)
Stern's *Dialect Monologues, Vol. II* (Afrikaans, English South African)
Trudgill and Hannah's *International English* (South African, West African)
Wells' *Accents of the English-speaking World* (South Africa, Nigeria)

Other tapes:
(Check the library for many CDs and taped authentic music of Africa like "Afro Beat
    Nigerian" by Fela Kuti, "The Lion Sleeps Tonight" by The Mahohalla Queens, and
    authentic Zulu music)

Books:
The Mind of Africa by W. E. Abraham (hailed by reviewers as probably the most impor-
    tant book written about Africans by an African)
Afrikaans by M. O. Bergers
The Africans: An Ethnological Account by Harold K. Schneider
South Africa   by Tom Hopkinson
Peoples of Africa   pub. by Diagram Group
Let's Visit North Africa by Frances Wilkins
Rwanda by J. K. Pomeray
Zaire by Rebecca Stefoff
(See other books listed under the heading for the specific region in Africa that you are
    studying.)
Afrikaans-Engels, Engels-Afrikaans Dictionary,   ed. by Abel Coetzee
*A Dictionary of Africanisms: Contributions of Sub-Sahanan Africa to the English Lan-
    guage* by Gerard M. Dalgish
A Place with the Pigs by Anthol Fugard (written in dialect)

AFRICAN-AMERICAN
(Southern/historic to urban/Ebonics)

(*Author's note*: African-American culture embraces a range of dialects due to it's complex history.
These dialects vary [as any do] from region to region, and through the eras. First I've included films
that are set in the South, several of which are historic. The *derivative* of what we recognize as a distinct
dialect has Southern roots, Southern sounds, even as African Americans moved north and west. In
several other U.S. regions, particularly the urban regions such as New York, Chicago, and L.A., the
speech of some African Americans has some noticeable patterns of grammar, pronunciation and slang
which would categorize it as a dialect, so I have included a list of just a few of the many examples of the
modern urban speech. Categorization of African-American dialects and "Vernacular Black English" as
a language ["Ebonics"] has been the controversial topic of many books and articles for the past forty
years. Some of these titles are listed below, under "Books.")

Films and TV series:
SOUTHERN and HISTORIC examples:
Roots (the mini-series, available on video; covers a very broad span of time, by
    beginning with the family's African ancestors)
Driving Miss Daisy   (period Atlanta setting; Morgan Freeman is from Tennessee)

The Color Purple (stars Ophrah and Whoopie Goldberg)
Glory (and other Civil War films)
Porgy and Bess (opera by Gershwin, the first opera to feature this type of speech)
(The portrayal of blacks in *Gone with the Wind* has come under heavy criticism)
North and South
Lady Sings the Blues (about Billie Holiday)
School Daze (Spike Lee production, set in a modern Atlanta college)
The Cotton Club
Purlie (musical)

URBAN/EBONICS/more contemporary:
Once Upon a Time When We Were Colored (critically acclaimed BET performance,
     starring Felicia Rachad, directed by Tim Reed)
Crooklyn (a Spike Lee production, about a girl that moves from Brooklyn
     to the South)
Tap (with Gregory Hines; features famous old-time tap dancers)
Raisin in the Sun (Chicago; late '50s)
Barbershop (south-side Chicago, with Ice Cube and Cedric the Entertainer; has
     received some criticism for political incorrectness)
Friday
Brown Sugar (about the hip hop industry)
Kids
Go Tell it On the Mountain (based on the book by James Baldwin)
Set it Off (with Queen Letifa, from New Jersey)
A Soldier's Story
Money Talks
Menace 2 Society
Freeway
I Spy (and other Eddie Murphy films where he plays excitable characters)
Bad Boys (stars Martin Lawrence, who has his own TV series, *Martin*; Lawrence
     uses stereotypically exaggerated hip slang of an urban accent; *Bad Boys* co-
     stars Will Smith, from the *Fresh Prince* TV series, who doesn't really have the
     urban dialect)
"The Jamie Foxx Show"; "The Wayans Brothers" (TV series; Jamie, and all of the
     Wayans, including Daman and Keenen Ivory, are from NYC, and often do cliché
     comic exaggerations of the urban dialect; check other films starring Jamie,
     Damon, andKeenen)
Can't Hardly Wait (white urban speech; see also *8 Mile*, with white urban rapper,
     Eminem)
Hollywood Shuffle (important parody of the "blaxploitation" film featuring urban
     African-American characters)
Airplane I (the "I speak Jive" scene is a parady of the '60s-'70s jive)
(Many, many other "urban" films have come out recently)

Dialect tapes and texts:
The Hermans' *American Dialects* (African-American) (no tape)
Lane-Plescia's *Accents for Black Actors* (African American)
Machlin's *Dialects for the Stage* (Black American)
Wise's *Applied Phonetics* (no tape)

Other tapes:
(Check for audiotapes of Lorraine Hansberry's plays on cassette, such as *A Raisin in the Sun* and *To Be Young, Gifted, and Black*.)

Books:
The Story of English (book and video, chapter on "Black on White")
Language in the Inner City: Studies in the Black English Vernacular by William Labov
Dialect Clash in America by Paul Brandes and Jeutonne Brewer (chapter on Black Amerenglish)
Juba to Jive: A Dictionary of African-American Slang by Charlene Major
Black Talk: Words and Phrases from the Hood to the Amen Corner by Geneva Smitherman 1994
Black Noise: Rap Music and Black Culture in Contemporary America by Tricia Rose 1994
The Rap Attack: African Jive to NY Hip Hop by David Toop 1984
"*Black Engliah and Rap Music*" by Mike Daly (www.finearts.yorku.ca/mdaly/blackenglish.html)
(See Alicia Banks' article: www.Afronet.com)
A Linguist Looks at the Ebonics Debate by Charles J. Fillmore 1997
Black English Vernacular (Ebonics) by Alondra Oubre, PhD. 1997
Black English; and *Perspective on Black English* by J. D. Dillard 1975
A Segmental Phonology of Black English by Philip Luelsdorff 1975
(Check for the many recent NY Times articles and other sources dealing with the controversial "Ebonics" issue)

ASIAN, East and Central
(China/Japan/Korea/Vietnam/Tibet)

Listen for: All evenly stressed syllables, small mouth opening, narrow range, dental sounds, difficulty with tip of tongue consonants, "l's" and "r's" sound like "an "rl" combination, qualities similar to their folk music

Practice sentence: "*Follow your heart when I tell you that I am not able to help you solve these two problems*"="*Forlow yo hot whe' I terl you da' I am no' abrl to herlp you sorlf deez two prlobrlm*" (no plurals)

(Note: Sources for the regions known as East India and Pakistan are listed under "India." Be aware that in many films that have specific Asian settings, a variety of Asian-born actors are often cast. For example, it is likely that not every Asian actor in Joy Luck Club is Chinese)

Films and TV series:
CHINA:
The Last Emperor (shot on location in the People's Republic of China)
Joy Luck Club
Farewell My Concubine
Flower Drum Song (stars Nancy Kwan; set in San Francisco's Chinatown)
M. Butterfly
Dragon: the Bruce Lee Story (starring Jason Scott Lee, who is actually Hawaiian)

Enter the Dragon; Chinese Connection (and many other Bruce Lee films; Chinese)
Dragon Fist; Supercop; Rumble in the Bronx (many other films starring Jackie Chan)
Legend of the Drunken Master (Jackie Chan's voice is dubbed into English, but Chinese
     actors are used for the looping)
Red Curtain (set in China)
King of Masks (set in China; subtitled)
Anna and the King (the recent *King and I* story starring Lin Yun-Fat)
Mortal Kombat
China Girl
The Road Home
Shadow Magic (Peking, subtitles)
Little Buddha (set in India, but real Tibetan Buddhist monks are cast)
Charlie Chan in Rio; Charlie Chan at the Wax Museum (and many other Charlie
     Chan films; considered by many critics a woeful example of Chinese steroetyping)
Young Dragons I and *2* (with Chen Shun Yun; Chinese)
They Call Me Bruce (with Johnny Yun; Chinese)
Fists of Fury (Bruce Lee)
Surf Ninjas (humorous title, but some good Asian sources)
(Hundreds of other Ninja movies)
Red Corner (Richard Gere film set behind the "Red Curtain")
The Wedding Banquet (Taiwan and Chinese-American characters)
Girl from Hunan (in Cantonese, with subtitles; one of the few films made in the People's
     Republic of China)
Distant Harmony: Pavarotti in China (documentary)

JAPAN:
Mishima (Ken Ogata stars)
"Shogun" (the miniseries, available on video)
Snow Falling on Cedars (stars Yuiko Kudo, first generation Japanese)
Gung Ho (authentic Japanese actors)
Ren
The Woman in the Dunes
Merry Christmas, Mr. Lawrence
Teahouse of the August Moon (with Michiko Kyo)
Karate Kid (with Noriyuki "Pat" Morita)
Rising Sun
That's the Way I Like It (Singapore; about the disco craze in 1977)
Picture Bride
Heaven's Burning
Come See the Paradise
Akira Kurosawa's Dreams (in Japanese with subtitles, about Van Gogh)
(Films directed by Akira Kurosawa, subtitled)
Dreams (subtitled; Martin Scorsese film about Van Gogh)
Bridge on the River Kwai (with Sessu Hayakawa as the Japanese prison commander)
You Only Live Twice (007 film with Japanese stars)
Jirohachi (documentary)

VIETNAM / KOREA / TIBET and others
Casualties of War (Vietnam)
Heaven and Earth (Vietnamese leading lady)
Good Morning Vietnam (a few native Vietnamese characters)
Full Metal Jacket (Vietnam)
The Scent of Green Papaya (set in Vietnam, with subtitles)
"China Beach" (TV series, set in Vietnam)
Indochine (Vietnamese characters, but they speak French)
M*A*S*H (film and TV series, set during the Korean War; listen for Rosie the barkeep)
Eat, Drink, Man, Woman (Korean; stars Ang Lee)
The Wedding Banquet (Taiwan and Chinese characters)
Kundun (about Tibet's 14th dalai lama)
Ossian: American Boy, Tibetan Monk (documentary shot on location in Nepal, about a four-year-old American boy who enters a Buddhist monastery)
Shadows Over Tibet (documentary)
Hearts and Minds (documentary about Vietnam and the effects of the war on the people)
Chang (pseudo-documentary action-adventure about primitive villagers in Thailand)

Dialect tapes and texts:
Blunt's *Stage Dialects* (Japanese)
Blunt's *More Stage Dialects* (Asia: China, Vietnam)
British Broadcasting Company Record *English with an Accent* (Chinese: Hong Kong)
The Hermans' *Foreign Dialects* (Japanese, Chinese, Pidgin English, Filipino) (no tape)

Books:
The Asians by Paul Thomas Welty
East Asia and the Western Pacific by Harold Hinton
Traveler's Guide to Asian Customs and Manners by Elizabeth Devine and Nancy L. Braganti
Malaysia and Her Neighbors by Bernard Newman
Coping with China by Richard King and Sandra Shatzky (excellent source, though the book title has a negative connotation)
The Chinese: A Portrait by David Bonaira
Beijing Photos by Beth Sabée and Roland Süssmann
Why the Chinese Are the Way They Are by Benjamin Appel
The Japanese Way: Aspects of Behavior, Attitudes, and Customs of the Japanese by Norika Takada and Rita L. Lampkins
Coping with Japan by John Randle and Mariko Watanabe (excellent source, though a negative title)
The Japanese Character: A Cultural Profile by Nyozekan Hasegawa
With Respect to the Japanese: A Guide for Americans by John C. Condon
Everyday Life in Traditional Japan by C.J. Dunn
Discover Japan, Vol. 2: Words, Customs and Concepts
Japanese Society Today by Tadachi Fukutake
Japan Unmasked by Ichiro Kawasaki
Japan by Beth Reilor
Japan by Library of Nations

The Japanese Islands, a Physical and Social Geography by Jacques Pezeu-Massabuau
Things Korean by Horace N. Allen
Coping with Korea by Gary P. Steenson (excellent source, though a negative title)
English Pronunciation for Japanese Speakers by Paulette Kate and Lillian Pons

AUSTRALIAN / NEW ZEALAND

*Listen for: Mouth is a pulled back wide slit, note similarities but differences from Cockney, nasal
        vowels so "map" is "mep," "better" is "bittuh," "there" is "theh," "Outback" is almost "etbeck"*
Trigger: Pull head slightly back, strong and straightfaced like Crocodile Dundee
*Practice sentence: "Good Day, Mate. Whenever you're here, I hope to meet your little son and daughter
        out there in the Outback"="Goo-dye Myte. Win-iv-uh yaw' hi', oy ha-uh-oop to muh-eet yaw' little
        son an' dawduh-ret theh-rin the etbeck." (notice they don't drop "h's" or glottal stop "t's" like Cockneys)*

<u>Films and TV series:</u>
Strictly Ballroom (excellent primary sources for Australian)
Muriel's Wedding (all characters; urban Australia)
A Cry in the Dark (Meryl Streep's accent is flawless, and most other characters are
        authentic; note that males and females have a bit different tone quality)
Crocodile Dundee I and *2* (Paul Hogan is the archtype, vocally and physically, of the
        Australian Outback male)
The Man from Snowy River; Return to Snowy River (set in rural Australia in the 1800s)
F/X and *F/X 2* (or any Bryan Brown film)
My Brilliant Career
The Thorn Birds (the miniseries available on video); *Against All Odds* (or any other
        Rachel Ward film)
The Crocodile Hunter: Collision Course, and the TV series (Steve Irwin's Aussie acent
        and manner is over the top)
Lantana
Down Under (the singer/actress Olivia Newton-John made this music/travel video,
        which is a wonderful overview of the country; she interviews several Australians.
        Newton-John has what is called the Anzac dialect—the Australian-New Zealand
        Army Corps dialect—which is educated Australian)
Down Under (different film than the one listed above; set in Australia)
The Adventures of Priscilla, Queen of the Desert
Breaker Morant
Malcolm
Gallipoli; Tim (and Mel Gibson's other early films, which show off his light accent)
Rain (New Zealand)
Don't Tell Them It's Me (New Zealand)
Heavenly Creatures (New Zealand; listen to Pauline and her family)
The Coca-Cola Kid; Once Were Warriors (for dialects of the aboriginal cultures, such as
        the Maori; also listen to some of the natives in *The Piano*)

Dialect tapes and texts:
Blunt's *More Stage Dialects* (Australia and New Zealand)
British Broadcasting Company Record *English with an Accent* (Australian, New Zealand)
The Hermans' *Foreign Dialects* (Australian, Australian Pidgin) (no tape)
Molin's *Actor's Encyclopedia of Dialects* (Australian and New Zealand/Anzoc)
Lane-Plescia's *Australian/New Zealand for Actors*
Stern's *Acting with an Accent* (Australian)
Trudgill and Hannah's *International English* (Australian)
Wells' *Accents of the English-speaking World* (Australia and New Zealand)

Books:
G'Day! Teach Yourself Australian by Collin Bowles
Let's Talk Strine (written in eye-dialect)
The Story of English (video and book, chapter on "The Echoes of an English Voice)
Australia: the Land and Its People by Elizabeth Cornelia
Coping with Australia by Eleanor Greet (excellent source, though the book title has a
        negative connotation)
We Live in Australia by Rennie Ellis
Australia: Enchantment of the World by Emilie U. Lepthien
Outback by Thomas Keneally
The Ribbon and the Ragged Square: An Australian Journey by Linda Christmas
Encyclopedia of Australia by Andrew and Nancy Learmonth
Australia by Nick Lush
Australian English by W. S. Ramson
The Australian National Dictionary, ed. by W. S. Ramson
Australian Words and Their Origins, ed. by Joan Hughes
Teach Yourself Australian in Twenty Easy Lessons by Louis Silvestro
A Personal Kiwi-Yankee Dictionary for the New Zealand Traveler by Louis S. Leland, Jr.
Journey Through a Timeless Land by National Geography an Roff Smith

Other tapes:
In a Sunburned Country by Bill Bryson (the book on tape)

BRITISH (Standard British*
to middle-class British)

*Standard (or upscale) British is also often called RP, or Received Pronunciation

Listen for: Wide, controlled inflection, smooth, articulate, crisp "t's," forward "aww" feel like on "Who would open all the boxes"

Trigger: Spitting marbles onto the outstretched hand; literally holding sides of face forward, head floats up with dignity, no fidgeting

Practice sentence: "Michael Caine was always here at my house, eating an O'Henry candy bar, dancing with a little spoon"="Michael Caine was awwlays he-rat my house, eating an eh-oo Henry candy bah, dahncing with a little spoon." (compare that to the Cockney version)

Films and TV series: (many of them also feature Cockney, Irish, Scottish or Welsh characters, so you need to be able to distinguish between RP and the different regional varieties of Great Britain)

Gosford Park (all classes of British, servants to rich, wannabees, Americans)

Mary Poppins; Star (and the many other films Julie Andrews has been in)

My Fair Lady (both Cockney and Standard British; Rex Harrison's Higgins is High British; Audrey Hepburn's Eliza Doolittle goes from low-class Cockney to elegant British. See also non-musical version, *Pygmalion* with Dianna Rigg, or the older one.)

Sherlock Holmes (all of the films and TV shows)

Deathtrap; Dirty Rotten Scoundrels (and dozens of other films Michael Caine has done)

For Your Eyes Only; View to a Kill; Octopussy (and all the many James Bond films that Roger Moore has been in; however, Sean Connery's 007 has a touch of Scottish, and Irish-born Pierce Brosnan's is very light)

Elizabeth (about the Queen, with Cate Blanchett)

Importance of Being Ernest (old and new versions)

Persuasion, Pride and Prejudice, Emma (any films of Jane Austin's works)

A Room With a View; Howard's End (and anything else with Helena Bonham Carter)

Shadowlands; Howard's End (and anything else Anthony Hopkins has done, in which he uses his British accent)

Reversal of Fortune; French Lieutenant's Woman; Damage; Dead Ringers (and any Jeremy Irons film; he aso voiced the evil "Scar" in *The Lion King* animated film)

Mary Shelley's Frankenstein (Kenneth Branagh's version)

Much Ado About Nothing (Shakespeare, with Emma Thompson and Kenneth Branagh)

Sense and Sensibility; Nine Months (and any of Emma Thompson's films)

The Madness of King George (in period)

An Ideal Husband (in period)

The Ruling Class (deals with issues of class in England; also, anything else starring Peter O'Toole, such as *Lion in Winter*)

Ten Little Indians (there are several versions of this Agatha Christie story)

Death on the Nile (and all of the many Agatha Christie films and TV shows)

Enchanted April

Without a Clue (Michael Caine plays a Sherlock Holmes impersonator, Ben Kingsley plays Watson)

Bedknobs and Broomsticks (with Roddy McDowell, who has been in dozens of other films)

Star Trek: Nemesis; Star Trek: First Contact; Star Trek: Generations (Patrick Stewart's Captain Picard has an elegant, classically-trained British accent, though he was born in the North Country; the TV series is called "Star Trek: The Next Generation")

"The Avengers" (the old TV series; also, anything Diana Rigg is in; she often hosts PBS specials)

Immortal Beloved; Scarlet Letter; Lost in Space (with Gary Oldman)

The Secret Garden (film uses RP though the book is place in Yorkshire)

Hamlet (all versions, including the one starring Mel Gibson, who did the accent well)

Richard III; Henry V; Pride and Prejudice (and other Laurence Olivier films)

Richard III (the newer version with Ian McKellen; any Shakespeare film cast with British actors will show all social classes)

Lord of the Rings (but listen for the royal or elevated characters)

Harry Potter (but listen carefully for different class levels and British varieties)

Rosencrantz and Guildenstern Are Dead (set in Shakespeare's England)

Topsy Turvy (about Gilbert and Sullivan, 1700s)

Valmont (period piece)

Tom Jones (the classic, period piece with Albert Finney)

Miss Julie (set in 1895; she speaks RP and her co-star is N. English)

The Browning Version (and anything else Albert Finney has been in)

License to Kill (Timothy Dalton plays 007)

Annie; Oliver Twist; Three Musketeers (any other Tim Curry film in which he uses his British accent; his accent may be considered upper middle class)

The Four Musketeers (the newest *Three Musketeers* doesn't use all British actors)

Taming of the Shrew (Michael York has a beautiful Standard British accent; Richard Burton is Welsh; Elizabeth Taylor's accent is upscale American, and shows just a hint of her English upbringing. Check for other Michael York films.)

Austin Powers (Michael York's accent and demeanor is upper class RP)

Camelot (with Vanessa Redgrave; Richard Harris is Irish, but does a British accent)

Georgie Girl (or any films with Lynn or Vanessa Redgrave)

Educating Rita (Michael Caine's educated British contrasts with Julie Walters's thick working-class accent)

A Fish Called Wanda (with John Cleese and the more Cockney Michael Palin, both of Monty Python fame; an excellent opportunity to watch how the British are contrasted with Americans)

Monty Python and the Holy Grail (and all of the many Monty Python films and TV shows, for all class levels)

Time Bandits (all classes; and anything else with John Cleese)

(Any documentaries or TV specials about the royal family; the Queen and Prince Charles speak "the Queen's English" but Fergie and Lady Di sound more upper middle class.)

CONTEMPORARY "MIDDLE-CLASS" BRITISH:
> *(Note: Several British varieties as well as "light" Cockney can sound similar to what I am calling middle-class British)*

Arthur 1 and *2* (Dudley Moore's accent is middle-class British, though he plays rich)
"Absolutely Fabulous" (TV series in syndication and on video; the leads are mostly middle-class British; several minor characters are of various regional varieties)
Time after Time (middle-class accent; check any Malcolm McDowell or David Warner films; McDowell was also in *Clockwork Orange* and *Star Trek: Generations*)
Fourth Protocol (Michael Caine often modifies his Cockney to a middle-class dialect)
"The Monkees" (Davey Jones, of the '60s boy band; TY series in syndication)
Austin Powers (Mike Myers is a great, clear secondary source)
This is Spinal Tap (Hackney, N. of East End; secondary but quite authentic)
"The Tracy Ullman Show" (Ullman has a more middle-class accent; in her TV series, currently syndicated, she does a number of dialects extremely well; she was also in the film *Ready to Wear*)
Sliding Doors (Gwenyth Paltro's accent is good)
"Are You Being Served?"; "Black Adder"; "Fawlty Towers"; "Drop the Dead Donkey"; "Whose Line Is It Anyway?" (and many other British shows that are regularly shown on TV; several British classes and varieties are represented)
"The Benny Hill Show" (reruns on TV feature the commedian doing a number of fabulous British accents from all classes)
"The Osbornes" reality TV series
About a Boy; Four Weddings and a Funeral; Two Weeks Notice; Nine Months (anything with Hugh Grant, contemporary upper middle-class British)

Dialect tapes and texts:
Blumenfeld, Robert *Accents of English* (text only, no tape)
Blunt's *Stage Dialects* (Standard British)
The Hermans' *Foreign Dialects* (British) (no tape)
Hughes and Trudgill's *English Accents and Dialects* (Received Pronunciation/RP)
Kur's *Stage Dialect Studies* (Standard British) (no tape)
Lane-Plescia's *Standard British for the Actor* (now in a new edition)
Machlin's *Dialects for the Stage* (Standard British)
Meier's *Accents and Dialects for Stage and Screen*
Molin's *Actor's Encyclopedia of Dialects* (British English)
Stern's *Acting with an Accent* (Standard British)
Trudgill and Hannah's *International English* (RP/British Standard)
Wells' *Accents of the English-speaking World* (RP)
Wise's *Applied Phonetics* (Standard Southern British) (no tape)

Other tapes:
(There are literally hundreds of British books and autobiographies on tape, read by prominent British actors. Many of them demonstrate several varieties of British accents.)
The Story of English (book and video, chapter on "The Mother Tongue")

Books:

English by David Frost (excellent source about the British people's national character, by the famous British talk-show host)

Coping with England by Jean Hannah (excellent source, though the book title has a negative connotation)

Exploring English Character by Geoffry Gorer

The British: Portrait of a People by Anthony Glyn

Brit-think, Ameri-think: A Transatlantic Survival Guide by Jane Walmsley

The English by Norman F. Cantor

British: A Portrait of an Indomitable Island People by Norman Gelb

Everyman's English Pronouncing Dictionary by Daniel Jones (the accepted authority for Standard British pronunciations; you can use this in researching the pronunciations of proper names and phrases in your play script)

English-English by Norman W. Schur (a dictionary translating British phrases and proper names)

British-American Language Dictionary by Norman Moss (translates British phrases and proper names)

British English: A to Zed by Norman W. Schur

Oxford English Dictionary by Oxford University Press

Chambers' English Dictionary

BBC Pronunciation Dictionary of British Names by G. E. Pointon

(Check J.C. Wells' web site for on-line articles regarding RP)

BRITISH (regional varieties)

Listen for: how the inflection varies from RP, often upward like Scottish, use of both the tapped and dropped r, how the "uh" vowel "luck" may become "look." Other British varieties sound close to what we would recognize as Cockney.

Practice sentence for Liverpudlian: "Ringo. He's my favorite Beatle. I love his drum playing" = "Ringuh-oo. 'e's moy favorite Buh-ee'l. Oy loov 'is droom playin'."

Films and TV series:

Hard Days Night; Help (and all of the Beatles films; Liverpool dialect, called Liverpudlian)

The Beat (the story of the early Beatles; Liverpool; excellent source)

The Beatles Anthology (TV documentary on video; Liverpudlian)

Let It Be (documentary that chronicles the last days of the Beatles)

Imagine: John Lennon (documentary which chronicles Lennon's public and private life)

Educating Rita (Julie Walters's accent is a perfect example of a working class Liverpool accent, and contrasts with Michael Caine's Standard British)

Shirley Valentine (Liverpool)

High Hopes (the girl has a Liverpool accent)

Mona Lisa (the girl lead is Liverpudlian)

Swing (Liverpool)

Gunga Din (Cary Grant's early film shows his native Bristol-Liverpool accent)

Little Voice   (on location in Scarsborough, North Country, especially the talkative mother)

"All Creatures Great and Small"   (the old series on TV is set in Yorkshire, in the British North Country; the lead character is a veterinarian from Glasgow, Scotland; the film of the same name is also on video, starring Anthony Hopkins)

Lock, Stock and Two Smoking Barrels   (the two thieves are modern Manchester; other characters are "Cockney")

Bellman and True   (main character and his son are from the North Country)

Still Crazy   (modern North Country)

Brassed Off   (modern Yorkshire; light with good slang and grammar changes)

Born Romantic   (modern N. Country and other regional varieties)

Mutiny on the Bounty   (1935 version has the Norwich accent; Trevor Howard, from Kent, is in the 1962 version, but Marlon Brando's British accent is poor)

Star Wars   (Peter Cushing is from Surrey)

Swiss Family Robinson; Dunkirk; Goodbye, Mr. Chips   (and other John Mills films; Mills is from Suffolk)

Cider with Rosie   (Gloucestershire)

Saturday Night and Sunday Morning   (authentic Nottingham; stars a very young Albert Finney)

"Frasier"   (TV series; Jane Leeves plays Daphne, the housekeeper, using the Manchester accent of Northern England; she was previously on "Murphy Brown," and "Eastenders" using more of a Cockney accent. She hails from East Grinstead.)

Waterland   (set in the Fen Country, but the dialects are not authentic)

The Secret Garden   (a musical version may have the Yorkshire dialect, but the film uses RP)

(Many films have characters that speak dialects other than Standard British or true Cockney, including *My Fair Lady*, the Sherlock Holmes and Agatha Christie movies, etc.)

<u>Dialect tapes and texts:</u>

Blumenfeld's *Accents of English*   (no tape)

Blunt's *More Stage Dialects*   (British Isles)

British Broadcasting Company Record *English with a Dialect*   (numerous regions)

Hughes and Trudgill's *English Accents and Dialects*   (various regions)

Karshner and Sterns' *Dialect Monologues, Vol. II*   (Liverpudlian)

Lane-Plescia's *North Country British*   (numerous regions)

Lane-Plescia's *Personalized British-based Dialect Service*   (call for a specific dialect)

Machlin's *Dialects for the Stage*   (North British)

Meier's *Accents and Dialects for Stage and Screen* (Northern Ireland, Liverpool, Hampshire, Yorkshire)

Stern's *Acting with an Accent*   (British North Country)

Wells' *Accents of the English-speaking World*   (the N. and S. of England/rural Norfolk)

CANADIAN
(see also "French Canadian" for separate listings)

Listen for: tendency to have flatfaced vowels, rhetroflex "r's," variant pronunciations, such as "drama" to "a" as in "can," and listen for the "eh" added for emphasis at the ends of phrases.

Films and TV series:
Margaret's Museum (Helena Bonham Carter does a great example of Atlantic Canadian)
Shipping News (Newfoundland; note, many original settlers were from Ireland)
The Hanging Garden
The Grey Fox
Men with Brooms
The Wars
The Red Violin
The English Patient (avoid, no good primary or secondary sources)
This Hour has Twenty-Two Minutes (comedy show based in Halifax)
CODCO (comedy show based in Newfoundland)
(Many actors, such as Michael J. Fox and Mike Myers hail from Canada, but do not have a dialect that would be recognized onstage as Canadian)

Dialect tapes and texts:
David Ferry's *"Canajun, eh"* (available through theatrebooks.com)
Allen and Rogers' *Tongues of the North American Project* (13 Canadian dialect samples)
Blunt's *More Stage Dialacts*
Karshner's *Dialect Monologues*
Trudgill and Hannah's *International English*
Wells' *Accents of English*

Other sources:
Check the Canadian Film Board on line. Tapes: sent by mail: Sandra Lindberg, School of Theatre Arts, Illinois Westleyan Univ., P.O. 2900 Bloomington, IL 61701 or slindber@titan.iwu.edu
Check ACTRA (the Alliance of Cinema, TV and Radio Artists union, like SAG).
Check CBC's web site for telephone interviews with native Canadians.

Books:
Canadian Faces and Places by Yves Marchand (includes French Canadian)
Canada and the Great White North, ed. by Rand McNally Publishers

COCKNEY

(Note: Several British regional varieties sound close to London Cockney, and more middle-class British
     speech sounds like a "light" Cockney, so see also sections on "Middle-class contemporary British"
     and British varieties)

*Listen for: Wide inflection, uncontrolled highs and lows, all vowels become diphthongs, especially
     A=I, EE=uhee, I=oy, ow=a-uh-oo, OO=uhoo*
*Trigger: Eating a big sloppy sandwich, open back and then forward (a-uh-oo), or use Stern's trick of an
     animal gulping an insect.*
*Practice sentence: "Michael Caine was here at my house, eating an O'Henry candy bar, dancing with a
     little spoon"="Moykel KIne was 'ee-rat me youse, uh-eetin an a-uh-oo wenruhee candy bah, dahncin'
     wif a li'le spuh-oon."*

Films and TV series:

Oliver (Jack Wild, who plays the Artful Dodger, was also one of the merry men in Kevin
     Costner's version of *Robin Hood*)
My Fair Lady (excellent example of the transformation from heavy Cockney to High
     British; the 1938 or the Dianna Rigg version of *Pygmalion* are even better
     examples of Cockney than the Audrey Hepburn musical version)
A Christmas Carol; Scrooge (all of the many versions of this, except for the modernized
     American ones, such as those starring Henry Winkler and Bill Murray)
"East Enders" (reruns of this popular British soap on TV)
This is Spinal Tap (secondary sources but accurate for Hackney, north of East End)
Little Voice; Alfie; The Man Who Would Be King (Michael Caine allows his natural
     Cockney to come through)
Sweeney Todd (the musical has very little dialogue, but most of the characters sing in
     Cockney dialect)
Mary Poppins (some Cockney characters; Dick Van Dyke's chimney-sweep character
     has a poor accent)
Last Orders (thick S. London dialect)
Spice World (with the Spice Girls)
Monty Python and the Holy Grail (and all of the many Monty Python films and TV
     shows)
Gosford Park (contrasts servants with upper classes; period)
Sherlock Holmes (all of the films and TV shows have characters from all British varieties
     and classes)
Chitty Chitty Bang Bang (several characters)
Passport to Pimlico (London suburb)
Naked (about the Cockney people)
Bellman and True (several levels of Cockney; also available on audiobook)
High Hopes (several levels of Cockney; also available on audiocassette)
Michael (Bob Hoskins' natural accent)
Mona Lisa (Bob Hoskins and Michael Caine demonstrate several levels of Cockney; the
     girl is from Liverpool; also available on audiocassette)
The Krays
Lock, Stock and Two Smoking Barrels (modern "Cockney;" the two theives are from
     Manchester)
Major Barbara (1941 film)

The Cook, the Thief, the Wife, and her Lover
Willy Wonka and the Chocolate Factory
Midsummer Night's Dream; Merry Wives of Windsor; As You Like It, Henry IV (and
     numerous other Shakespeare productions on film have lower-class Cockney
     characters to contrast with the royalty)
(See under "British" for contemporary middle-class accents that sound like a light Cockney)

Other tapes:
(Try original London and Broadway albums of *My Fair Lady, Oliver, Sweeney Todd*)
(Many audiobooks of the classics will have clear Cockney and British varieties)

Dialect tapes and texts:
Blumenfeld's *Accents of English* (no tape)
Blunt's *Stage Dialects*
British Broadcasting Company Record *English with an Accent* (London/Cockney, and
     other regions in England with dialects similar to Cockney)
The Hermans' *Foreign Dialects* (no tape)
Hughes and Trudgill's *English Accents and Dialects* (London/Cockney, and other regions
     in England)
Kur's *Stage Dialect Studies* (no tape)
Lane-Plescia's *Cockney for Actors*
Machlin's *Dialects for the Stage*
Meier's *Accents and Dialects for Stage and Screen*
Molin's *Actor's Encyclopedia of Dialects*
Stern's *Acting with an Accent* (Cockney)
Wells' *Accents of the English-speaking World* (London: Cockney)
Wise's *Applied Phonetics* (Standard Southern British/Cockney) (no tape)

Books:
The Cockney by Julian Franklyn (excellent source)
Cockney Past and Present: A Short History of the Dialect of London by William Matthews
     (good chapter on characteristic grammar)
Cockney Dialect and Slang by Peter Wright
(The script of the play, *Pygmalion*, has the Cockney dialogue written in George Bernard
     Shaw's phonetics for pronunciation)
(Check the dictionaries listed under the heading for British sources, to find books that
     will give you definitions and pronunciations of Cockney phrases and proper names.)

DUTCH (the Netherlands or Holland; also Pennsylvania Dutch)

(*Note*: You will hear the Dutch influence in some of the South African dialects)

Listen for: The similarities and contrasts from Germanic and Scandinavian sounds, dental "this, that" to "dis, dat," hard r's--"mother" is "mudderrr"

Trigger: Bit of a pursed lipped mouth shape, like Swedish

Films and TV series:
The Hiding Place (good secondary sources)
Witness (Pennsylvania Dutch)
Deathtrap (the character of Helga, the psychic is Dutch)
Antonia's Line (Dutch subtitled)
Hans Christian Andersen (Danny Kaye plays the title role without the appropriate Danish accent, but it is filmed in Holland and a few minor characters are Dutch)
Goldmember (Mike Myers plays the highly exaggerated Dutch character in the 3rd Austin Powers film)
Roy Rogers, King of the Cowboys (documentary; follows the exploits of Dutch director Thys Ockersen who had a boyhood interest in Roy Rogers; has some Dutch subtitles)

Dialect tapes and texts:
Blunt's *More Stage Dialects* (West Europe—The Netherlands)
British Broadcasting Company Record *English with an Accent* (Dutch)
The Hermans' *American Dialects* (Pennsylvania Dutch) (no tape)
Wise's *Applied Phonetics* (Pennsylvania Dutch) (no tape)

Other tapes:
Corrie (a behind-the-scenes look at the making of the film *The Hiding Place*, based on the book written by Corrie ten Boom, who is Dutch; find this source at Christian bookstores or a Christian film service; also check for the short video, *Jesus, the Victor*, a personal portrait of Corrie ten Boom)

Books:
The Dutch by Ann Hoffmann
The Land and People of Holland by Adriaan J. Barnouw and Raymond A. Wohlrabe
The Oxford Duden Dutch-English Dictionary
Dialects and Levels of Language, ed. by Joseph Littell (chapter on Pennsylvania Dutch)

EASTERN EUROPEAN
(Czech, Slovak, Hungarian, Rumanian, Yugoslavian)
(*Note*: "Rumania" is a variant spelling for "Romania." For Finland, see under Russia)

Listen for: *Restrained melody and passion compared to Russian, "weather" is "vedderrrr" with "r's" almost rolled, the 5 Latin vowels of "mah, meh, mee, moh, moo."*

Trigger: *Breathing through a very small mouth opening, as if lips are frozen, thick butterscotch pudding in the throat.*

Practice sentence: *"I want to suck your blood"= "I vant too sock yourr blahd"*

"Look into this crystal ball and I will tell you why, when and where to find love."="Luke eentoo dees crreestal ball and I veel tale you vhy, vehn, and vehrr too find lahf."

Films and TV series:
Dracula (and the many other films Bela Lugosi was in; his accent was authentic Transylvanian; other versions of Dracula portray the character well as a Transylvanian)

Bram Stoker's Dracula (good secondary source)

Ed Wood (Martin Landau plays Bela Lugosi; great secondary source for Hungarian)

Her Alibi (stars the supermodel Paulina, who is Czech)

A Shot in the Dark; The Pink Panther Strikes Again (Herbert Lom plays Chief Inspector Dreyfuss, whom Klousseau slowly drives insane; Lom's native Czech accent comesout most strongly when he gets upset)

I Love You to Death (the older mom, played by Joan Plowright, is a good secondary source for Czech)

The Saint

Divided We Fall (Czech, about Nazi's)

Immortal Beloved (Isabella Rosellini is Italian, but adopts a fair Hungarian accent)

Stripes (the comedy's plot leads to Czechoslovakia, where some minor characters sound authentic)

Touch of Evil; Death of a Scoundrel (and other Zsa Zsa or Eva Gabor films; Budapest-Continental accents)

Gotcha (the female lead, Linda Fiorentino, attempts a Czech accent; her character says she is Czech with a Berliner accent)

My Fair Lady (Rumanian character, Zoltan Korpathy, who appears in the party scene)

Czechoslovakia: Triumph and Tradition (travelogue)

Road Scholar (documentary; follows Rumanian poet Andrei Codrescu on a coast-to-coast drive)

Dracula: A Cinematic Scrapbook (documentary about Bela Lugosi and other stars who played Dracula)

(Check for documentaries about the Serbo-Croatian conflict.)

Dialect tapes and texts:
Blunt's *More Stage Dialects* (Greece and Eastern Europe—Yugoslavia, Hungary, Rumania, Czechoslovakia, Lithuania)

British Broadcasting Company Record *English with an Accent* (Czech, Hungarian, Slovak)

The Hermans' *Foreign Dialects* (Middle European—Lithuanian, Yugoslav, Czech, Finnish, Hungarian) (no tape)

Molin's *Actor's Encyclopedia of Dialects* (Lithuanian, Czechoslovakian, Yugoslavian, Hungarian)

Books:
Eastern Europe by Library of Nations
Eastern Europe: Czechoslovakia, Hungary, Poland by Godfrey Blunden
Slavophilia: Slavic and East European Resources (see www.Slavophilia.net)
The Land and People of Romania by Julian Hale
Let's Visit Romania by Julian Popescu
Bulgaria by Julian Popescu
Hungaria: A Country Study by Eugene Keefe, et. al.
Let's Visit Czechoslovakia by Julian Popesco (More updated books will reflect the nation's split into the Czech Republic and Slovakia.)
Czechoslavakia: Crossroads and Crises

FRENCH

Listen for: Melodic smoothness, nasality, dental sounds like "zis" and "zat," tendency to say "-air" for "-er" endings, the treatment of the uvular "r," nasal "n", soft treatment of "ch" to "sh" and "j" to "zh"

Trigger: Kissy-lips; spitting out grape seeds from deep in your throat, both throaty and dental; a feel of proudly "waving the French flag" at the ends of lines to get the stress to flip up at the ends.

Practice sentence: "Well, this is the challenge for Jack's father--going in one direction forever"= "Whale, zees eez zee shall-awnzh' for zhahk's fah-zair'--go-ing' een wahn di-rec-shaw' fo-reh-vai' (stressing final syllables)

Films and TV series:
Green Card; My Father the Hero (with Gèrard Depardieu, who provides an excellent example of a clearly-spoken French accent)
French Kiss (primary sources and Kevin Kline's accent and manner are very good)
Gigi (with Maurice Chevalier and Leslie Caron, who has a perfectly clear, light accent; also, the little boy in it is French)
An American in Paris (and any other Leslie Caron films)
Fanny (starring Maurice Chevalier, who has a very clear, somewhat heavy accent; also stars Louis Jordan)
Addicted to Love (excellent source, Tcheky Karyo, born in Turkey but raised in Paris, is one of France's most popular stars)
Chocolat (with Juliette Binoche)
Ronan; Just Visiting (with Jon Renault)
Can Can; Swamp Thing; Octopussy (Louis Jordan has a Parisian aristocratic dialect, but in roles where he shows anger or excitement, his native Marseilles-Nice dialect shows through)
Love Songs; *The Hunger*; *Indochine* (or any Catherine Deneuve film)
White; *Killing Zoe*; *Europa Europa*; *Before Sunrise* (with Julie Delpy)
On a Clear Day You Can See Forever (for the lead male, Yves Montand)

Ready to Wear/Prêt-à-Porter (the fashion show is set in France, so several characters are authentic)

The Thief, The Cook, the Wife and Her Lover

Is Paris Burning? (Alan Delon and other authentic French)

Queen Margot (with Isabella Adjani and John Hughes Anglade)

The Other Side of Midnight (stars Marie France Pisier)

Paris Holiday (French comic Fernandel plays opposite Bob Hope)

Octopussy (007 film)

The Professional

Frantic

Love in the Afternoon

The Pink Panther (Peter Sellers fakes a broadly comic Parisian accent for his Inspector Klousseau in several Pink Panther films; other characters in the sequel, *A Shot in the Dark*, are authentic)

Beauty and the Beast (in the Disney animated version, the character voice for the "candle-stick," who sings "Be Our Guest" is a very light, fairly decent secondary source)

Last of the Mohicans (the French soldiers)

The City of Lost Children (subtitles, Ron Perlman does a good accent)

Moulin Rouge (hardly any French accents, secondary sources)

Clue (character of Yvette)

Lost and Found (two characters have a very light French accent)

Golden Jubilee, Salute to Chuck Jones (Pepe Le Pew, the French skunk, is on this Warner Brothers cartoon video; an exaggerated stereotype)

The Little Mermaid (one song, "Le Poisson")

"Poirot" television series (he's the Belgian inspector, sort of a Sherlock Holmes type; this Belgian accent is very close to the French)

"Jacques Cousteau" TV specials and undersea documentaries

Monty Python and the Holy Grail (an outrageous spoof of a French character)

Cyrano (the Depardieu version, with subtitles)

Babette's Feast (in French, with subtitles)

Manon of the Spring (in French, with subtitles)

Amelie (in French, with subtitles)

In Love with Paris; If These Walls Could Speak (travelogues)

Dialect tapes and texts:
Blunt's *Stage Dialects*
British Broadcasting Company Record *English with an Accent*
The Hermans' *Foreign Dialects* (no tape)
Kur's *Stage Dialect Studies* (no tape)
Lane-Plescia's *Major European Accents*
Machlin's *Dialects for the Stage*
Molin's *Actor's Encyclopedia of Dialects*
Stern's *Acting with an Accent*

Other tapes:
Poirot Investigates by Agatha Christie (read by David Sachet; check the many other Poirot tales; Poirot is Belgian, which sounds very much like French)
Concrete Blonde (French band)
Lucky Stiff (the musical has a great song called "Speaking French")

Books:

French or Foe? by Polly Platt (a must-read)
France and the French by Harvey Edwards
Coping with France by Fay Sharman (excellent source, though the book title has a
      negative connotation)
The French by Theodore Zeldin
A Portrait of France by Lee Server
The Land and People of France by Jonathan Harris
The French: Portrait of a People by Sanche de Gramont
France by S. A. Nyon
France by Time-Life Books Library of Nations
French Culture Since 1945, ed. by Malcolm Cook
When in France by Christopher Sinclair-Stevenson
Wicked French for the Traveller by Workman Publishing   (amusing guide to phrases)
Handbook of Popular French Culture, ed. by Pierre L. Horn
France in the 20th Century by Philip Ouston
France Observed by Henri Gougaud and Collettee Gouvion
Paris by John Russell
The Frenchman and the 7 Deadly Sins by Fernando Diaz-Playa (a Spanish author's
      biased but interesting look at the French)
Paris, Past and Present by M. Ercole Pozzoli

FRENCH CANADIAN

Listen for: The hard "r's" and how it sounds compared to light French; the "eh" filler

Films and TV series:
A Strange Brew
Slapshot
Albino Alligator
"Twin Peaks" (TV series on video; the character of John Rinault pl;ays French Canadian)
Jesus of Montreal (with subtitles)

Dialect tapes and texts:
Machlin's *Dialects for the Stage*
Wise's *Applied Phonetics* (no tape)

Other tapes:
Audiocassettes of Bob and Doug MacKenzie from SCTV shows (the Second City troupe);
      French Canadian
L'Anglaise, Funny You Should Say That (French Canadian radio comedy team of Joan
      Stuart and Peter Cullan)
(Celine Dion interviews and concerts)

Books:
The French Canadians 1760-1967 by Manson Wade
Canadian Faces and Places by Yves Marchand (includes French Canadian)
Speaking Canadian French by Mark M. Orkin (describes the people)
Quebec by Anthony Hocking
A Canadian Myth: Quebec Between Canada and the Illusions of Utopia by William
        Johnson
French Canadian Society /Vol. 1 by Rioux and Martin
Canada and the Great White North, ed. by Rand McNally Publishers
Les Canadiens by Rick Salutin (a play)

GERMAN /AUSTRIAN /SWISS

Listen for: Inflection differences depending on the region of Germany; the uvular "r," "father" becomes
        "fazuh" OR "fadduh," depending on the region; strong delilberate consonants project through a
        small slit mouth opening, which affects the uvular "r" and softens voiced consonants to become
        voiceless, i.e., "Germany was good in those days"="Chuhmany vass gooot in dose dayss"
Trigger: Pinch sides of lips together and suck them in to your lips, so that "w" becomes like "v,"
Practice sentence: "There was nothing I wanted to say to you, and so you might as well go away"=
        "Zeh-uh ees nussink I vantet to zay too you, unt zo you might ass vell gaw avay." (with Berliner
        narrow range and a feel of strict discipline)

Films and TV series:
Cabaret
Goldfinger (James Bond's adversary is German)
A View to a Kill (several other Bond films use Germans as the antagonists)
The Hindenburg
Fahrenheit 451 (a number of other dialects are represented as well)
Dr. Strangelove (Peter Sellers adopts an excellent accent)
Run, Lola, Run
Varion's War (WWII Jewish-German prison camp)
Victory
Odessa File
Das Experiment (subtitles)
Diary of Anne Frank (only the father speaks in dialect)
Indiana Jones and the Last Crusade (Jones's adversaries)
Top Secret
The Girl and the General
Unfaithfully Yours; Paris Texas (and other early Nastassja Kinski films)
Touch of Evil; Blonde Venus (and the dozens of other Marlene Dietrich films; she speaks
        with a proper Berliner accent; also see the documentary about her, called *An
        Evening with Marlene Dietrich*, or *Marlena*)
"Hogan's Heroes"; "Rat Patrol" (old TV shows possibly in reruns; "Hogan's Heroes"
        has the exaggerated comical Germans, but Werner Klemperer's Colonel Klink had
        a very consistent accent, which he learned by mimicking his German father)

Those Daring Young Men in Their Jaunty Jalopies (one of the many foreign characters is German)
Marathon Man (Laurence Olivier adopts a consistent German)
I.Q. (Walter Mathau does a great job as Albert Einstein)
The Girl and the General (Rod Steiger adopts a consistent German)
Hart's War (WWII prison camp, but leads aren't German)
(There are many World War II movies featuring Germans, but many may not be authentic.)
The Swing Kids (not a good source, as hardly any of the characters speak in a German accent)
Schindler's List (not the best source for German, as most of the authentic accents are spoken by the Polish characters)
The Empty Mirror (psychological portrait of Hitler; the lead actor uses his British dialect; co-star Joel Gray does a nice light German; lots of clips of Hitler speaking German)
(Watch early Arnold Schwarzenegger films, or his comedies, where his Austrian accent comes through; later, when he filmed *Twins*, he studied a High German accent.)
Julia (Maximilian Schell is Austrian-German)
The Boys from Brazil (Lilli Palmer's Austrian-German is authentic; Laurence Olivier learned the Germanic Yiddish)
Now, Voyager; Casablanca (and other films with Paul Henreid; Austrian)
Death Watch; The Hero; The Trial (and other films with actress Romy Schneider; Austrian)
Ship of Fools (and other films with Oskar Werner; Austrian)
The Enemy Below (and other films with Curt Jurgens; Bavarian-Munich accent)
Casino Royale; Dr. No (and other films with Ursula Andress; Swiss-German)
Fedora (Marthe Keller; Swiss-German)
The World at War (and many other documentaries about WWII and the fall of the Berlin Wall)
Triumph of the Will (now-infamous German documentary about the rise of Hitler's Third Reich)
Anne Frank Remembered (documentary)

Dialect tapes and texts:
Blunt's *Stage Dialects*
Blunt's *More Stage Dialects* (Germany and Austria)
British Broadcasting Company Record *English with an Accent*
Chambers and Trudgill's *Dialectology*
The Hermans' *Foreign Dialects* (no tape)
Kur's *Stage Dialect Studies* (no tape)
Lane-Plescia's *Major European Accents*
Machlin's *Dialects for the Stage*
Molin's *Actor's Encyclopedia of Dialects* (German and Austrian)
Stern's *Acting with an Accent* (German)
Wise's *Applied Phonetics* (no tape)

Books:
The German Way by Hyde Flippo (fantastic resource)
Coping with Germany by John A. S. Phillips (wonderful book about the people and their customs, though the title has a negative connotation)
Getting Along with the Germans by Bob Larson (another excellent and amusing source)
The German People by Robert H. Lowie

Of German Ways by LaVern Rippley
Travel the World: Germany (and other travelogues)
Germany by Time-Life Books
Germans by George Bailey
The Germans by Adolph Schalk
East Germany: A Country Study, ed. by Stephen R. Burant
Embarrassing Moments in German and How to Avoid Them by Noah J. Jacobs
German National Identity After the Holocaust by Mary Fulbrook
The German People and Social Portrait to 1914 by Robert H. Lowie
The Land and People of Austria by Raymond A. Wohlrabe
Austria by Siegner
Collin's Pocket German-English, English-German Dictionary
German Phrase Book by I. Colemen and R. Nash Newton

GREEK

Listen for: Similarities to Italian, but without a tendency to use the intrusive "uh" like "foot-a-ball"

Films and TV series:
My Big Fat Greek Wedding (Greek-American family, most are secondary sources)
Zorba the Greek (shot in Crete; Irene Papas is the only authentic lead; Anthony
      Quinn is Mexican-American but did a good Greek accent; and Lila Kedrova
      is actually Russian and French)
The Greek Tycoon (shot on location)
McKenna's Gold; Dirty Dozen; Balaras File (with Telly Sevalas)
Guns of Navarone (set in Greece; stars Irene Papas, a good example of non-Athenian
      Greek; she has also done a number of other films)
The Trojan Women (starring Irene Papas)
Phaedra; Never on a Sunday (and other Melina Mercouri films; educated Athens accent
Onassis (based on "The Greek Tycoon"); possibly other TV movies based on his
      marriage to Jackie Kennedy)
(Check travelogues)

Dialect tapes and texts:
Blunt's *More Stage Dialects*
The Hermans' *Foreign Dialects* (no tape)

Books:
Portrait of Greece by Nicholas Gage
A Greek Portfolio by Constantine Masos
Let's Visit Greece by Garry Lyle
Eperon's Guide to the Greek Islands by Arthur Eperon
Greece: Aegean Island Guide by Gordan Rietvold
The Living Past of Greece by Mary Burn

HAWAIIAN/South Sea Islands

Listen for: similarities to Asian speech, but lighter, all even syllables

Films and TV series:
Hawaii (the princess was Tahitian)
"Hawaii 5-0"; "Magnum P.I." (TV series in reruns, set in Hawaii)
Lilo and Stitch (animated, teenage surfer character by Jason Scott Lee)
(Jason Scott Lee is Hawaiian, in the live action *Jungle Book, Soldier* and other films)
Once on This Island (musical)
The Bounty; Mutiny on the Bounty (the first one is the most historically accurate)
Ring of Fire (Indonesia; documentary about the mysterious primitive tribes in Borneo,
       Krakatoa, and other South Sea islands)
Moana of the South Seas (documentary about the Samoan culture; also billed as *Moana,
       a Romance of the Golden Age*)
(Many travelogues feature natives speaking)

Dialect tapes and texts:
The Hermans' *Foreign Dialects* (Hawaiian, Filipino)
Henrickson's *American Talk* (section on Hawaiian and Gullah; check Bibliography)

Other tapes:
Poi Dog and *Crab Dreams* (albums by Hawaiian comedian Rap Replinger, who speaks
       Pidgin Hawaiian)
(Look for comedy albums performed by Andy Bumatai, who speaks Pidgin Hawaiian)
(Find albums by the popular Hawaiian singer Don Ho.)

Books:
Hawaii Pono by Lawrence H. Fuchs
Hawaii: The Sugar-Coated Fortress by Francine du Plessix Graham

Indian/Pakistani (South Asian)

Listen for: Choppy, all equal syllables, up and down inflection pattern, very narrow mouth opening.jaw
set, lips barely touching, "thick" tongue placement for "L," dental sounds like "fadduh" for 'father,"
"r" taps for medial, linking and initial "r's" but possibly more the British dropped "r"s at ends of
syllables.

Practice sentence: " I would love to help you bring your only brother back from India quickly"="I vood Lahf
too heLp you brreeng yourr-rrawn'Ly' brrah'derr' bahk frrahm EEn'-dee'-ah' kvick'Ly'."

Films and TV series:

Monsoon Wedding (excellent primary sources of Indian)
Kamasutra (same writer as above, excellent primary sources of India)
Mississippi Masala (Indian)
Ghandi (Ben Kingsley's accent is good; others in the movie are primary sources)
The Mystic Masseur (Indians in Trinidad in 1940s-50s, secondary and primary sources)
A Passage to India (with Victor Banerjee, his Indian is authentic, but very light)
Jewel in the Crown (video of the PBS miniseries, India under British rule)
City of Joy (stars Patrick Swayze as an American; other characters are authentic Indian)
Snow Falling on Cedars (India; with actress Youki Kudoh)
Earth; Fire (Two recent films from India)
Mission Kashmir (India)
My Beautiful Launderette (Pakistani immigrant character)
East is East (Pakistanis in Northern England)
Little Buddha (Keanu Reeves's accent is questionable, but real Tibetan Buddhist monks
        are cast)
The Millionairess (Peter Sellers does an excellent Indian accent)
Short Circuit I and *2* (Fisher Stevens plays a comical, exaggerated Indian character; it's
        a consistent secondary source)
Baji on the Beach (for a study of all classes in India)
Bollywood (about the film community in India; all ranges of dialects; subtitled)
Rudyard Kipling's The Jungle Book (the live-action version, not as good a source; stars
        Jason Scott Lee, who is Hawaiian; very few of the native Indians have lines)
Phantom India (a five-star documentary tour of the nation)
(Also check with your city's South Asian Cultural Association about the many South
        Asian Film Festivals that are held each year.)

Dialect tapes and texts:
Blunt's *More Stage Dialects*
British Broadcasting Company Record *English with an Accent*
The Hermans' *Foreign Dialects* (no tape)
Molin's *Actor's Encyclopedia of Dialects*
Stern's *Dialect Monologues, Vol. II* (Asian Indian)
Trudgill and Hannah's *International English*
Wells' *Accents of the English-speaking World*

IRISH   (North and South)

Listen for: Upward lilt for Northern, downward wide lilt for Southern Irish, very hard "r's," (but not rolled like Scots), all vowels influenced by a held jaw

Trigger: "Grrrrr"

Practice sentence: "Do you hear me, now? My brother and I come all the way from Ireland, doncha know, where we were born and raised"="Do ya heerr me noo? Me broodderr an' oy coom Al the weh froom Oyrrlind, dahncha nah, wehrr we werr barrn an' rehzd."

Films and TV series:

The Field (Richard Harris uses his real accent; many others are authentic rural Northern Irish; this is an excellent film to study the culture of the people)

My Left Foot (urban Dublin; all dialects are authentic, except for Daniel Day-Lewis; but his accent is perfect)

In the Name of the Father (Belfast; with Peter Postlethwaite and Daniel Day-Lewis)

Da (urban Dublin; many primary sources; Martin Sheen's character has an accent that goes in and out, but this can partly be explained by the fact that his character moved away from Ireland)

Far and Away (Tom Cruise and Nicole Kidman do admirable Southern Irish accents; excellent film to study the culture and attitudes of the Irish people)

Michael Collins (set in Ireland, 1916-22; primary and secondary sources for Northern Irish; Liam Neeson plays the title role but not the appropriate West Cork dialect; the man who killed Collins in the ambush is from Cork, and Ian Hart adopts the Cork accent well)

American Women (set in Donegal, NW Ireland)

Patriot Games (Northern Irish characters)

The Crying Game (Northern Irish characters, with the exception of Forest Whitaker's)

Circle of Friends (Dublin)

The Commitments (urban Dublin)

The Playboys (with Irish-born Aidan Quinn and several primary sources)

Playboy of the Western World (County Mayo, in northwest Ireland)

The Secret of Roan Inish (set in County Donegal, northwest Ireland)

Riders to the Sea (western Ireland)

Angela's Ashes (Limerick; leads are secondary but boys are all locals--listen for slushy s/sh/st as in 'out of it' bcomes 'oush of ish')

Widow's Peak (stars several native Irish actors; Mia Farrow does a pretty fair job)

Bloody Sunday (N. Ireland in Derry)

The Magdelene Sisters

The Brothers McMullen (the mother is authentic, but the sons aren't)

Hear My Song (Dublin)

Prayer for the Dying (Northern Ireland)

The Dead (Southern Ireland)

Dancing at Lughnasa (NW Ireland, Donegal; secondary sources for leads, Meryl Streep's is good; narrator played by Gerard McSorley is from County Tyrone; Agnes, played by Brid Brennan is the only lead that is Irish)

The Gangs of New York (about Irish immigrants to New York in 1862)

The Quiet Man (stars John Wayne; Maureen O'Hare is Irish, the vicar is authentic)

Darby O'Gill and the Little People (the Disney film)

Evelyn (with Pierce Brosnon who was born in Ireland; leads are secondary sources)
Frankie Starlite (based on Chet Raymo's book, *The Dork of Cork;* listen to the son)
The Devil's Own (avoid; about the IRA, but Brad Pitt's accent is poor)
(Check Sherlock Holmes and Agatha Christie stories that have Irish characters, and
        skits of Monty Python and Benny Hill TV shows)

Dialect tapes and texts:
Blunt's *Stage Dialects* (teaches the Southern Irish)
Blunt's *More Stage Dialects* (British Isles/Ireland)
British Broadcasting Company Record *English with an Dialect* (Ulster and Eire)
The Hermans' *Foreign Dialects* (teaches the Southern Irish) (no tape)
Hughes and Trudgill's *English Accents and Dialects* (Belfast—Northern Irish)
Kur's *Stage Dialect Studies* (no tape)
Lane-Plescia's *Irish for Actors* (teaches North, West, and Belfast varieties)
Machlin's *Dialects for the Stage*
Meier's *Accents and Dialeclts for Stage and Screen*
Stern's *Acting with an Accent*
Stern's *Dialect Monologues, Vol. II* (Northern Irish)
Trudgill and Hannah's *International English*
Wells' *Accents of the English-speaking World* (Northern and Southern)

Other tapes:
(You can probably find audiobooks, record albums, or videotapes of plays done at the
        famous Abbey Theatre in Ireland, especially plays by Sean O'Casey, John Millington
        Synge, Brian Friel, and Brendan Behan.)
The Chieftans (this modern band does traditional Irish music; they have a number of
        albums listed under the same name as their band)
Irish/Gaelic (the Language Teaching Cassette #30, Educational Services; this covers the
        Ulster dialect)
Watermark (Enya sings in Irish/Gaelic on her album)
(Sinead O'Connor's accent comes through in her singing.)
(The band, The Proclaimers, have the Northern Irish dialect)
(Listen to albums by the recording artists The Pogues; they have a concert video called
        The Pogues Live at the Town and Country.)
(For the Limerick dialect, try local radio station at www.95fm.ie, with a live feed on the net)
"Live and Kicking--The People of Ireland: from Dubliln to Kerry and In Between" live
        comedy tour of Ireland by stand-up comic, Niall Toibin
(Try web site www.gbfm.galway.net for the Galway county dialect

Books:
The Story of English (book and video, chapter on "The Irish Question")
The Irish by Donald S. Connery
Ireland: A Terrible Beauty by Jill and Leon Uris
The Irish Mystique by Max Caulfield
The Irish: Portrait of a People by Richard O'Connor
Dublin: A Portrait by V. S. Pritchett and Evelyn Hober
Irish Traditions, ed. by Kathleen Jo Ryan and Bernard Share
Slanguage--a Dictionary of Irish Slang by Bernard Slane

My Village, My World by John M. Feehan (about Northern Irish village life; Feehan also wrote *The Secret Places of Donegal, The Secret Places of The Burren, The Secret Places of the West Cork Coast,* and *The Secret Places of the Shannon*)
How the Irish Saved Civilization by Thomas Cahill
(British dictionaries will help you with pronunciations and definitions of Irish phrases.)

ITALIAN

Listen for: Dental placement is key, very open, expressive, melodic, "r" is tapped, there are only 5 Latin vowels: mah, meh, mee, moh, moo--"Father let Eve go too," intrusive "uh" between consonant syllables, let it flow with a loose spine and big sweeping gestures.

Trigger: Dental on "Dees, dat and dee udderr ting," or tongue click on back of teeth: "nt, nt, nt, no, no, no, no" Try loudly with lots of gesturing: "You don' eattuh you vegetables, I gonna tella you Papa."

Practice sentence: "No! This is the truth, there will never be another good day for me without you, my love"="No! (quick, no diphthong) Dees eess dee trrut, derrr weel nayferr be anahderr gooood-a deh forr-a mee weetout-a you, my lahv." (w/tapped "r's")

Films and TV series:
The Godfather (about the Sicilian-New York Mafia, but Coppola cast authentic Italians from all across America, so you'll hear a variety of dialects)
Brief Encouner (with Sophia Loren and Marcello Mastroianni; Loren was also in *Man of La Mancha, El Cid, Houseboat,* and many other films; check other films with Mastroianni)
Silence of the Hams (spoof, narrated by Ezio Greggio; his narration is not exaggerated)
Summertime (set in Venice; with Katherine Hepburn, her leading man is Italian)
Ready to Wear/Prêt-à-porter (set in France, but Marcello Mastroianni and Sophia Loren star)
It Started in Naples (set in Naples and Capri, starring Sophia Loren and Vittorio De Sica)
8 1/2; La Dolce Vita (and other Fellini films; subtitled)
Swept Away (lead actor Adriano Giannini and famous father, Giancarlo)
The Last Kiss
White Knights; *Blue Velvet* (early Isabella Rossellini uses a light Italian)
Sleepers (Vittorio Gassman, familiar Italian-American actor, plays the restaurant owner)
The Bridges of Madison County (Meryl Streep's Italian American is excellent)
Orpheus Descending (Vanessa Redgrave does a wonderful Italian American in her role as Lady; see also an earlier version called *The Fugitive Kind*)
Moonstruck (New York-Italian family, secondary sources; good source for culture study)
I Love You to Death (New York-Italian family; Kevin Kline is a fair secondary source)
Prizzi's Honor (New York-Italians; even the secondary sources are good)
Goodfellows (New York-Italians)
Married to the Mob (New York-Italians)
Used People (Italian and Jewish-New Yorker characters)
Boy Meets Girl (Little Italy, NY; a guy trying to learn Italian to impress a girl)
The Nude Bomb (Vittorio Gassman is from Genoa, which has a lighter Northern Italian dialect, similar to the Milano subdialect)

The Other Side of Midnight (Raf Vallone is from Turlin and uses a light Northern Italian;
     also starring Marie France Pisier)
Big Night (good secondary sources for Italian Americans)
The Most Happy Fella (musical; characters of Tony and Rosabella; Italian American)
The Sheik (and other Rudolph Valentino silent films from the '20s for body language)
Mussolini and I (not a good source, as it was played with British accents)
(For more Italian-New Yorker examples, see the listings under "New York")

Dialect tapes and texts:
Blunt's *Stage Dialects*
Blunt's *More Stage Dialects*
British Broadcasting Company Record *English with an Accent*
The Hermans' *Foreign Dialects* (no tape)
Kur's *Stage Dialect Studies* (no tape)
Lane-Plescia's *Major European Accents*
Machlin's *Dialects for the Stage*
Molin's *Actor's Encyclopedia of Dialects*
Stern's *Acting with an Accent*
Wise's *Applied Phonetics* (no tape)

Books and articles:
The Italians: How They Live and Work by Andrew Bryant
The Italians: A Full-Length Portrait Featuring Their Manners and Morals by Luigi Barzini
The Art of Living Italian Style by Edmund Howard
Italy by Muriel Grinrod
Italy: A to Z by Robert S. Kane
Italy: A Country Study, ed. by Rinn S. Shinn
Mannen, Edward W., and Robert Sonkin. "A Study of Italian Accent," *Quarterly Journal
     of Speech*, 22 (February 1936): 1-12. (article in a journal)
Italian-English, English-Italian Dictionary by Collins Sansoni
Wicked Italian for the Traveler by Workman Publishers (amusing guide to phrases)

JAMAICAN
(and other islands in the West Indies)

*Listen for: all syllables equal stress, upward lilt at ends of most words because of the French influence,
the distinctive rolling melody, lips open wide and glide forward almost like fish, dropped initial
"h" like French dental on "th" to a "t" or "d," very open "er" to "uh, so "father thinks" becomes
"fah-duh tinks"; compare this accent to African,*

Trigger: "Welcome to Jamaica, mon"="Wale-cum' too Juh'-may'-cuh', mon" with a very relaxed spine.

*Practice sentence: "Eh, mon, in Jamaica, everything you cook at home will be worth eating"="Eh, mon,
een Juh'-may'-cuh' ev'-ree'-ting' you coook at 'oh-um weel be wurt ea-ting' "*

"I think he's my brother, and that is that"="I tink eem my brudduh, ahn dot eez dot"

Films and TV series:

Marked for Death (Steven Seagal film with many primary-source speakers, including a
white Jamaican female)

Lunatic (Jamaican)

Live and Let Die (Haitian and Jamaican; a James Bond film)

The Harder They Come (with reggae star Peter Tosh)

Serpant and the Rainbow (Haiti)

The Mighty Quinn (supporting cast are Jamaican)

Island in the Sun (Harry Belafonte, who spent his early years in the West Indies, allows
his accent to come through)

The Comedians (stars Roscoe Lee Browne; if you can find the play *Dream on Monkey
Island*, which starred Browne, you may use it as a good source about the Haitian
culture)

Clara's Heart (not as good a source, as Whoopi Goldberg's accent is not always consistent; not many others in the film with native accents have lines)

(Check Whoopi Goldberg's one-woman show on video, where she does a Jamaican
character.)

Cool Runnings (not as good a source, as the African-American actors are not authentic
Jamaicans)

Bitter Cane; Dreams of Democracy; Haiti: Killing the Dream; Pig's Tale; Razistans
(documentaries on Haiti)

Dialect tapes and texts:

Blunt's *More Stage Dialects* (Jamaica and Trinidad)

Hendrickson's *American Talk* (Gullah)

The Hermans' *American Dialects* (Gullah and Virgin Islands) (no tape)

The Hermans' *Foreign Dialects* (Bermudan) (no tape)

Lane-Plescia's *Accents for Black Actors* (including Jamaican, Trinidadian, Haitian)

Molin's *Actor's Encyclopedia of Dialects* (British West Indian)

Stern's *Acting with an Accent* (West Indian/Black African)

Trudgill and Hannah's *International English* (West Indian and Jamaican Creole)

Wells' *Accents of the English-speaking World* (West Indies)

Other tapes:

Uprising (One of Bob Marley's albums in which he sings in his native Jamaican accent; look also for interviews with him)

Simple Pleasures (Bobby McFerrin's album includes the song "Don't Worry, Be Happy" in his clear Jamaican accent)

Valley of Decision (reggae CD includes the song "Christofari")

(You might be able to find interviews with the Jamaican singer Elaine Cole.)

(Check other reggae albums.)

(Harry Belefonte sings in a light accent of his native West Indies.)

For Trinidad and Tobago, check some of the TNT radio stations broadcasts online for local announcers. Also on the National Public Radio website, a story about steel pan music; also, some musical recordings made during TNT carnival, with native speakers.

Books:

How to Speak Jamaican by Ken Maxwell

Roots of Jamaican Culture by Mevyne Aeleyne

Dominican Republic and Haiti by Scott Doggett and Leah Gordan

The Land and People of the West Indies by Phillip Sherlock

Let's Visit the West Indies by John C. Caldwell

Changing Jamaica by Adam Kuper

Playboy of the West Indies by Mustapha Natura (the play is written somewhat "in dialect")

MIDDLE EASTERN
(Arab, Persian/Farsi, Isreal)

Listen for: Dental placment (thick "rh's," "t's" and "d's," tapped "r"s), similarity to Mediterranean, but more restrained, glottal stops on words starting with vowels, making it sound choppy and all even syllables

Practice sentence: "This is your Arabian and American friend's purpose--to be very involved"=

"Zis 'ees yo-rrah-rray-bi-ahn 'ahnd 'Ah-may-rree-can frrend's purr-pose--too be ferry 'een-folft."

Films and TV series:

Black Stallion 2 (Arabian)

Satin Rouge (Arab)

Protocol

Steal the Sky (Isreali and Iraqi characters)

Raiders of the Lost Ark (secondary characters)

Lawrence of Arabia (with Egyptian-born Omar Sharif was schooled in the British system in Alexandria, so he sounds crisper and more Mediterranean)

Funny Girl (Omar Sharif)

The English Patient (sequences filmed in Tunisia)

Rose Tattoo (1953, with Egytian actress Anna Magnani)

Not Without My Daughter (Iran)

Delta Force (Arab)
Iron Eagle 1 and 2
Wedding in Galilee (in Hebrew/Arabic; foreign film)
(Any films Tarek Ali or Ismail Bashbag were in)
The Mummy 1 and *2* (secondary sources)
Ishtar (set in a fictional Middle Eastern country)
Robin Hood: Prince of Thieves (Kevin Costner's version; listen to Morgan Freeman's
        Muslim character)
Arabian Nights (about the legendary tale, actors are secondary sources, like Jason Scott
        Lee and Tcheky Karyo)
Aladdin (the Disney cartoon doesn't really use Arabic voices, but you might be able to
        find an old movie about the Aladdin character that features authentic Arabians)
(The many films about Jesus are not done in the appropriate Hebrew or Middle Eastern
        dialects; neither are many of the films—older or recent—about other Biblical
        characters, such as David, Joseph, or Moses.)
Grass (documentary about Persian nomads)
(Documentaries about the Gulf War/Desert Storm)
(There are many guest stars on current TV shows who are Middle Eastern, particulary
        the political dramas, like "The Agency"; also on CNN.)

Dialect tapes:
Blunt's *More Stage Dialects* (Near East-Saudi Arabia)
Stern's *Acting with an Accent* (Arabic)
Stern's *Acting with an Accent* (Persian/Farsi)
Stern's *Dialect Monologues, Vol. II* (Hebrew)

Other tapes:
Getting By in Arabic (two tapes and booklet by Barron's Publishing with native Arabic
        speakers)
Sheva (Isreali band)
"Call to Prayer," sung by Baaba Maal, on *The Compact Realworld Album*
Shaday (album by Persian singer Ofra Haza)
(You might be able to find audiotapes of *The Arabian Nights*, *Aladdin*, or *Ali Baba and
        the Forty Thieves*.)

Books:
A Traveler's Guide to Middle Eastern and North African Customs and Manners by Elizabeth
        Devine
Middle East Patterns: People, Places and Politics by Colbert C. Held
Coping with Turkey by Simon Cole (good source, although the title has negative conno-
        tations)
Working in the Persian Gulf: Survival Secrets for Men and Women, The Real Story
        by Blythe Camenson
Kuwait by S. and P. J. Hassall
(Check under the specific country's name for additional sources.)

MIDWESTERN U.S./Chicago/ Detroit/Cleveland/Cincinnati/ Minnesota

Listen for: *"R's are not dropped like in Brooklynese, may be rhetroflex for "farm" midwestern dialects, but nasality is present like New Yorker, no internal lilt is an important trait*

Films and TV series:
Hoop Dreams (urban or "street" Chicago)
Bugsy; Baby's Day Out; Godfather Part 3; Airheads (Joe Mantegna is from Chicago)
The Untouchables (about Al Capone in Chicago during the Prohibition)
Palazzola's Chicago (documentary about the people of Chicago)
(Check films with these actors with middle-class Chicago speech: John Belushi, Bill Murray, Jeremy Pivens, John Joan Cusack. John Malkovich and Gary Sinise are also from Chicago, though often upscale their speech depending on the role. Dennis Franz, still on the TV series "NYPD Blue," previously in "Hill Street Blues" and other films speaks in his urban Chicago dialect.)
Blues Brothers 2000 (Dan Ackroyd exaggerates his Chicago accent as Elwood)
8 Mile (Detroit)
Glengarry Glen Ross (set in Chicago)
Fargo (Minnesotan; the cops and residents of Brainerd are good primary and secondary sources for that distinctive American dialect)
"Bobby's World" (Minnesotan; TV cartoon featuring the talent of Howie Mandell; Bobby's Mom speaks with a Minnesotan dialect, using many colloquialisms)

Dialect tapes and texts:
Allen and Rogers' *Tongues of the North American Project* (5 Chicago and 1 Ohio sample)
Hermans' *American Dialects* (Middle Western)
Machlin's *Dialects for the Stage* (Midwestern)
Stern's *Acting with an Accent (Chicago; and Midwest Farm/Ranch)*

Other tapes:
Farewell My Lovely (Joe Mantegna, of a blue-collar Chicago background, reads this audiobook by Raymond Chandler)
 "Saturday Night Live" skits about "da Bears" are broad versions of working class Chicago.
(Talk show host Phil Donahue is from Cincinnati--which is a neutral Midmwestern dialect),
(Martin Sheen is from Dayton, Ohio)
Prairie Home Companion (the charming Lake Wobegone series, about life in a small Minnesotan town; Garrison Keillor narrates, but does not have a distinctive Minnesotan dialect)
How to Talk Minnesotan by Howard Mohr (this lighthearted book was employed by the dialect coach of the film *Fargo*)
(Check in the library under "Scandinavian Americans" for more listings for the Minnesotan derivative.)

Books:
Dialects and Levels of Language, ed. by Joseph Fletcher Littell (ch. on "Mark Twain"/
    Missouri dialect)
The Story of English (chapter on "O, Pioneers!" and the BBC video)
(Check for resources under the name of the U.S. city or state)

NATIVE AMERICAN*

*Referred to as Native American Indian, or North American Indian in older sources.

(Note: The term "Eskimo," may be politically incorrect. Though the term is still embraced
by some of these native peoples of North America, others prefer to be called by their
regional names of Inuit, Aleutian, Greenlandic, Inuktitut, and others. Linguists might
still call them "Eskimo-Aleut.")

Listen for: restraint and dignity in inflection and manner, equally stressed syllables, slight retroflex "r's"

Films and TV series:
Last of the Mohicans (with Native American actors)
Dances with Wolves (with Floyd Red Crow Westerman; Mary McDonnell's lead character
        is an excellent secondary source for Sioux; the Sioux tribe congratulated Kevin
        Costner on the authenticity of this film in its attention to detail)
Smoke Signals (authentic contemporary Native American)
Last of the Dogmen (Cheyenne tribe in Colorado)
Little Big Man (stars Dustin Hoffman; Cheyenne tribe in Colorado)
A Man Called Horse; Return of a Man Called Horse (realistic depiction of the Sioux)
Thunderheart (set in a Sioux reservation in South Dakota)
Geronimo (with Joseph Running Fox), and *Geronimo: An American Legend* (with
        Wes Studi as the Apache warrior)
Squanto: A Warrior's Tale (about the events leading up to the first Thanksgiving)
Legends of the Fall (the narrator is Native American, actor Gordan Tootoosis, who
        seems to follow the typical vocal patterns of Chief Dan George)
Johnny Greyeyes
Grey Owl (with Pierce Brosnan as a white boy raised by Native Americans)
Skins (S. Dakota natives)
Koyaanisqatsi and the sequel *Powaqqatsi* (Hopi Indian tribe)
Windtalkers (Navaho; about the use of Native American code during the war)
Crazy Horse (about the battle with Custer)
Clearcut (stars Graham Green)
The Outlaw Josey Wales (Clint Eastwood production, set in Missouri)
Indian in the Cupboard (Litefoot plays the lead)
Pocahontas (the Disney cartoon; no attempt at authentic dialects)
(Many old western shows on TV feature "Indians" but seldom don't use Native Ameri-
        can actors.)
The Fast Runner (Intuit tribe in Alaska)

Map of the Human Heart (Inuit/Aleutian)

Incident at Oglala (documentary; interviews with Native Americans, about the American Indian Movement; director Michael Apted ficitionalized the conflicts between traditionalist Native Americans and their "mixed-blood" tribal leaders in his film *Thunderheart*)

Nanook of the North (documentary; Eskimo; see also the new film documentary on "the making of . . ." this film, listed under *Nanook of the North*)

The Native Americans (TBS video series, as told by Native Americans from across the U.S.)

More Than Bows and Arrows (award-winning documentary narrated by Kiowa author Dr. N. Scott Momaday, the first Native American to win a Pulitzer Prize; call The Southwest Indian Foundation at 1-505-863-4037 and ask for #7211)

Set of four *"Ancient Americans"* videos narrated by Cherokee actor, Wes Studi; and *"America's Great Indian Leaders"* video, narrated by members of native tribes, available at www.southwestindian.com

Dialect tapes and texts:

(None known)

(Do a Google search on "Eskimo Inuit accent dialect" for helpful links. Be aware that the word "Eskimo" is considered politically incorrect to some.)

Other tapes:

Legends of the Native American (two-cassette tape set, read by Cherokee Indian Jackie Crow Hiendlmayr; call The Southwest Indian Foundation at 1-505-863-4037 and ask for #735)

Navaho Place Names: An Observer's Guide (book and tape, read by Navaho speakers; call The Southwest Indian Foundation 1-505-863-4037 and ask for #5008)

Books:

Indian America Guide Book: A Traveler's Companion (where to find over three hundred Native American tribes in the U.S.; call The Southwest Indian Foundation at 1-505-863-4037 and ask for #5460)

The Book of Elders (life stories of thirty Native Americans from nineteen different tribes)

The Indians in America by Wicome Washburn

Letters and Notes on the Manners , Customs and Conditions of North American Indians by George Catlin

Indian Sign Language by Robert Gray-Wolf Holsinde

The Indian Sign Language by W. P. Clark

"Native Peoples" Magazine at www.nativepeoples.com, or call (714) 693-1866

Encyclopedia of Native American Tribes; *American Indian History to 1900*; *Atlas of the North American Indian,* all by Carl Waldman

Introduction: The Handbook of American Indian Languages by Univ. of Nebraska Press

(Contact the American Indian Association in your area for other resources.)

(Look in the library under the tribe name, e.g., Sioux, Pawnee, Navajo [also spelled Navaho], Crow, etc.; look also under "Indians of North America.")

NEW YORK/Brooklynese
and Other Northeastern Urban Accents

(*Author's note:* I've tried to divide the films into several categories to help you focus your research, however be aware that several speakers are difficult to categorize with absolute definity and there is much crossover. Plus, the older regionalisms like what I am calling "older Bronx," are fading.)

Listen for: Humped up tongue, as in a "nyah," causing nasal tone and lazy tip of tongue, dropped "r's"
Trigger: Chewing gum, saying "Lawn Guyland" and "Noo Yawk,"
Practice sentence for Brooklynese: "Call my mother for more coffee talk"="Call moy mudduh fo' mo'uh coffee talk" (with "oo-ah's")

<u>Films and TV series:</u>

General New York—Brooklynese and regional varieties, "Noo Yawk," Long Island, New Jersey, Staten Island, Lower East Side, and Bronx:

Taxi (the film, and also the TV series in syndication, has characters from all the ethnic and socioeconomic backgrounds of New York)
"Welcome Back, Kotter" (this TV series in syndication also features characters from all ethnic backgrounds)
A League of Their Own; Sleepless in Seattle (Rosie O'Donnell is from Long Island; also catch her on TV doing stand-up, or possible reruns of her daytime talk show)
Sleepers (authentic dialects of "Hell's Kitchen," a neighborhood in New York)
My Cousin Vinny (Joe Pesci and Marisa Tomei provide perfect examples of the dialect)
Ten Tiny Love Stories; Beethovan's 2nd (Debi Mazar has small roles in many films; charming example of this dialect)
Amazing Stories (Rhea Perlman was also in the TV series "Cheers" as Carla)
City Slickers, Good Morning Vietnam (with Bruno Kirby; he played Barry Scheck in "The OJ Story" on TV)
The Adventures of Ford Fairlane (Stand-up commedian Andrew Dice Clay provides a stereotypical example; he has several stand-up comedy videos)
"The Amy Fisher Story" (and the other TV specials about "The Long Island Lolita;" features her strong Long Island accent)
(Billy Crystal is from Long Island)
L.I.E. (exaggerated Long Island)
Pushing Tin (Brit, Cate Blanchett does a pretty good "Lawn Guyland" accent)
(Comedian Jerry Lewis is from New Jersey)
The Bowry Boys; East Side Comedy (features the 1930s type of New York accents)
Sidewalks of New York (Manhattan and surrounding burroughs)
A Bronx Tale
Fort Apache (on location in the Bronx)
Owl and the Pussycat (Comedian Robert Klein uses Bronx vowels)
The Gangs of New York (set in 1862, Daniel Day-Lewis' early New Yorker is good)
(Older New Yorker: James Cagney, Humphrey Bogart, Groucho Marx, Three Stooges)

Nuyorican:

White Men Can't Jump; Fearless (actress Rosie Perez has a strong Bronx-Puerto Rican
     accent)
Maid in Manhattan (Jennifer Lopez is Bronx-Puerto Rican, nowadays called "Nuyorican")
Empire (S. Bronx, with John Leguizamo and Latino rapper, Fat Joe)
Piñero (about the Nuyorican actor-playwright, played by Benjamin Bratt)

New York-Italian

Twins; War of the Roses; Romancing the Stone; Other People's Money; and old
     "Taxi" episodes on TV (and anything Danny deVito has done)
Lethal Weapon 2 and *3; Home Alone 1* and *2; Goodfellas* (or anything else with Joe Pesci)
My Cousin Vinny (Joe Pesci and Marisa Tomei provide perfect examples of the dialect)
"Who's the Boss" and "Taxi" (Tony Danza's characters in his early TV shows, which
     can still be seen in syndication, are excellent examples of the New York-Italian
     accent; note that his accent is greatly diminished for his more recent film roles)
Bullets Over Broadway (with Chazz Palminteri, also in *Jade* and *The Usual Suspects*)
Summer of Sam /S.O.S (Italian-Americans in N.Y.)
Saturday Night Fever; Grease (early John Travolta for strong New York-Italian accent;
     also the television series "Welcome Back, Kotter"; a lighter version of his accent
     is in the *Look Who's Talking* film sequels)
Dick Tracy (many of the actors cast as mobsters do an authentic New York-Italian)
Goodfellows (New York-Italians)
Prizzi's Honor (New York-Italians; even the secondary sources are good)
Moonstruck (New York-Italians; secondary sources, starring Cher)
I Love You to Death (New York-Italians; Kevin Kline is a fair secondary source)
The Pope of Greenwich Village (N.Y.-Italians; with Eric Roberts and Mickey Rourke)
Used People (Italian and Jewish-New Yorker characters)
Sleepers (Vittorio Gassman, familiar Italian-American actor, plays the restaurant owner)
Boy Meets Girl (Little Italy, N.Y.; a guy trying to learn Italian to impress a girl)
Married to the Mob (N.Y.-Italians; many of the supporting characters speak with au-
     thentic accents; Michele Pfeiffer's accent is a questionable secondary source)
(See also the Italian section)

New York-Jewish*:

   (**Author's Note:* Many people of the Jewish religion and culture who live in New York area have a
   recognizable accent that is commonly referred to as the New York-Jewish accent. This is a Brooklyn or
   Bronx dialect that has the distinctive lilt characteristic of the Yiddish language of Eastern Europe
   of going up at the ends. So, here I call it the "New York-Jewish" accent. See also my notes and other
   sources under "Yiddish.")

Funny Girl (Barbra Streisand, from Brooklyn, speaks with a strong accent of Lower
     East Side, Manhattan)
Brighton Beach Memoirs; Broadway Bound (from the semi-autobiographical Neil Simon
     trilogy)
Torch Song Trilogy (and anything with Harvey Fierstein)
"Laverne and Shirley" (the syndicated TV series; Laverne, Penny Marshall's character,
     provides a great example of a Brooklyn-based dialect; also listen to Squiggy)

The Hard Way; Challenge of a Lifetime (Penny Marshall's characters; she performs
     small roles in these films)
The Producers, High Anxiety, etc (Mel Brooks is from Brooklyn; in many comedies; in
     History of the World Part I, he satirizes Jews during the Inquisition)
My Favorite Year
Kissing Jessica Stein
Quiz Show (John Turturro's character)
"The Nanny" (TV series; Fran Drescher's accent has a Queens "honk"; listen to her
     autobiography book on tape, "Enter Whining")
Back to School; Ladybugs; Easy Money; Caddyshack (Rodney Dangerfield's accent has
     its source in the Brooklyn dialect)
Life with Mikey (Brooklyn accent, which the character has to tone down when he goes for
     a commercial casting)
(Adam Sandler is from Brooklyn; in *Billy Madison*, the cartoon *One Crazy Night*, and
     other comedies)
Once Upon a Crime (comedian Richard Lewis also has a stand-up comedy video)
(Joan Rivers uses some of her Yinglish slang in her TV appearances)
"Seinfeld" (TV series; George's parents)
The Ritz; Hairspray (Jerry Stiller was once part of the Stiller and Meara comedy team
     along with Anne Meara; Stiller plays George Castanza's dad on TV's "Seinfeld")
My Little Girl; Out-of-Towners (with Anne Meara)
(Woody Allen's characters in all of his films, although his speech is idiosyncratic)
(W.C. Fields, George Burns, Jack Benny and Bert Lahr grew up in the burlesque era)

New York—"older" Bronx and Queens (in which "ur"="oy", i.e., "certainly"="coytainly" and "third"="toid")

Little Shop of Horrors (Ellen Green performs with a heavy Bronx accent for the role of
     Audrey)
Guys and Dolls (listen to the character of Adelaide, who sings "A Person
     ("poyson") Could Develop a Cold"; the film as a whole is not recommended for
     N.Y. accent study)
"All in the Family" (both Archie and Edith Bunker on the old TV show set in Queens)
(Curly, of The Three Stooges, had a Bronx accent)
(The "third" to "toid" sound is also found in several of the Jewish-New Yorker speakers
     above, especially the older speech, like Groucho Marx and W.C. Fields)

OTHER NORTHEASTERN DIALECTS—Boston, New England, Maine
*(Listen for: these don't use the "oo-ah" sound for "ah" when upscale but listen for the "Pawk the caw in
     Hawvad yawd" sounds, flat internal lilt, and Maine's distinctive inflection dip within vowels and
     possible use of the British "cahnt ahsk" for "can't ask")*

JKF (features what is called the Kennedyesque accent of Massachusetts)
The Ref; cartoon voice for *Ice Age* and *A Bug's Life* (stand-up comedian, Denis Leary is
     from Boston)
In the Bedroom (with Sissy Spacek; listen to ex-husband of Marisa Tomei's character)
Catch Me if You Can (Tom Hanks' New England dialect has gotten critical acclaim)
Quiz Show (Rob Morrow's Massachusetts accent comes and goes)

"Simpson's" cartoon character, Mayor "Diamond Joe" Quimby is a stereotype for the Massachusetts/Kennedyesque dialect

Pet Cemetary (Fred Gwynn's character has a Maine accent; he was also in the old "Car 54" show on TV; he doesn't use the accent for "The Munsters" show on TV)

On Golden Pond (set in Maine; Katherine Hepburn calls herself a Yankee-New Englander)

"Murder She Wrote" (TV series, featuring some Maine accents)

"Newhart" (the early series had a mailman from Maine)

(For the old Pepperidge Farm commercials, the spokesman uses a classic Maine dialect)

Cape Cod and the Islands (one of several good travelogues with Nantucket locals)

Dialect tapes and texts:
Blunt's *Stage Dialects* (Brooklynese)
Blunt's *More Stage Dialects* (Down East/New England)
Hermans' *American Dialects* (New York City and upper New York state, Philadelphia, New England, Pennsylvania Dutch) (no tape)
Kur's *Stage Dialect Studies* (New York, New England) (no tape)
Machlin's *Dialects for the Stage* (New York-Brooklynese and Yankee/New England)
Stern's *Acting with an Accent* (New York City)
Stern's *Acting with an Accent* (Kennedyesque: Upper-class New England)
Stern's *Acting with an Accent* (Down East New England)
Stern's *Acting with an Accent* (Boston)
Trudgill and Hannah's *International English* (New England)
Wise's *Applied Phonetics* (New York City and Eastern American) (no tape)

Other tapes:
How to Talk Yankee—A Down East Foreign Language Record by Bob Bryan and Tim Sample (witty dialogue that helps you learn the Down East Maine dialect)
Comedian Vaughn Meader's remarkable impression of JFK in *"The First Family,"* an album of JFK-inspired satire (!962), available on CD online.
(For the New Hampshire dialect, you might be able to find a recording of a professional production of the play *Our Town*, written by Thornton Wilder.)
Ted Kennedy live on C-SPAN or on RealAudio files
Enter Whining (audiotape of Fran Drescher's autobiography; Jewish-New Yorker)
(Find Maine storyteller, Tim Sample on CD and Maine comedian, Bob Marley on CD.)

Books:
Maine Lingo by John Gould (for the slang, lingo, and special pronunciations)
Dialect Clash in America by Paul Brandes and Jeutonne Brewer (chapter on the Big City dialect)
Dialects—USA by Jean Malmstrom and Annabel Ashley (chapter on New England)
Spoken Records by Helen Roach (descriptions of the speeches of the Kennedys)

POLISH

Listen for: similarities to Russian/Slovak, only more restrained into the back of the throat, "wv" for "w"
Trigger: thick butterscotch pudding in the back of the throat, it's as if the lips are frozen on the face

Films and TV series:

Europa, Europa; Olivier, Olivier; Fever (3 films set during WWII)
Sophie's Choice (Meryl Streep is a very good secondary source)
Schindler's List (several characters are Polish-Jewish, including Ben Kingsley as a strong
        secondary source)
The Tenant; Back in the U.S.S.R. (Polish director Roman Polanski starred in a few films)
Invincible (set in Poland and Berlin; with Finnish star, Jouko Ahola)
Generation A (in Polish, with subtitles)

Dialect tapes:

Blunt's *More Stage Dialects* (the Polish accent is listed under Greece and Eastern Europe)
British Broadcasting Company Record *English with an Accent*
The Hermans' *Foreign Dialects* (no tape)
Molin's *Actor's Encyclopedia of Dialects* (no tape)
Stern's *Acting with an Accent* (Polish)

Books:

The Polish Way by Adam Zavoyski
Eastern Europe: Poland by Godfry Blunder
Polish Traditions and Surveys by Dustin Barlow
Poland: A Country Study, ed. by Harold D. Nelson
Slavophilia: Slavic and East European Resources (see www.Slavophilia.net)
Warsaw by Malgorzata Omilanowka
Hunting Cockroaches, the Polish play by Janus Glowacki, has a list of pronunciations
        of Polish words and names in the glossary

PORTUGUESE and BRAZILIAN

Listen for: similarities to Latin/Italian dental sounds, tends to be smoother than Spanish

Films and TV series:

Amazon Burning (on location in Brazil; stars Sonia Braga who is Brazilian; the film also stars Raul Julia who is Puerto Rican; Braga also stars in *Moon Over Parador* and *The Rookie*)

Mystic Pizza (about a Portugese-American family in Mystic, Connecticut; actors are secondary sources)

Boca (set in Rio de Janeiro, Brazil)

Copacabana; Springtime in the Rockies (Carmen Miranda is Brazilian)

The Mission (with Portuguese and Spanish aboriginal South Americans)

Brazil (*not* a source; don't be fooled by the title, as the movie has nothing really to do with Brazil)

It's All True (one of these three unfinished Orson Welles documentaries is about Brazil)

Dialects texts and tapes:

Blunt's *More Stage Dialects* (Portuguese)

The Hermans' *Foreign Dialects* (Portuguese) (no tape)

Books:

The Selective Traveler in Portugal by Ann Bridge and Susan Lowndes

The Last Old Place: A Search Through Portugal by Datus C. Proper

Let's Visit Portugal by Ronald Seth

Portugal by Hanns Reich

Brazil: A Country Study, ed. by Richard Nyrop

Brazil: A Travel Survival Kit by Mitchell Schoen and William Hertzberg

The Land and People of Brazil by Norman P. Macdonald

RUSSIAN (and Finland)

Listen for: Rolled "r's," dental placement, passion from deep inside that must be restrained, "wv" sound for
"w," voiced consonants are softened, like "going" becomes "goink"

Trigger: Nearly closed-mouth deep breathing, as if not wanting cold to get in, or like breathing through
plegm in throat, lips are frozen on face but still struggling against the difficulty to pronounce English

Practice sentence: "I come from Russia where I work hard there to make a living in the book store"=
"I cahm frrahm Rahshuh, vehrr I verrk harrt derre too mek leeveek een boook storr." (they often
leave off "a" and "the")

Films and TV series:

White Knights (Mikhail Baryshnikov's Russian accent is a great example; several other
characters are primary sources; the female ballet dancer, played by Helen Mirren,
is a secondary source but has an excellent accent)

Company Business; Turning Point (or any other Baryshnikov film)

The Russia House (Klaus Maria Brandauer, who plays the character of the writer is an
excellent source; Michelle Pfeiffer's Russian accent is excellent)

Reds (Warren Beatty's film, in which he includes interviews with Russians who've lived
through the Bolshevik Revolution)

To Russia With Love (James Bond film; other 007 films have Russian antagonists)

GoldenEye (the '90s Bond film has many good primary and secondary sources)

Back in the U.S.S.R. (first American film shot entirely in Moscow; several authentic Russians; Roman Polanski is Polish)

Citizen X (based on a true story)

Moscow on the Hudson (Robin Williams does a pretty convincing Russian)

East-West (with Sergei Bodrov, Jr.)

Police Academy: Mission to Moscow

The Adventures of Buckaroo Bonzai (Russian commedian Yakov Smirnov has small
roles in several other films as well)

The Russians Are Coming, The Russians Are Coming (Alan Arkin does a good Russian)

Gorky Park (only the leading lady, Joanna Pacula, is really Russian; William Hurt's
Russian accent is not consistent; check other Pacula films)

Dr. Strangelove

Dr. Zhivago

Red Heat (several authentic accents, although Arnold Schwarzenegger uses his own
Austrian accent)

Spies Like Us (several of the antagonists who chase Chevy Chase)

(Boris and Natasha on the old Rocky and Bullwinkle cartoons; also check the live action
Rocky and Bullwinkle)

Invincible (with Finnish actor, Jouko Ahola; set in Poland and Berlin)

Hunt for Red October (not a good source, as Russian accents are not used)

Three Songs of Lenin (documentary epitaph to Lenin; in Russian with subtitles)

Behind the Kremlin Wall; Post Soviet Russia (and other documentaries)

(Check for other documentaries about WWII.)

Spirit of a People: New Portrait of Russia (on video)

Dialect tapes and texts:
Blunt's *Stage Dialects*
British Broadcasting Company Record *English with an Accent* (Russian and Slovak)
The Hermans' *Foreign Dialects* (Russian, Middle European: Finnish) (no tape)
Kur's *Stage Dialect Studies* (no tape)
Lane-Plescia's *Major European Accents*
Machlin's *Dialects for the Stage*
Molin's *Actor's Encyclopedia of Dialects* (Russian and Lithuanian)
Stern's *Acting with an Accent* (Russian)
Wise's *Applied Phonetics* (no tape)

Other tapes:
Joseph Brodsky Reads his Poetry

Books:
Coping with Russia by Robert Daglish (excellent source, though a negative title)
Put Your Best Foot Forward: Russia by Mary Murray Busrock
Portraits of Soviet Life by Alan Bookbinder, Olivia Lichtenstein, and Richard Denton
A Day in the Life of the Soviet Union by A. Collins
Soviet Union by Silver Burdett
The Soviet Union Today by the National Geographic Society
Why They Behave Like Russians by John Fischer (written in 1946)
(Look for newer sources that reflect the country's current political reorganization.)
English-Russian Dictionary by V. K. Müller
Oxford Russian-English Dictionary by Marcus Wheeler
Wise, Claude Merton. "Russian and English Speech Sounds," *Journal of Speech and Hearing Disorders*, 14:4 (December 1949), pp. 332-4. (article in a journal)
The Russian Way by by Zia Dabaro and Lilia Vokhmina
The Land and People of Finland by Erick Berry

SCANDINAVIAN
Western Europe: Sweden, Norway, Denmark

(also included here are Iceland, Greenland, Nordic countries)

(*Note*: the Minnesotan dialect is an American derivative; see listings under "New York and Other Northeastern Dialects." For Finland, see "Russian." For "Newfoundland" see "Canadian.')

Listen for: *The unique upward internal lilt, unique retroflex "r" aimed at the front teeth, the "w" to "v" sound, a distinctive sing-song up and down lilt within vowels and entire phrases (Norwegian being more reserved),*

Trigger: *With an umlaut or kiss or whistle lips, say "Swedish' and "Norway" as "Sveedishh" and "Norrvay"*

Practice sentence: "Ja, the weather in Sweden and Norway in June is never too sweltering"=
   "Yah, da vedderr een Sveden and Norrvay een Yoon (an umlaut) iss neffer too (umlaut) sveltering."

Films and TV series:
The Emigrants (Southern Swedish and Norwegian; with Max Von Sydow and Liv Ullmann)

The Exorcist; Hannah and Her Sisters; A Kiss Before Dying (starring Max Von Sydow; slight "Uppsala Graduate" Swedish)

The Unbearable Lightness of Being (with Lena Olin from Stockholm)

Enemies: A Love Story (with Lena Olin from Stockholm)

The Dive (starring Norwegian actor Bjorn Sundquist)

Out of Africa (Meryl Streep's Danish accent is flawless)

Mifune (Danish)

(Victor Borge, the comic pianist, is from Denmark; there are tapes of his many concerts and TV appearances.)

Shipwrecked (authentic Norwegian actors, filmed in Norway)

I Remember Mama (Norwegian)

My Life as a Dog (Swedish; subtitled)

Casablanca; For Whom the Bell Tolls; Intermezzo (Ingrid Bergman's earliest films show her Stockholm accent; early Greta Garbo films do, as well; both lost their accents later)

Persona (and other Swedish films, directed by Ingmar Bergman; subtitled)

The Farmer's Daughter (with Loretta Young; not very consistent Swedish accent)

(Tim Conway, the comedian, did a funny, exaggerated Swedish character on the old "Carol Burnett Show.")

The Vikings (no Swedish accents are used, but the scenery helps your research)

No Such Thing (Iceland, authentic)

Dancer in the Dark (stars pop singer, Bjork from Iceland; and check for possible interviews)

Smilla's Sense of Snow (Greenland; excellent source)

Dialect tapes and texts:
Blunt's *More Stage Dialects* (West Europe—Sweden, Norway, Denmark)

British Broadcasting Company Record *English with an Accent* (Danish)

The Hermans' *Foreign Dialects* (Swedish, Norwegian) (no tape)

Stern's *Acting With an Accent* (Norwegian and Swedish)

Wise's *Applied Phonetics* (Norwegian) (no tape)

Other tapes:

O, Pioneers! (the play on video, not the film version; stars Mary McDonnell, who does a wonderful Swedish accent; several others in the play do fairly good Swedish accents as well)

I Remember Mama (any recording of this Norwegian play)

(Any recording of an August Strindberg play actually done in Sweden)

Books:

Dahl, Thomas. "The Scandinavian Dialect in American Speech," *Speech Teacher* 6:3 (September 1957):247-49. (article in a journal)

The Swedes by Paul Britten Austin

The Land and People of Norway by Elvajean Hall

Swedish Folktales and Legends, ed. by Lone Thygesen Blecher and George Blecher

Prisma's Modern English-Swedish Dictionary, ed. by Bror Danielsson

SCOTTISH

Listen for: Upward lilt, held jaw in a "grrrr" like Irish, but with a rolled "r," glottal stops for some "t's" like Cockney

Trigger: "grrrrr," and digging in like the warrior Braveheart

Practice sentence: "Oh, I tried to tell you before, lad, but you were a wee bit cross"="Och, aye! Oy troid ta till ya befarr lad, boo' ya werra wee bi' crraws."

Films and TV series:

Rob Roy (excellent primary and secondary sources)

Braveheart (some good primary and secondary sources, though not accurate for period, and some actors are Irish)

Trainspotting (contemporary)

Shallow Grave (leads are authentic)

Chariots of Fire (the young minister and his sister)

Gregory's Girl

The Big Tease (Glasgow)

Born Romantic (anything with Craig Ferguson)

The Piano (Holly Hunter's narration in Scottish is wonderful)

The Man Who Would Be King (in this film, Sean Connery's native Scottish shows through, though it is light)

The Name of the Rose; Indiana Jones and the Final Crusade (Sean Connery sounds more Scottish in these productions than in his 007 films; he also provided the voice for the dragon in *Dragonheart*)

Upstairs, Downstairs (with Gordon Jackson as Mr. Hudson, the butler)

The Prime of Miss Jean Brodie (with Gordon Jackson; check other films Jackson was in)

Local Hero

Comfort and Joy

Shrek; So I Married an Axe Murderer; Austin Powers: The Spy Who Shagged Me (Mike Myer's version of Scottish is fun and quite good)

Tight Little Island (1949, but a good source for locals)

Lady and the Tramp (the Scotty dog, Jacques, in the Disney cartoon is a stereotype)
("The Simpsons" cartoon groundskeeper is a stereotype)

Dialect tapes and texts:
Blunt's *Stage Dialects*
Blunt's *More Stage Dialects* (British Isles)
British Broadcasting Company Record *English with a Dialect* (Edinburgh, Glasgow,
        Inverness, Ayrshire)
The Hermans' *Foreign Dialects* (no tape)
Hughes and Trudgill's *English Accents and Dialects* (Edinburgh)
Kur's *Stage Dialect Studies* (no tape)
Lane-Plescia's *Scots for the Actor*
Meier's *Accents and Dialects for Stage and Screen*
Molin's *An Actor's Encyclopedia of Dialects*
Stern's *Acting with an Accent*
Trudgill and Hannah's *International English*
Wells' *Accents of the English-speaking World*
Wise's *Applied Phonetics* (no tape)

Other tapes:
Kidnapped by Robert Louis Stevenson, read by Bill Simpson (book on tape with several
        varieties of Scottish)
Let Sleeping Vets Lie (listed under the title *All Things Bright and Beautiful* in the
        U.S., read by author James Herriot, who was raised in Glasgow)
Upstairs, Downstairs (on cassette, with actor Gordon Jackson as the butler)
Too Deep for Tears (stories set in Scotland)

Books:
The Story of English (book and video, chapter on "The Guid Scots Tongue")
Scotland: An Intimate Portrait by Geddes MacGregor
Of Scottish Ways by Eve Begley
The Scots by Clifford Hanley
The Scotch by John Kenneth Galbraith (who claims that the Scottish people were never
        called 'Scots')
Scotland for Beginners: Bannockburn an' a' That
Scotland: The Light and the Land by Colin Baxter
Scotland by Magnus Linklater
World in View: Scotland by Doreen Taylor
The Scottish World: History and Culture of Scotland by Harold Orel
A Companion to Scottish Culture by David Daiches
People and Society in Scotland, Vol. II by Hamish W. Fraser
Scottish Clan and Family Encyclopedia by Collins
Pocket Guide to Scottish Words by Isabel Macleod (pronunciation guide and glossary for
        commonly used words, first and last names, and place names of the Scots/Gaelic
        dialect, published in Glasgow by Richard Drew Publishing in 1986)
Scots Dictionary by Alexander Warrack
Scottish Tongue by William Craigee
The English Languages by Tom McArthur (chapter on Scotland)
Englishes Around the World, ed. by Edgar W. Schneider, Vol. 1, British Isles

SOUTHERN DIALECTS (American)

Listen for: how they vary in tone placement and inflection, all vowels become diphthongs except "I"="a" as in "cat," some dialects drawl, some twang, note if they harden or drop their "r's" (called rhotic or non-rhotic "r's"), vowels are very flatfaced and the tongue is humped up

Trigger: Tongue humping up, bucking like a bucking bronco

Practice sentence: "I reckon there's only two men strong enough to handle horses, sheep and cows right here in River Junction"="Ah ricken therrr's uh-oonly tuh-oo min strowng enuhhf ta hayndle horrrses, shuh-eep ayn' ca-yuhs rat herrre in Riverrr Juhhnction."

APPALACHIAN / MOUNTAIN DIALECTS (Kentucky, Tennessee, Arkansas, The Ozarks, parts of Virginia and the western Carolinas; these Southern dialects seem to get stuck in the back of the throat and behind the lower teeth, with very hard "r's," and thin mouth opening, and the most nasality of all the Southerns. Watch for arms held in closer to body, no fussy movements, deeper, more masculine, earthy feel, straight-talkin' flatter inflection, tendency to have lots of slang and less careful articulation if it's a less educated, folky mountain person or "hillbilly.")

Films and TV series:
Coal Miner's Daughter (Sissy Spacek plays Loretta Lynn, who was raised in the Appalachian mountains; good secondary source)
The Songcatcher (late 1800s; authentic Appalachian folk singers)
Nine to Five; Best Little Whorehouse in Texas; Rhinestone (Dolly Parton; Tennessee)
Sommersby (Jodie Foster received professional coaching to develop the Tennessee accent she used in the film)
In Country (Kentucky)
Tobacco Road (portraying "Georgia crackers")
Ernest Saves Christmas, Daddy and Them, Beverly Hillbillies: the Movie, and all of the Jim Varney *Ernest* films (Varney was from Lexington, Kentucky)
O Brother, Where Art Thou (the soundtrack is legendary; secondary sources for a prison break from Mississippi north towards the Ozarks)
Comprimising Positions (and other Judith Ivey films)
"Grace Under Fire" (TV series starring commedienne Brett Butler, who is from Georgia; Butler also made a stand-up comedy video)
"Empty Nest" (TV series in reruns; Park Overall, who plays the nurse Laverne, provides a great example of a Tennessee dialect)
"The Critic" (TV cartoon in reruns; Park Overall provides the voice for Jay's girlfriend, using her natural Tennessee accent; Overall also plays Rowena in the film *Biloxi Blues* and is in *Tainted, The Gambler Returns, Fifteen and Pregnant, etc.*)
The River (with Sissy Spacek; set in Tennessee)
"Beverly Hillbillies" (TV series; characters are from the Ozarks; the movie version has fair secondary sources)
Christy (set in Appalachian Mountains)
"Hee Haw" (reruns on TV; various mountain and hillbilly dialects)
(Tapes of the musical *Li'l Abner* depict the feuding hillbillies, Hatfield's and the McCoys)
(Billy Bob Thornton and "early" Bill Clinton, for Arkansas)
(Any of the dozens of Elvis films; Memphis, Tennessee)

Elvis—That's the Way It Is; *Elvis '56*; *This is Elvis* (documentaries)
Harlan County, USA (documentary about Kentucky coal miners)

Dialect tapes and texts:
Blunt's *More Stage Dialects* (Border States—Appalachia, Tennessee, Ozark, Arkansas)
The Hermans' *Foreign Dialects* (Mountain) (no tape)
Lane-Plescia's *American Southern, Vol 1 & 2* (with many samples)
Stern's *Acting with an Accent* (American Southern)

Other tapes:
(Many country-western singers are from Nashville; listen to tapes or check TV shows
     featuring talent from Nashville, Tennessee—shows from Opryland, for example.)
(Any old shows featuring Tennessee Ernie Ford)
(Country singers Glen Campbell and Johnny Cash are from Arkansas.)
(Any audio or video of the play collection *The Kentucky Cycle* by Robert Schenkkan)
Deliverance (the book on tape, read by the author)
"O Brother, Where Art Thou" (soundtrack)

Books:
Down in the Hollar: A Gallery of Ozark Folk Speech by Vance Randolph and
     George Wilson
Mountain-ese: Basic Grammar for Appalachia by Aubrey Garber
Dialect Clash in America by Paul Brandes and Jeutonne Brewer (chapter on the
     Appalachian dialect)
Dialects and Levels of Language, ed. by Joseph Fletcher Littell (chapter on
     the Kentucky dialect)

DEEP SOUTH / PLANTATION (also called the Tidewater dialect or "non-rhotic
     modern Southern, or "Junior League," which is the upscale neighborhoods of the
     South, spoken in some of the coastal and Delta states of Mississippi, Louisiana,
     parts of Georgia and Alabama, excluding the Piedmont area which has rhotic,
     or "hard r's"; this dialect has dropped "r's" like British. Listen and watch for
     many similarities to British manner, pronunciations, and the "r's.")

Films and TV series:
Gone with the Wind (also see *Scarlett*, the sequel)
Forrest Gump (Tom Hanks and Sally Field do the Greenbow, Alabama accent
     flawlessly; the young Forrest is a primary source)
Orpheus Descending (with Vanessa Redgrave as the Italian character, Lady,
     but several others have the Plantation accent)
Cat on a Hot Tin Roof (set on a modern plantation in Mississippi; many other
     Tennessee Williams plays are set in the Deep South, but they are not always
     done with the proper Southern accent; the character of Big Daddy is a
     great example of a proud modern-day plantation owner)
Streetcar Named Desire (New Orleans; Blanche DuBois's character; in the
     Jessica Lange version, both sisters do a fair Plantation accent)
The Glass Menagerie (Paul Newman's production; set in St. Louis, but the

character of Amanda, who is originally from Mississippi, is a good secondary source)

In the Heat of the Night (set in a Mississippi town; Rod Steiger's character and others demonstrate the dialect well; Sidney Poitier doesn't have the accent; the old TV series of the same name, with Carroll O'Connor, is a good source, too)

"Golden Girls" (old TV series in reruns; actress Rue McClanahan has the perfect Plantation accent; she's been on a number of TV shows and specials)

Ruby's Bucket of Blood (about a '60s Louisiana nightspot)

Memphis Belle, Hope Floats, Copy Cat, Little Man Tate (early films of New Orlean's-born Harry Connick, Jr.)

The Client (Susan Sarandon does a fair accent; Tommy Lee Jones's is flawless; the TV series has some good sources and some bad)

The Long, Hot Summer (Mississippi; both the 1958 Paul Newman and the 1986 versions; Judith Ivey is in the 1986 version with Don Johnson)

Heaven's Prisoners (with Alec Baldwin; Louisiana)

Midnight in the Garden of Good and Evil (Savannah, not always consistent)

The War (Kevin Costner and Elijah Wood attempt the accent; this is not the best source)

Mississippi Burning

Ghosts of Mississippi

Driving Miss Daisy (good secondary sources)

Deliverance (Georgia)

"Designing Women" (TV reruns; set in Atlanta; Dixie Carter's character does an upscale Atlanta accent, though she is originally from Tennessee)

Golden Jubilee, Fractured Funnies (Foghorn Leghorn, the rooster in the Bugs Bunny cartoons, is featured in several Looney Toons videos, with all his great Southern expressions)

Great Balls of Fire (Dennis Quaid plays Jerry Lee Lewis, from Louisiana)

I Am What I Am (Jerry Lee Lewis stars; Louisiana)

French Quarter (New Orleans)

King Creole (set in New Orleans; Elvis film)

Mississippi Blues (documentary about the Deep South)

The Louisiana Story (documentary dramatizing the effect of oil development on the lives of a boy and his family members)

American Traditions Videos: Life Along the Mississippi and *The Great Steamboat Race* (both documentary videos are narrated by Loretta Young)

(Check the films listed under "Cajun" that were shot in New Orleans.)

Dialect tapes and texts:

Allen and Rogers' *Tongues of the North American Project* (3 Virginia dialects)

Blunt's *Stage Dialects* (American Southern)

Lane-Plescia's *American Southern, Vol 1 & 2*

Machlin's *Dialects for the Stage* (Southern)

Other tapes

Deliverance (the book on tape read by the author, excellent source for Georgia, with the dropped "r's")

Books:
Southern Stuff: Downhome Talk and Bodacious Lore from Deep in the Heart of Dixie by Mildred Jordan Brooks
Dialects—USA b y Jean Malstrom and Annabel Ashley (chapter on the Inland Southern dialect)
Whistling Dixie: A Dictionary of Southern Expressions by Robert Hendrickson

CAJUN   (the French-based Southern dialect of the Delta bayou; also Creole—both spoken in parts of Louisiana)

Practice sentence: "I guarantee, you're going to put some onions in that there stew before long, cher"="Ah gua-rohn-tee' yo gunna put sahm ah-ni-onz' in dat day-uh stew befoe lowng, cheh."

Films and TV series:
Scorchers (excellent examples of Cajun, though mostly secondary sources; especially the daughter and the preacher)
No Mercy (Cajun)
Belzaire the Cajun (Armand Assante's Cajun is questionable; other character's dialects are good)
Passion Fish
The Big Easy (Dennis Quaid adopts an accent that is not always consistent, but there are a few realistic Cajuns in the film, including Dave Petitjean. See under "Other tapes" for Petitjean's stand-up acts on tape)
Candyman 2
Angel Heart (New Orleans and other Southerners)
Louisiana Cookin' (TV show hosted by Justin Wilson, who exaggerates his Cajun accent; he tells stories and uses all kinds of colorful expressions) Also check his: "Cooking with Justin Wilson" video, and his cookbooks written in dialect with lots of slang.
Delta Heat (several colorful characters from the Louisiana bayou)
Shy People (set in the Louisiana bayou)
Zydeco Nite 'N' Day (musical video with interviews and performances by several Zydeco legends)
Hot Pepper (documentary about Cajun-French zydeco music legend Clifton Chenier)
Celebrating Cajun Culture; Cajun Country; Portrait of America: Louisiana (travelogues)
Gator Tale; French Louisiana (documentaries.)
Yum, Yum, Yum; Chef Paul Prudhommes Louisiana Kitchen Cooking (cooking videos)
(See the Plantation/Deep South dialects for other New Orleans sources.)

Dialect tapes and texts:
Blunt's *More Stage Dialects* (Cajun)
The Hermans' *American Dialects* (Louisiana French, Cajun, and New Orleans Creole) (no tapes)
Stern's *Dialect Monologues, Vol. II* (Cajun)
Trudgill and Hannah's *International English* (English-based Creole)
Wise's *Applied Phonetics* (Louisiana French) (no tape)

Other tapes:

(Cajun stand-up comedian, Dave Petitjean [who played Randy Quaid's uncle in *The Big Easy*] has a series of great tapes, available through KOM-A-DAY Recording at, P.O. Drawer 10, Ville Platte, LA 70586, (318) 363-2184. Get his earliest tapes for his thickest dialect.)

Cajun Fairytales, Cajun Folktales (wonderful audiobooks by storyteller J.J. Reneaux)

The Cajun Way (possibly only on phonograph record; check your library)

Cajun Party (one of the most popular music albums in Louisiana, performed by the Cajun Playboys)

(There are many Zydeco and Mardi Gras and "Best of Louisiana" albums.)

Books:

The Cajuns: From Acadia to Louisiana by William Faulkner Rushton

Cajun Life by Jo-el Sonncer

Cajun Country by Barry R. Ancelet

Cajun Home by Raymond Bial

Being Cajun isn't a Picnic, But the Coffee's Good by Verne Pitre

The Face of Louisiana by Elemore Morgan

Louisiana Images by George Francois Mugnier

Cajun Household Wisdom by Kenneth Agullard Atchity

Cajun Night Before Christmas by Trosclair (written "in dialect")

Clovis Crawfish and the Orphan Zo-Zo by Mary Alice Fontenet (written "in dialect")

Cajun Dancing by Ormonde Plater, and Cynthia and Rand Speyrer

Cajun Music, a Reflection of a People by Ann Allen Savoy

Cajun Alphabet by James Rice

Cajun Sketches, from the Prairies of Southwest Louisiana by Lauren C. Post

Pidgin and Creole Languages by Susanne Romaine

Modern Englishes: Pidgins and Creoles by Loreto Todd

Speaking Louisiana: A Cajun Dictionary by Jennifer and Ed Martin

Creole: The History and Legacy of Louisians's Free People of Color by Sybil Kein

Our People and Our History: Fifty Creole Portraits by Rodolphe Lucien Desdunes

TEXAN / OTHER SOUTHERNERS (Texas accents have rhotic hard "r's" with tone focus placed in the middle to the back of the mouth, lots of variety in rhythm, volume and hands-on-hips proud attitude.

For Oklahoma/Panhandle Texas, listen for choppy, quick, clipped rhythm and disctinctive adenoidal-nasal-throaty placement.

This list includes the Piedmont area, the foothills region of North Carolina and Virginia, which has tone focus aimed right at the hard palate, and hard "r's.")

Films and TV series:

Broadcast News; Miss Firecracker; Raising Arizona (Holly Hunter is from Georgia; her accent is strongest in these films; she can portray a great Texan character)

Fool for Love (Kim Basinger is from Georgia but does a great Texan; the playwright, Sam Shepard, also stars)

Nadine (Kim Basinger; others attempt a Texan accent; Jeff Bridges's isn't accurate)

Perfect Harmony (East Texas)

True Stories (East Texas)

The Man from Left Field; Tremors; Reba McEntire Live (and other films with country singer Reba McEntire with, a thick Oklahoma accent)

Tombstone (many good examples of Arizona/Texan accents; plus Val Kilmer's Doc Holliday has a good Deep South accent)

Wyatt Earp (good secondary sources for Arizona/Texan, though Kevin Costner's accent isn't consistent)

Wild Bill (Jeff Bridges and other secondary sources for Deadwood, South Dakota) (Hundreds of old cowboy films have Texan accents.)

Places in the Heart (Sally Field does a good Southern in several of her films)

Crimes of the Heart (Sissy Spacek's accent is appropriate for this play's Mississippi setting; Jessica Lange's accent is good)

Trading Mom; Badlands (and other Sissy Spacek films; Texan)

Lone Star (with white, black, Mexican and Native American South Texans)

Fried Green Tomatoes (Birmingham, Alabama)

Sweet Home, Alabama (Secondary sources; set in Greenville and Pigeon Creek, Alabama; Reece Witherspoon is originally from Nashville)

Steel Magnolias (Dolly Parton is from Tennessee; Julia Roberts's accent is Alabama; others are using a variety of Southern accents, though the film is set in northwest Louisiana)

Nell (Carolinas)

"Andy Griffith Show" (Griffith is from Mt. Airy, N.C.); "Mayberry RFD"; "Gomer Pyle" old TV series (Carolina foot-hills" accents; the Mayberry folk are also featured on several film spin-offs)

"King of the Hill" (animated series set in Arlen, Texas; great secondary sources)

"Petticoat Junction"; "Green Acres" (old TV series)

"Designing Women" (catch the TV reruns; each woman has a slightly different upscale Southern accent; it's set in Atlanta)

(Jeff Foxworthy, a rural Georgia-born stand-up commedian, famous for his "redneck" comedy routine, had his own sitcom on TV; check for comedy videos)

Across the Wide Missouri (listen to the character actor, not Kirk Douglas for the accent)

Annie Get Your Gun (musical)

Oklahoma! (musical)

The Grapes of Wrath (Oklahoma)

Everybody's All-American (features 3 different Southern accents)

Wild West (a five-volume set of documentary videos)

American Traditions Videos: Life Along the Mississippi and *The Great Steamboat Race* (documentary videos, narrated by Loretta Young)

Bound for Glory (about Woody Guthrie, who is from Oklahoma; starring David Carradine)

Woody Guthrie—Hard Travelin' (documentary tribute to Guthrie)

Dialect tapes and texts:

Allen and Rogers' *Tongues of the North American Project* (15 North Carolina samples, one Texas, 3 Virginia)

British Broadcasting Company Record *English with an Accent* (Southern American)

The Hermans' *American Dialects* (Dalmarva Peninsula, Tidewater, East Texas) (no tape)
Kur's *Stage Dialect Studies* (Southern) (no tape)
Lane-Plescia's *American Southern, Vol 1 & 2* (with many samples)
Machlin's *Dialects for the Stage* (Southern; Midwestern/Oklahoma; SW/Texas)
Stern's *Acting with an Accent* (Four Texas dialects)
Stern's *Acting with an Accent* (Midwest Farm/Ranch)
Wise's *Applied Phonetics* (Southern American) (no tape)

Other tapes:
Texas Bound: 8 by 8, edited by Kay Cattarulla (two cassettes of stories by Texas writers, read by Texas actors; available from SMU Press, Distribution Center, Drawer C, College Station, TX 77843-4354)
Woodie Guthrie, Library of Congress Recording (three hours of conversations and songs by the Oklahoman folk singer; excellent source)
(Ross Perot, presidential candidate in '92 and '96, provides a great example of an Oklahoma accent, with his colorful use of slang and imagery.)
Will Rogers' America, In His Own Voice (Oklahoma; the famous cowboy speaks out about American politics)
A Season for Justice (John Dees's book on tape; Alabama)

Books and articles:
Dialect Clash in America by Paul D. Brandes and Jeutonne Brewer (chapter on Southern)
Holmes, J. "On Speaking Texan," *Publication Weekly*, 223 (May 20, 1983):154. (article in a periodical)
Dialects—USA by Jean Malmstrom and Annabel Ashley (chapter on Texan)
Country Talk by Dick Syatt
Cowboy Slang by Edgar R. "Frosty" Potter
You-All Spoken Here by Roy Wilder, Jr. (Southern slang and pronunciation)
Down-Home Talk: An Outrageous Dictionary of Colorful Country Expressions by Sutherlin Smith
Happy Trails: A Dictionary of Western Expressions by Robert Hendrickson
Whistlin' Dixie: A Dictionary of Southern Expressions by Robert Hendrickson

SPANISH
(Mexico, Spain, Puerto Rico, Cuba, Central and South America)

Listen for: dental placement like Italian with hard "th's" as "d's," syncopated rhythm with equally stressed syllables, 5 vowels: mah, meh, mee, moh, moo, some ends of words are light, "r's are Latin tapped or may be distinctively rhotic, inflections vary depending on Spanish culture,with the lilt and rhythm following the music of that region i.e., Mexican tends to have a down-turned mouth placement and downward inflection, Cuban and Puerto Rican are quicker than Mexican, Spain and Argentina have a nobility, etc.)

Trigger: "d-d-d-d" horse race with dental placement; and with mouth slightly turned down.
"Hello. My name is Inigo Montoyo. You killed my father. Prepare to die." (from *Princess Bride*)

Practice sentence: "I don't want to kiss you, you pig, but I will be selling you this, that and the other little thing tomorrow, my love"="I don' wan' too kees you, you peeg, baht I weel bee sale-een you dees, dat and dee udder leetle ting too-maw-rroh, my lahv."

<u>Films and TV series:</u>
My Family/La Familia (good primary and secondary sources for Mexican-American)
La Bamba (Mexican)
Stand and Deliver; American Me; The Chico Mendez Story (Edward James Olmos is a primary source for Mexican)
Traffic (Mexico; check other films with Benacio del Toro)
Real Women Have Curves (contemporary Los Angeles Latinos)
Rules of Attraction (starring Mexican-American actor Clifton Collins)
Woman on Top (Penelope Cruz is Mexican)
Frida; Wild Wild West; Fools Rush In; Death to Smoochy (Selma Hayek is Mexican)
Batteries Not Included; Down and Out in Beverly Hills; Fugitive Among Us; Jacob's Ladder (all starring Mexican actress Elizabeth Peña)
Three Amigos (several supporting roles are Mexican; set in Mexico)
The In-laws (supporting roles; set in Mexico)
Fantasy Island; Return to Fantasy Island; Naked Gun (and other Ricardo Montalban films, or the old TV series "Fantasy Island"; educated Mexico City accent)
Wrath of Khan (Star Trek film; Ricardo Montalban is Khan)
Tie Me Up, Tie Me Down
All About My Mother
Cheech and Chong's Next Movie; Nice Dreams (or any other Cheech and Chong movie; comically exaggerated Mexican)
Golden Jubilee, Salute to Fritz Freleng (Speedy Gonzales cartoons, voiced by Mel Blanc, are comic exaggerations of Mexican; this is a video of several Looney Toons)
Like Water for Chocolate (in Spanish, with subtitles; Mexican)
"George Lopez" TV series, stars the Mexican-American stand-up commedian
"Greetings from Tuscon" TV series about a Mexican-Irish family
(Many other old cowboy films are set in Mexico, including *Butch Cassidy and the Sundance Kid*.)
(Actress, Charo, is a stereotype)

The Joy of Talking . . . Spanish (instructional video for English speakers traveling to a Spanish country)
A Mexican Colonial Tour (travelogue)

PUERTO RICAN:
Addams Family; Addams Family Values; Kiss of the Spider Woman (or any other Raul Julia film; Raul was Puerto Rican)
West Side Story (Puerta Rican characters)
Seems Like Old Times (Puerta Rican)
Piñero (about Nuyorican actor-playwright Miquel Piñero, starring Benjamin Bratt)
Super Mario Brothers (John Leguizamo's character is New Yorker-Latino; he's originally from Colombia; he does a comic exaggeration of his accent in the film *To Wong Fu, Thanks for Everything, Julie Newmar*)

SPAIN:
Mambo Kings; Desperados; Mask of Zorro (anything with Antonio Banderas, who is from Spain)
Rain Man (the character of Susanna is from Spain)
Eight Million Ways to Die (Spain; stars Andy Garcia)
The Princess Bride (Mandy Patinkin plays a great character from Spain)
Monsignor (Fernando Rey speaks Iberian Spanish; his accent is more suppressed in *The French Connection*)
Of Love and Shadows
Si, Spain! (travelogue)

CUBA:
The Perez Family (Cubans in Miami; Marisa Tomei does a good Cuban accent)
Predator 2; Colors; Extreme Prejudice; Running Man; Moscow on the Hudson (Cuban-born Maria Conchita Alonzo stars)
"I Love Lucy" (Desi Arnaz, who plays Ricky Ricardo on the television series, is Cuban, though an exaggerated stereotype)
Fidel (biographical drama about Fidel Castro of Cuba)
Improper Conduct (documentary about Fidel Castro's regime through the Cuban Revolution; in Spanish with English narration and subtitles)
Cuba Amor; Cuba: Portrait of Castro's Cuba; Cuba: Holding Back the Tide (documentaries)

SOUTH AND CENTRAL AMERICA:
Noriega: God's Favorite (about Manuel Noriega of Panama)
Bananas (Woody Allen film about San Marcos, with authentic Latin Americans)
Death and the Maiden (set in Chile, but no Spanish accents are used)
1492 (Gèrard Depardieu plays Christopher Columbus, but not with an authentic-sounding Italian accent; not many Spanish characters have lines)
Jurassic Park (supposed to be set in Costa Rican area, but secondary characters are mostly Mexican, rather than Costa Rican actors)
It's All True (three unfinished short documentaries by Orson Welles about Latin America)

Dialect tapes and texts:

Blunt's *More Stage Dialects* (Spain, Portugal, and Spanish in America—Chicano, Latino-Costa Rica)

British Broadcasting Company Record *English with an Accent*

The Hermans' *Foreign Dialects* (Spanish, Mexican, Portuguese) (no tape)

Kur's *Stage Dialect Studies* (no tape)

Machlin's *Dialects for the Stage*

Molin's *Actor's Encyclopedia of Dialects* (American Spanish, European Spanish)

Stern's *Acting with an Accent* (distinguishes between Spain and Mexico)

Wise's *Applied Phonetics* (no tape)

Books:

Dialect Clash in America by Paul Brandes and Jeutonne Brewer (chapter on Mexican)

Coping with Spain by Garry Marwin (excellent source, though the book title has a negative connotation)

The Spanish Character by Bartolome Bennassar

The Spaniards by Michael Perceval

The Spanish Temper by V.S. Pritchett

The Spaniards and Their History by Mendendez Pidal

A Day in the Life of Spain by Collins Publishers

Spain by Library of Nations, a Time-Life Book

Spain by Hugh Thomas and the editors of Life World Library

Spain by Robert Goldston

Distant Neighbors: A Portrait of the Mexicans by Alan Riding

The Land and People of Mexico by Elsa Larralde

Hello Mexico by Morris Weeks, Jr.

Mexico by Walter Hanf

Mexico Through Foreign Eyes by Carole Neggar

The Mexicans by Harold Coy

Tepoztlán: Village in Mexico by Oscar Lewis

Life in a Mexican Village: Tepoztlán Restudied by Oscar Lewis

Ten Keys to Latin America by Frank Tannenbaum

Adventurer's Guide to Puerto Rico by Harry S. Parisier

Puerto Rico/St. Thomas Travel Guide by Antonio Villa

A Pocket Guide to Puerto Rico by the American Forces Information Service Department of Defense

The Oxford Duden Pictorial Spanish-English Dictionary by Oxford Unversity Press

The New World Spanish-English Dictionary by Salvatore Ramondino

The Official Spanglish Dictionary by Bill Cruz, Bill Teck, and eds. of "Generation n" Magazine

WELSH

Listen for: how it sounds similar to Liverpudlian, a cross between Scots and Cockney, with burred Scots "r's" like in "brright, brring, trry" and "verry nice pair-rof-shoes," but dropped "r's" at ends of syllables like Cockney, with the Gaelic throaty sounds, a held jaw and more flatfaced sounds, jaw hardly moving, can be smooth and sedate or rather clipped and quick, with a feel of being weighted down at the shoulders like with the heaviness of a life working in the mines.

Practice sentence: "I made my very own brown pair of shoes out of fresh cranberries"="Oy med me virry oon brroon pirra shooz oot of frrrish crrrahnbrreez."

Films and TV series:

The Englishman Who Went Up a Hill and Came Down a Mountain (set in Wales, excellent narrator voiceover, but Hugh Grant and the other leads are British)

The Corn is Green

Twin Towns (1990's, strong dialect, set in urban Swanson in the Black Hills)

August (version of Chekhov's *Uncle Vanya*, set in Wales with an authentic cast; directed by and starring Welsh native Anthony Hopkins)

Dancing at Lughnasa (an authentic Welsh actor, Rhys Ifans, plays Gerry)

(Richard Burton is Welsh, but just a flavor of his accent shows through in his films, as he is a British-trained actor.)

Dialect tapes and texts:

Blunt's *More Stage Dialects*

British Broadcasting Company Record *English with a Dialect* (Wales, North and South)

Hughes and Trudgill's *English Accents and Dialects* (South Wales)

Lane-Plescia's *Welsh for Actors*

Machlin's *Dialects for the Stage*

Meier's *Accents and Dialects for Stage and Screen*

Stern's *Dialect Monologues, Vol. II*

Trudgill and Hannah's *International English*

Wells' *Accents of the English-Speaking World*

Other tapes:

Under Milkwood (read by author Dylan Thomas)

(Singer Tom Jones is from Cardiff; you may be able to find interviews with him, and he has small roles in films like *Mars Attacks* where he plays himself.)

A Child's Christmas in Wales by Dylan Thomas (read by Welsh actor Richard Burton)

Books:

The Matter of Wales by Jan Morris

In Search of Wales by H. V. Morton

Dylan by Sidney Michaels (the play)

The Corn is Green by Emlyn Williams (the play)

Welsh-English, English-Welsh Dictionary by H. Meuirg Evans

(Check J.C. Wells' web page for his on-line article on Welsh phonetics)

YIDDISH

(*Author's note*: several texts inaccurately label this dialect as Jewish. The Yiddish dialect has a complicated history, with a mixture of regionalisms—Russian, Polish, German, Brooklynese, Hebrew, etc. The following sources contain dialects that have the distinctive melody, word choices, and tone of what we would recognize as Yiddish.)

Listen for: the upward swing at ends like the Temple songs; variances in consonants depending on what country the character lives in, like a rolled "r" or dropped "r," and possible use of "dis, dat" for "th's," both chewy and gutteral tone like dairy caught in your throat.

Trigger: "Oy, gevault! Beautiful, she's not. But rich, they are! Again with the rich! Rich-shmich, but can she cook, or what?"

Films and TV series:
Fiddler on the Roof (the Russian variety)
The Jazz Singer (the Neil Diamond version)
Yentl (with Barbra Streisand)
Eli, Eli (in Yiddish, with English subtitles)
The Boys from Brazil (Laurence Olivier learned the Germanic-Yiddish dialect for this film)
Funny Girl (Barbra Streisand's character and several others)
Invincible (pre-war Jewish life, set in Poland and Berlin; mostly secondary sources)
Varion's War (about Jews in a WWII prison camp)
The Frisco Kid (Yiddish-Polish, comical character with Gene Wilder as a rabbi)
A Stranger Among Us (about a Hasidic-Jewish community in New York)
Used People (New Yorker)
Cemetary Club (New Yorker)
Madhouse (New Yorker)
Shindler's List (not a good source, as the Jewish characters have Polish accents)
(See films and TV shows with commedians Carl Reiner, Mel Brooks, Milton Berle, and Jackie Mason, who have a strong Yiddish flavor to their New York accent. Mason's ethnic background is the source of much of his own humor, and some people find his routines about Jewish culture to be offensive. He wrote a book called *How to Talk Jewish* with Ira Berkow.)
(See other examples under "New Yorker" for the New York-Jewish variety.)
(Check your city's Jewish Community Center for Jewish film festivals in your area)

Dialect tapes and texts:
Blunt's *More Stage Dialects* (Jewish)
The Hermans' *Foreign Dialects* (Yiddish) (no tape)
Stern's *Acting with an Accent* (Yiddish)
Wise's *Applied Phonetics* (Yiddish) (no tape)

Other tapes:
Gimpel the Fool (Yiddish stories, read by Theodore Bikel, who played Tevya in the film *Fiddler on the Roof*)

Books:

Yinglish by Leo Rosten

Hooray for Yiddish b y Leo Rosten

Jewish as a Second Language by Molly Katz

A Dictionary of Yiddish Slang and Idioms by Fred Kogos

Instant Yiddish by Fred Kogos

How to Talk Jewish by Jackie Mason (amusing book by the comedian)

Dialects and Levels of Language, ed. by Joseph Fletcher Littell (chapter on Yiddish)

Dialect Clash in America by Paul Brandes and Jeutonne Brewer (chapter on Yiddish)

Gates to Jewish Heritage by Robbi David E. Lipman (on the web)

The Provincials: A Personal History of Jew is the U.S. by Eli N. Evans

Jewish Literacy by Rabbi Joseph Telushkin

Essential Judaism by George S. Robinson

Tevye the Dairyman and The Railroad Stories translated by Hillel Halkin

INDEX *(Dialect Directory entries are in italics)*

ORDER FORM

PLEASE SEND ME THE FOLLOWING:

_____Copies of this book, **THE DIALECT HANDBOOK**
    ISBN 0-9655960-6-0 $19.95

_____Copies of **ACCENT REDUCTION WORKSHOP**
          for Professional American Speech $35.00

A 3-CD set with book, to improve the clarity and fluency of your American speech. Guides actors in learning a Neutral American dialect, and business professionals to improve their image. In each exercise, Ginny gives coached instruction, demonstrates the words and sentences several times, and then leaves a space for you to repeat the phrase. Includes warm-ups for jaw and tongue, consonant drills for the major troublespots, vowel drills and sentences, and pronunciation lists. There are also sections to help to work on American inflection and stress patterns. Copyright 2000.

Name:_____

Address:_____

City:_____

Telephone:_____

Sales tax: Please add 6% for orders shipped to Florida addresses.

Shipping and handling: $4.00 for first book and $2.00 for each additional book. For orders outside the U.S., or for bulk orders, please make shipping arrangements through the publisher.

Total enclosed:_____

Mail your order with check enclosed to: Voiceprint Publishing
                                            3936 S. Semoran Blvd., PMB 243
                                            Orlando, FL 32822

Phone inquiries: (407) 381-5275
      FAX orders: (407) 381-5276
E-mail: <zazu@gdi.net>

You may purchase through PayPal on Ginny Kopf's web site:

www.voiceandspeechtraining.com